P9-CQG-451

STOCKTON STATE COLLEGE LIBRARY
POMONA, NEW JERSEY 08240

Reflections of Nature

FLOWERS IN AMERICAN ART

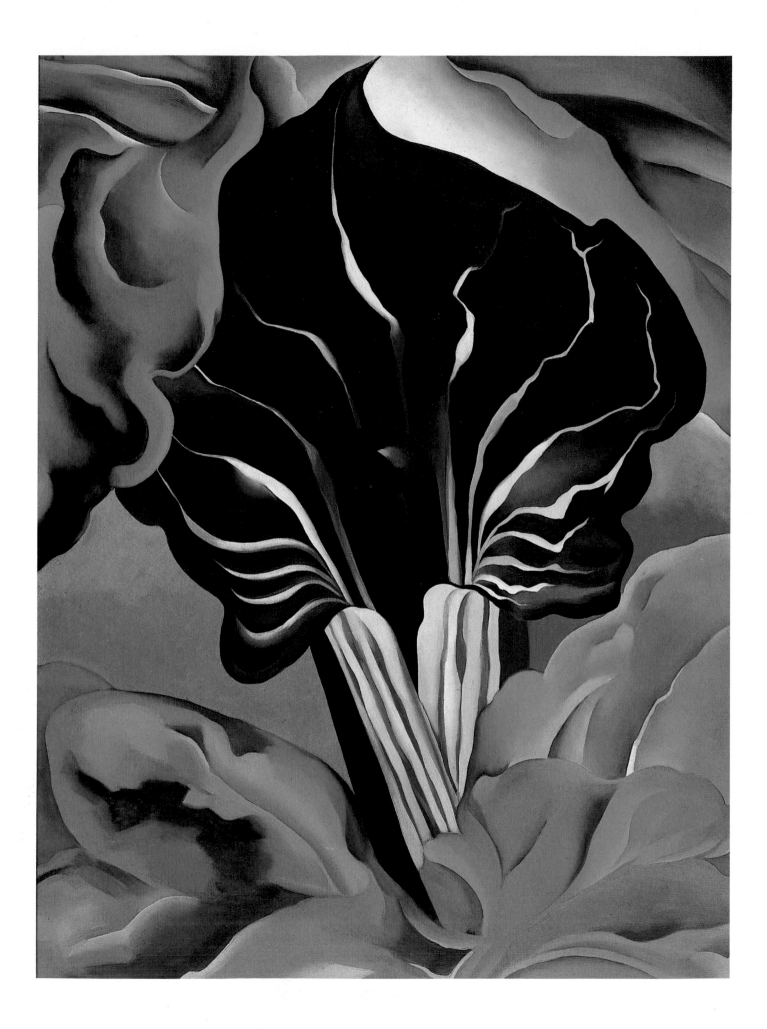

Reflections of Nature

FLOWERS IN AMERICAN ART

Ella M. Foshay

Alfred A. Knopf   New York   1984

in association with the Whitney Museum of American Art

THIS IS A BORZOI BOOK
PUBLISHED BY ALFRED A. KNOPF, INC.

Copyright © 1984 by Whitney Museum of American Art
All rights reserved under International and Pan-American
Copyright Conventions. Published in the United States
by Alfred A. Knopf, Inc., New York, and simultaneously
in Canada by Random House of Canada Limited,
Toronto. Distributed by Random House, Inc., New York.

Library of Congress Cataloging in Publication Data

Foshay, Ella M.
Reflections of nature: flowers in American art.

Catalog of an exhibition held at Whitney Museum of
American Art.
    Bibliography: p.
    Includes index.
    1. Art, American—Exhibitions. 2. Flowers in art—
Exhibitions. I. Whitney Museum of American Art.
II. Title.
N6505.F67 1984 758'.42'097307401471 83-48823
ISBN 0-394-53490-5
ISBN 0-87427-046-4 (Whitney Museum pbk.)

This book was published on the occasion of the exhibi-
tion "Reflections of Nature: Flowers in American Art"
at the Whitney Museum of American Art, March 1–
May 20, 1984, organized by Ella M. Foshay, Guest
Curator, and supported by grants from the Equitable
Life Assurance Society of the United States and the
National Endowment for the Arts. The publication
was organized at the Whitney Museum by Doris Palca,
Head, Publications and Sales; Sheila Schwartz,
Editor; James Leggio, Associate Editor; and Amy
Curtis, Secretary/Assistant.

Frontispiece: Georgia O'Keeffe. *Jack-in-the-Pulpit II*, 1930.
Oil on canvas, 40 × 30 inches (101.6 × 76.2 cm).
Collection of the artist.

Manufactured in Italy
First Edition

Contents

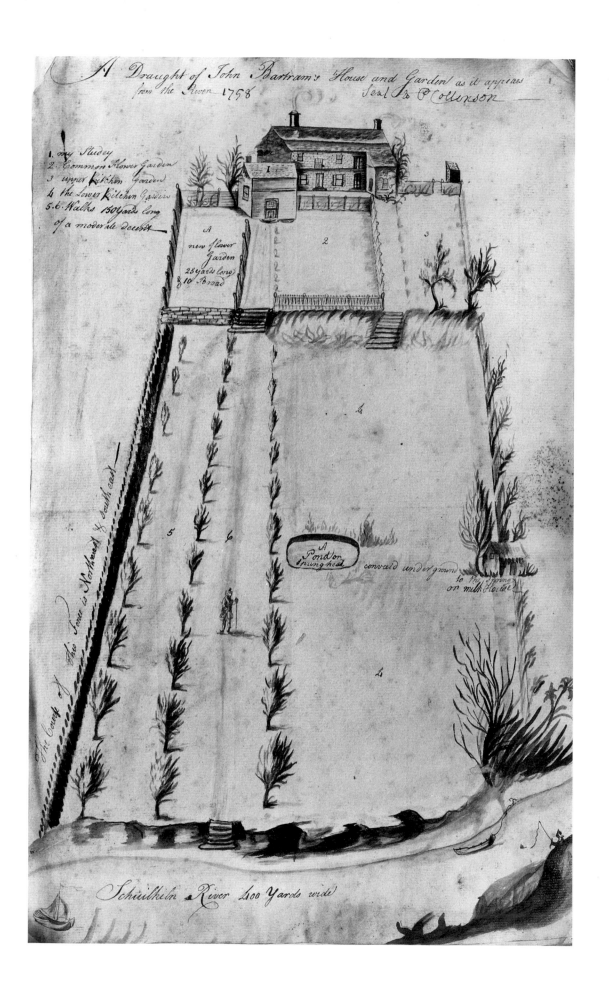

A Draught of John Bartram's House and Garden as it appears from the River 1758   Sent to P Collinson

1. my Studey
2. Common Flower Garden
3. upper Kitchen Garden
4. the Lower Kitchen Gardens
5.6. Walks 150 Yards long of a moderate decent

A new flower Garden 25 yards long & 10 Broad

A Pond on Spring head   conveid under ground to the Spring or milk House

The Course of This Some is Northwest & south east

Schuilkiln River 400 Yards wide

Foreword

THE EXHIBITION PROGRAM of the Whitney Museum of American Art has traditionally covered the full range of American art. Although the Permanent Collection concentrates on art of the twentieth century, with an emphasis on the work of living artists, through changing temporary exhibitions the Museum has always attempted to present to the public the most significant American art from its earliest known images to contemporary works. Thus we are very pleased to be able to offer the first major exhibition, and related publication, devoted to American flower painting from the eighteenth century to the present.

The idea of focusing on the flower in American art is not, however, entirely unprecedented in the history of the Whitney Museum. The spring 1930 exhibition at the Whitney Studio Galleries showed the work of early twentieth-century artists who used floral themes in a wide variety of media, including sculpture and stained glass. *Reflections of Nature: Flowers in American Art* is, in a sense, a sequel to that installation. Organized by Guest Curator Ella M. Foshay, Assistant Professor of Art and American Culture at Vassar College, this exhibition encompasses a larger time period and defines the relationship of flower imagery to changing attitudes toward nature. Ella Foshay's research and her approach to the subject affirm that flowers have a relevance to the most serious concerns of artists, reflecting in a unique manner their aesthetic and cultural priorities.

We are very grateful to the institutions and individuals who have lent these often fragile works of art for the exhibition associated with this book. They have been extremely generous, and we appreciate their cooperation. The exhibition would not have been possible without the generous support of the Equitable Life Assurance Society of the United States. This is the first project they have assisted at the Whitney Museum and we look forward to working together on many future endeavors for the benefit of the public. We are also grateful to the Garden Club of America, whose leadership has endorsed this project and whose encouragement and support have enabled us to reach a wide audience.

Tom Armstrong
Whitney Museum of American Art

JOHN OR WILLIAM BARTRAM, *A Draught of John Bartram's House and Garden as It Appears from the River,* 1758 (see Fig. 17).

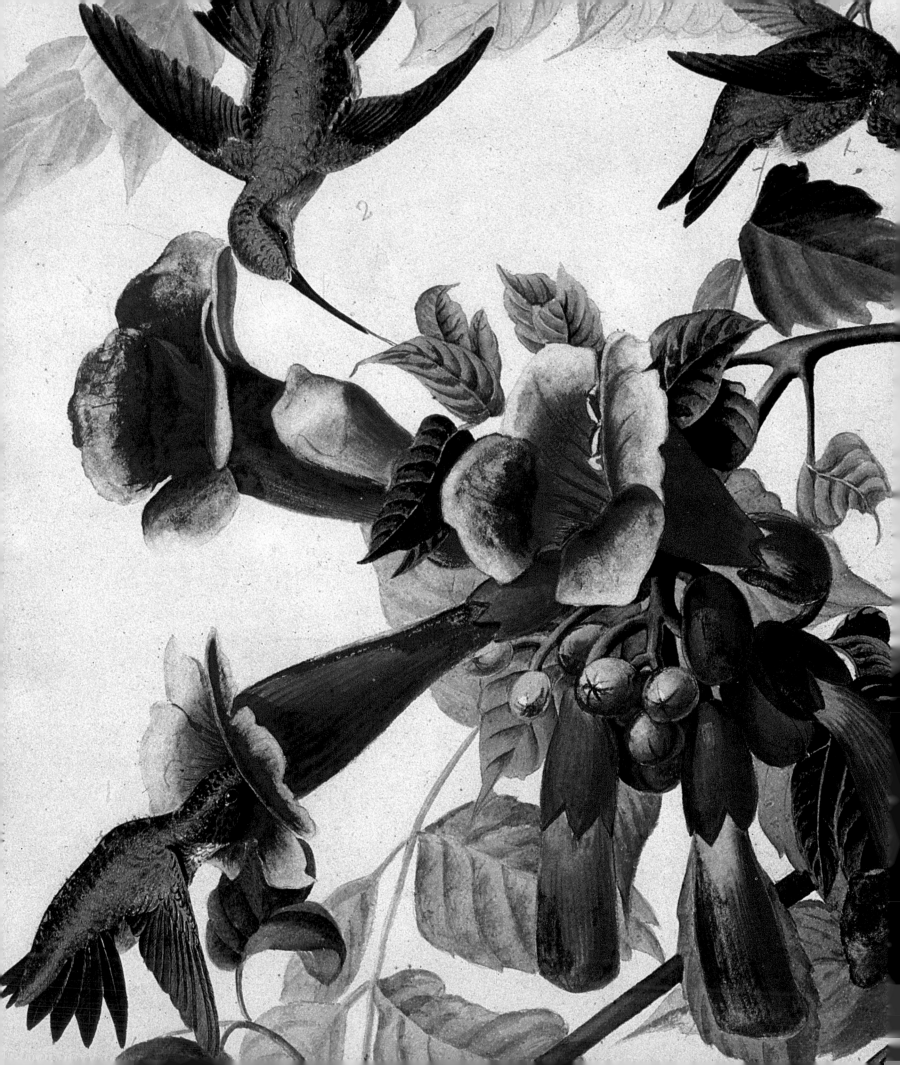

Sponsor's Letter

The Equitable Life Assurance Society of the United States is pleased to assist the Whitney Museum of American Art in presenting the first major museum survey of American flower painting. This exhibition and book offer the public an opportunity to see an extraordinary group of works. They also enrich our understanding of American culture by presenting these works of art within the context of the scientific and philosophical ideas about nature that prevailed during the times in which they were created.

Over the years, Equitable has established its own arts programs to assist individual artists as well as arts institutions. This is our first endeavor with the Whitney Museum, which throughout its history has brought to its audiences new insights into American art of all periods. The people at Equitable are delighted to become a part of that tradition of commitment to American art, and we hope to continue our association long into the future.

We join the Whitney Museum in extending our sincere thanks to the lenders to the exhibition, whose generosity and cooperation throughout the organization of this project have been extraordinary.

John B. Carter
President and Chief Executive Officer
Equitable Life Assurance Society of the United States

JOHN JAMES AUDUBON, detail of
Ruby-throated Hummingbirds, c. 1825
(see Fig. 78).

Preface and Acknowledgments

Reflections of Nature: Flowers in American Art explores the boundless wealth of flower imagery produced in America, and seeks to establish links between modes of floral representation and scientific and philosophical attitudes about nature. The word "flower" is employed here as a generic term for the vegetable world of plants, trees, and shrubs, although most of the works selected feature flowers— "nature's gems," as the nineteenth century was wont to call them.

To highlight the relationship between art and nature, I have placed limits on the media discussed. With a few notable exceptions, prints, drawings in pencil and watercolor, oil paintings, and collage seem to represent American flower imagery best. Within these categories, however, the folk art tradition has been largely omitted: the works under discussion have been chosen not only for their aesthetic quality, but for their shared dedication to "naturalism," as the term was understood during the periods in which they were produced.

This volume is divided into two parts: the first is an interpretative essay; the second comprises four short sections. The division provides a dual perspective on the subject of flowers in art. The essay views flower imagery through a wide-angle lens to encompass a broad cultural landscape. The scientist's, philosopher's, and aesthetician's ideas about the character and order of the natural world played a fundamental role in directing artists' responses to nature. The essay explores the connections between these ideas and the development of flower imagery in American art.

The sections, arranged in thematic and chronological groupings, provide a close-up perspective on individual works of art. Botany, still life, and landscape create the framework for works produced before 1900; while these types of images continue to be produced after that date, the diversity of styles and approaches among twentieth-century artists seemed most appropriately treated by a separate final section.

The two-part division is not intended to be rigid. Rather, the essay and the sections should be considered as complementary, often overlapping, perspectives on the same subject, since the development of flower painting in America owes as much to the talents and stylistic tastes of individual artists, and to their engagement in traditional artistic genres, as it does to the cultural ideas they embraced. Viewed together, I hope that the two parts of this volume capture an accurate picture of flowers in American art.

THE PREPARATION of this volume involved the cooperation and goodwill of many individuals and institutions both in this country and abroad. Although only a sprinkling of footnotes acknowledges debts to Barbara Novak, her inspiration as a scholar, mentor, and friend is engraved on every page. During my approach to this subject in its first incarnation as a doctoral dissertation, Tom Armstrong spotted the possibilities of an exhibition and has kept a supportive eye on the project ever since. Jennifer Russell deftly guided it through its labyrinthine development. The creative efforts of Sheila Schwartz, James Leggio, Nancy McGary, and Jane Heffner, to name only a few of the cooperative and genial members of the Whitney staff, have been invaluable. I was very pleased to have Alfred A. Knopf, Inc., join in the publication of this book. Their cooperation with the Whitney gained for me the talents of Susan Ralston, Betty Anderson, and Joe Freedman.

In Karen Stiefel and Mina Roustayi, I have had the benefit of the finest organizational assistance and creative research. Gloria-Gilda Deák supported my work and my spirit in ways too numerous to mention. Robert Rainwater and David B. Combs at the New York Public Library were always ready to provide assistance. Several of my colleagues and students at Vassar College took time from their busy schedules to help: Professors Eugene Carroll and Susan Donahue Kuretsky read sections, and Meg Golodner, Leith Gaines, and John Lee did research.

The generosity of lenders, both public and private, was unstinting, and each credit line should be read also as a note of thanks. It was my good fortune that this project led me into the world of flowers as well as art; there I benefited from the acute botanical judgments and gracious support of Mrs. Judith Diment, British Museum (Natural History); Mrs. Lothian Lynas, Dr. Rupert Barneby, and Mr. Thomas Everett, New York Botanical Garden; James White, Hunt Institute for Botanical Documentation; and Miss Margaret Stones, botanical artist.

I am deeply grateful to my husband, Michael Rothfeld, for his unfailing help from beginning to end. And my daughter, Ella, kindly timed her arrival to suit me.

E.M.F.

Introduction

GEORGIA O'KEEFFE once wrote: "When you took time to really notice my flower you hung all your own associations with flowers on my flower and you write about my flower as if I think and see what you think and see of the flower and I don't."

O'Keeffe poses us a hard task: to forgo our associations. For the manifold associations of flowers extend from symbolism to sentiment, from science to poetry, from religion to medicine. Great names and events crowd in: Linnaeus working out his taxonomic system, Goethe searching for the *Urpflanze*, Darwin writing about the fertilization of orchids, Thoreau using his hat as a botany box, Emerson wandering around the Jardin des Plantes in Paris, Asa Gray arguing with Louis Agassiz about species.

Can we imagine a universal garden, spread across acres of time and tended by gardeners of different beliefs—Oriental and Christian, classical and Near Eastern, Renaissance and Victorian, medieval and Rococo? Flowers, both exotic and commonplace, are transfused by meanings which often mutate in an image of species: the rose, attribute of Venus, goddess of love, becomes for Christian symbolism the sign of pure love and sacrifice; the grapevine, the vine of the true Christ; the classical laurel, dedicated to Apollo, the symbol of success; the jack-in-the-pulpit, painted in series by O'Keeffe, reads in the floral dictionary as ardor and zeal.

Meaning and syntax alter by culture and period, shifting with the ebb and swell of civilizations that have themselves been held to subscribe to organic principles of bud, bloom, and decay. Life, death, resurrection, mortality, immortality, growth—all are implied by the flower, whose constant presence on a planet filled with living things has invited culture after culture to deposit this rich palimpsest of references.

One is tempted to resort to the flowery language of the Victorians: the flower is life incarnate. Tough stuff, this, for an artist to deal with. Yet the strength of the American flower-painting tradition lies precisely in its ability to interfuse spirit and floral shell in an image of Emerson's fact as the "end or last issue of spirit."

We are not really surprised that the seventeenth-century Dutch, with their appetite for the particular, should have produced one of the world's great traditions of flower painting; nor that Oriental cultures (especially the Sung painters) should have done so as well. But it may come as a surprise that the humble tradition of flower painting in America rivals these in quality and endurance.

The reasons are rooted in the American cultural landscape: a unique protectiveness toward God's earthly furniture, and a respect for the integral wholeness of object identity within the work of art. There is an urge to reconstruct that identity—its weight in space, its surface skin and texture—and then to float to that surface the "spirit" residing in the Emersonian fact. This delicate enterprise was encouraged by the strong transcendental strain that permeated American art and literature in the nineteenth century and that continues to resonate in the twentieth.

There was, then, a fervent belief in the simplest aspect of nature as God's revelation. American flower painters were mandated to respect God's floral kingdom and to suggest the spirit within the outer shell or envelope. This can be seen as part of a larger cultural aim—nothing less than the spiritualization of matter and, at times, of American materialism. Flowers were neither decorative adjuncts nor scattered evidence of a relaxed Deity at play. They were cultural metaphors within which larger issues intersected.

THE EXACT MORPHOLOGY of the organic envelope became available early on through the growing botanical sciences. There is an arc from Mark Catesby's gathering of specimens in the eighteenth century through the apogee of the great Audubon and his assistants to the elegantly incised line engravings of Isaac Sprague for Asa Gray's botany texts in the mid-nineteenth century. Sprague's work tutored the Hudson River painters on plant anatomy even as their own eyes wrested empirical observations from the "real" thing. The empirical perception and the idea begin their long seesaw relationship in the history of American art. It is the balance of that dialectic, cross-referenced with another dialectic between spirit and matter, that generates the American tradition of flower painting.

The American sense of the specific picked up the characteristic bend of a leaf, the vector of a stem, the inclination of a petal. Into this empirical understanding, based on close observation, was conflated an ideal concern for a type that would reflect the perfection of God's creation—part of an overall aesthetic search for the essence that defines species. But over and above all this spiritual engineering, the artists were conscious of the organic principle underlying living things: the growing flower contains in small all the vulnerability of the organic world, which we ourselves share.

Where do we look for influences? The seventeenth-century Dutch, of course. But Dutch art, with its sheen and wetness, is an art in which the senses establish their own kingdoms. It can be seen as an art of appetite or at best of epicurean lusts. Dutch flowers cater to the eye as if it were a mouth; multiplicity of detail itself stuffs space. But the American works, even those directly influenced by the Dutch, merge real and ideal with a more abstract sense, one that distances the subject for contemplation even as it offers it for a consumption more spiritual than physical. There is a sense of indwelling spirit, more closely allied (in another of those mysterious Oriental affinities we happen upon in American art) to the Tao than to anything else. If we posit American flower painting as a great tradition, it is situated somewhere between West and East, between the Dutch simulacrum of appetite and the Oriental simulacrum of life—ch'i, breath, spirit. And it comes from a culture as consistent as those traditions, a culture it reflects and creates in that mysterious ambiguity with which art relates to culture.

One of the key issues in flower painting is the metaphorical overlap between paint and juice. Paint, in one European tradition, is an "exudate" of personality, and a substance which sucks into it some of the great issues of pre-modern art before it becomes one of the heroes, as it were, of modernism. In the French nineteenth-century mainstream tradition, we are often as conscious of paint and formal innovations as of the flower as subject. With Fantin-Latour, for instance, we are teased by a great flower painter with ambiguous references to paint as paint, and paint as petal and floral texture. The floral still life is also a miniature theater in which to ring formal changes—to exercise pre-modern concerns with design and color which prepare the way for the exalted status the still life assumes in the modernist era. Paint as an ambiguous metaphor of sap and juice, and formal arrangement as a forecast of the picture's modernist autonomy—these, it seems to me, are more European than American.

The Americans, including many of the moderns, were after something else. Their paint and their compositions show it. Without invoking Bergsonian vitalism, we might speak of a special organic energy that invigorates the American flower-painting tradition, so that it is hard to call its products *natures mortes*. These *natures vivantes* are of such intensity that they leap across one of the great barriers of the time without noticing it—from the idea of God's creation to Darwin's stringent concept of organic growth. Somewhere in this leap, organicism and spirit prevail, though God, a casualty, is left behind. American flowers embody, if you will, creationist and evolutionary ideas in one. Even before Darwin, American artists' intense pragmatic encounters forced this quality of growth, of life, of becoming, into their paintings, drawings, and prints.

This is a key paradox. Despite their pragmatic encounters with the specific, these American artists also implicitly held in their minds the Neoplatonic notion of an ideal type—a perfect flower toward which all other flowers in their infinite variety aspired. Species, in a larger sense, were also kept separate. The artists, more attracted philosophically to the naturalist Agassiz than to the botanist Gray, held as long as they could to the belief that species had been formed by a "thought of God." Floral perfection, God-conceived through a creational omnithought, had to be respected.

How profoundly the idea of nature changed in the later nineteenth century in the shadow of great scientific insights! The century began with the earth limited to a biblical history of about six thousand years, with all species calmly residing in their categories and, like ranks of angels, praising the Lord that had conceived them. By the end of the century, the age of the earth had extended into pre-human twilights, and mutability of species now served the idea of an autonomous and headstrong nature. Organicism, stripped of its metaphysics, was part of a world infinite in time and newly emergent through evolutionary process. For American artists, the idea of a life-force, initially symbolic and spiritual, could very easily be converted into a "botanical" spirit that satisfied Darwinian tenets and looked forward to a world based on the conditional and relative rather than on Newtonian cosmic "clockwork." This is the context in which the works here might be seen. With one somewhat ironic addendum: the portrayal of the organic in pre-modern art is replaced, in one theory of modernism, by the autonomous "organicism" of the work of art itself. The image of process becomes, as in much modernism, its own reciprocal metaphor. The organic model, assimilated by one aspect of modernist aesthetics, is transposed and relayed into the modernist era.

"THE PAINTER STRIVES and competes with nature," wrote Leonardo, who was closely read by the American artists. Flowers are surely one of the most difficult arenas in which to stage that competition. Flowers are perhaps nature's most perfect artifacts, in form, color, texture, and aroma—a property the painter can only encourage the viewer to conceptualize through the painted image. They are also some of its most evanescent. It is this contrast, profound but easily sentimentalized, between the life-spark and its imminent dissolution, that bestows on flowers—and flower painting—a sense of gentle urgency. Process and its medium, time, are often denied access to the planar dimension where flowers endlessly bloom in the hothouse of art. There is a particular irony, again, in the exclusion of the artist, the organic artificer, from the botanical paradise he or she makes permanent. Indeed, the artist immortalizing the flower engages in a complicated metaphor of his or her own mortality. No wonder that flowers, a mere phase in a reproductive cycle that we find aesthetically pleasing, have generated a formidable archaeology of feelings.

Yet do we exaggerate the fragility of the flower? Growth will out, the seed will split, its preservation cycles exploit birds and insects to maintain its universal regeneration. The flower is the epitome of the life-spark, vitalism's archaic proof. The flower equally demands to be left alone *in situ* and invites amputation, cunningly provoking in us that subtle guilt that persuades us that a cut flower is a butchered process. Yet the organic survives, despite our depredations. In our own time, we can extend our discourse from the floral still life to its model, and from its model to ecosystems and survival, and even to Thurber's last flower. Flowers, perhaps, have now become a symbol of something else.

Barbara Novak
Professor of Art History
Barnard College and Columbia University

The simplest particle of vegetable life, presents
an unbounded space for contemplation....

— DAVID AND CUTHBERT LANDRETH,
The Floral Magazine and Botanical Repository,
Philadelphia, *1832*

Reflections of Nature

FLOWERS IN AMERICAN ART

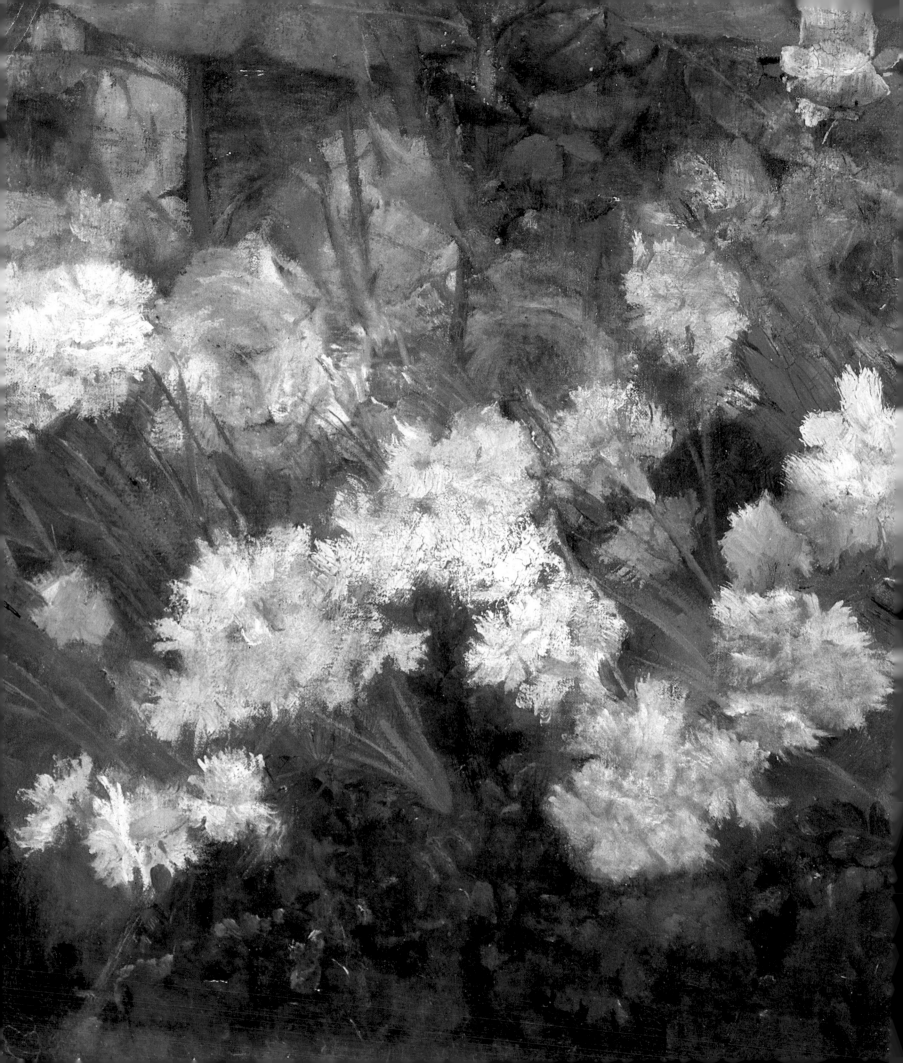

Flowers as a subject for art have been as often maligned as they have been praised. To some artists and critics of the past, the plant world seemed to lack the intellectual content and formal complexity deemed necessary for significant aesthetic expression. Foremost among the denigrators of the floral subject was Sir Joshua Reynolds, the influential British artist and theorist of the eighteenth century. In his *Discourses on Art* (1797) he presented a hierarchy of subjects for art, describing the challenges and pitfalls of the various categories—in order of importance, history painting (including historical, religious, and literary themes), landscape, portraiture, and still life. He judged still-life painting a distinctly "lower exercise" for a painter: its content offered none of the elevating moral lessons through which art gained stature as a lofty intellectual pursuit. Flowers, a subcategory of still life, were considered to be lovely but meaningless subjects, suitable only for training the hand of the aspiring artist. According to Reynolds, no mature artist should waste his brush on the lowly subject of flowers.[1]

Not all critics agreed with Reynolds. Even among his own countrymen, there have been staunch supporters of flowers as worthy themes for aesthetic expression. John Ruskin, whose *Modern Painters* (1851–60), a multivolume treatise on aesthetic principles, guided numerous American artists of the mid-nineteenth century, promoted the flower as a very appropriate but much neglected subject for painting. In contrast to Sir Joshua, Ruskin suspected that it was the *difficulty* of painting flowers, rather than the subject's alleged insignificance, which accounted for its neglect. Indeed, he felt that the challenge of transferring petals to paper might even be a task too great for successful accomplishment. Warning aspiring artists that "the best beauty of flowers being wholly inimitable and their sweetest service unrenderable by art," Ruskin offered them the discouraging conclusion that "the picture [of flowers] involves some approach to an unsatisfying mockery."[2] In light of such an admonition, the profusion of flower paintings produced in America during the period of Ruskin's strongest influence would appear to be a rise to the challenge of producing a "satisfying" mockery.

Maria Oakey Dewing, detail of *Garden in May*, 1895 (see Fig. 45).

Theoretical stances aside, the painter of flowers—like the poet or even the botanist—chooses a subject for his art which is more than just a thing of beauty designed for appeal to the eye. It is, instead, a multidimensional subject which lends itself to a variety of artistic sensibilities. The flower is beautiful, but it is also a vital organism, an embodiment of nature, and a fact of science, as well as a potent vehicle for symbolism. In creative hands, it can even become the provocation for stirring speculations on the character of life itself.

> Little flower—but *if* I could understand
> What you are, root and all, and all in all,
> I should know what God and man is.
> —Tennyson, "Flower in the Crannied Wall," 1869

EUROPEAN BACKGROUND

Long before the discovery of America, the floral world had proved itself to be a garden of curious and attractive delights. The history of recording plant life, in both verbal and visual form, includes some important precedents for the development of the flower genre in America.

Undoubtedly, the earliest interest in the vegetable kingdom was inspired by practical considerations—the potential of plant life for food and medicine. By the fourth century B.C., Aristotle had taken the study of botany beyond objective observation to include speculation about the "psyche" or "soul" of the plant. Not long after the Greek philosopher had systematized his inquiries, colored illustrations began to be included in herbal texts to illuminate both the physical and the spiritual properties of each plant.

By the first century A.D., the tradition of botanical illustration was well established, and Pliny the Elder evaluated the results. In his *Natural History*, he noted that there were a number of adept botanical artists in his own time whose sole "aim is to copy Nature," and who devoted themselves to painting "likenesses of the plants," which they enhanced with written descriptions of their properties. But Pliny warned against believing in the truth of these images: "Not only is a picture misleading when the colours are so many . . . but besides this, much imperfection arises from the manifold hazards in the accuracy of copyists." He also recognized that a single image of a plant could not capture a lifelike portrait, since the artist was limited to one stage in the plant's development: "It is not enough for each plant to be painted at one period only of its life," he pointed out, "since it alters its appearance with the fourfold changes of the year."[3] Pliny concluded, just as Ruskin would many centuries later, that the limner of flowers almost inevitably fell far short of the mark in creating a truthful image.

1. ANDREA AMADIO. *Papaver rhoeas* (corn poppy), in Benedetto Rinio, *Liber de simplicibus*, 1419. Tempera on parchment, 9⅜ × 7⅝ inches (23.8 × 19.4 cm). Biblioteca Nazionale Marciana, Venice.

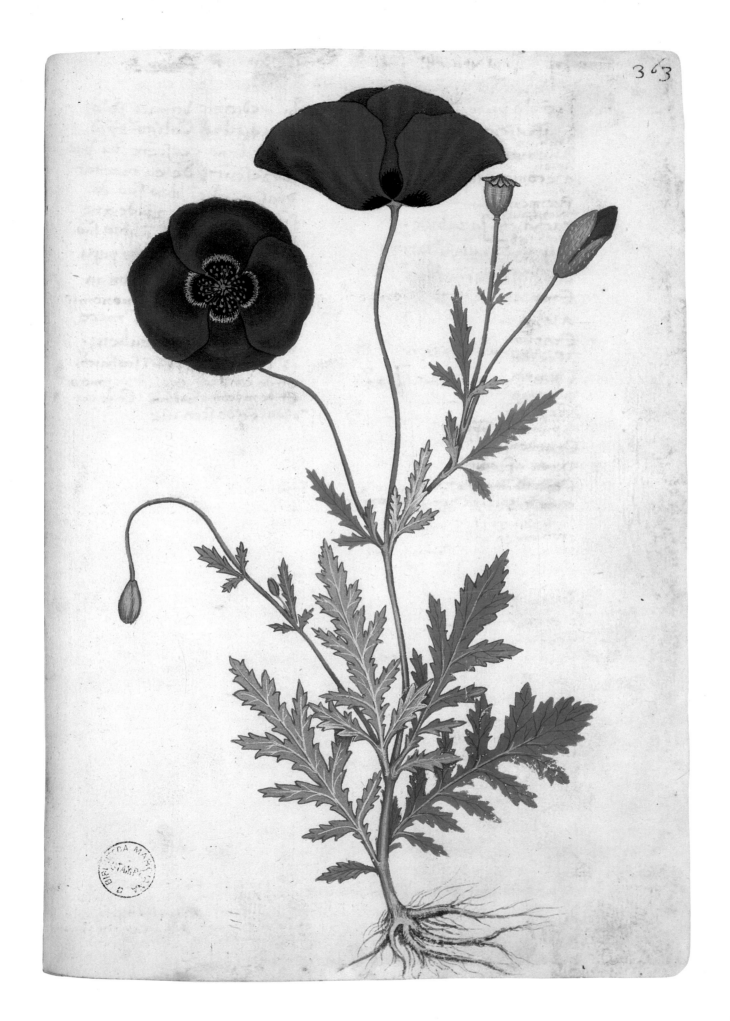

BIBLIOTHECA MARC STAMP

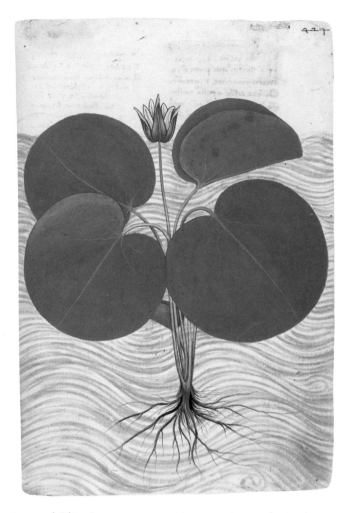

The botanical illustrations of Pliny's contemporaries survive only in later copies, such as those in the sixth-century copy of *De materia medica*, a pharmacopoeia written in the first century A.D. by the Greek physician Dioscorides. Despite Pliny's disclaimer, it is evident even from this copy that classical artists rendered plant life with a vivid naturalism based on close observation.

In the centuries that followed the classical period, naturalistic renderings of flowers and plants, sometimes in the service of science and sometimes in the service of art, did occasionally emerge. While "naturalism" can only be interpreted as a relative term, we assume that the naturalistic flower artist aimed at an accurate depiction of his subject based upon observation. These representations could appear in a variety of artistic contexts. A simple plant portrait suspended on the blank page of an herbal or botanical treatise could capture the lifelike quality of the specimen. In connection with the landscape genre, accurate portrayals of flowers began to appear in the seasonal settings of medieval Books of Hours, and culminated in some extraordinary sketches and flower-filled landscapes of the Renaissance period. What is often considered the apogee of realistic floral depiction—the seventeenth-century Dutch flower piece—developed in the context of still-life painting.

2. ANDREA AMADIO. *Nymphaea alba* (water lily), in Benedetto Rinio, *Liber de simplicibus*, 1419. Tempera on parchment, 9⅜ × 7⅝ inches (23.8 × 19.4 cm). Biblioteca Nazionale Marciana, Venice.

"Naturalism," however, is a complex issue that requires further definition. The floral bouquets in Dutch art, for example, included accurate renderings of individual flowers but inorganic combinations of specimens. Representations of flora which are botanically correct may also project a variety of symbolic associations, sometimes personal, sometimes mythical, and often religious. Moreover, nature itself was not a static concept: the perception of nature could change according to current scientific notions about its character and order. As a result, flower paintings of every type contribute to our understanding of the relationship between the cultural and the aesthetic attitudes of a given generation of artists.

The empirical approach to nature that dominated the classical period lost currency during the Christian Middle Ages. Consequently, illustrations in herbals, the principal type of book devoted to the study of plants in Europe, became highly stylized.[4] Illustrators relied upon the images in earlier texts rather than on direct observation of specimens to produce their plant portraits. However, a naturalistic approach to plant drawing never completely disappeared. A remarkable exception to the generally rough and schematic images of plants in medieval herbals can be found in the illustrations for the *Liber de simplicibus*, a pharmacological treatise compiled in Venice in 1419 by Benedetto Rinio, a medical doctor at the University of Padua.

The naturalism and vitality of the drawings—made by Andrea Amadio, an otherwise unknown artist—probably owe a debt to the preservation in the Islamic world of the empirical legacy of the ancients. The teachings of Greek philosophy, natural science, and particularly medicine, lived on in Arabic culture, and were gradually reintroduced into Europe during the twelfth century and influenced the development of medieval flower imagery. Of the almost five hundred full-page paintings of plants in the *Liber de simplicibus*, the *Papaver rhoeas* (corn poppy; Fig. 1) exemplifies Amadio's rare talent. His keen perception of the live specimen surfaces in his careful re-creation of the plant's dense and hairy root structure, the delicate crenulated lines of the leaf contours, and their textural veining. Evidence of Amadio's desire to capture a total portrait of the plant's life is his inclusion, on a single plate, of four images of the corn poppy's vivid scarlet blossom, each at a different stage of growth and from a different vantage point.[5] Amadio's visual projection of a water lily for the same volume goes even further to enliven its subject (Fig. 2). The artist includes a background pattern of wavy blue-green lines to indicate the appropriate aquatic setting for the plant.

Some herbals did not call for the accurate eye of an Amadio because they were not strictly scientific records. An early definition describes the herbal as a book devoted to the "virtues" no less than to the "properties of plants."[6] Their pages were filled with a curious blend of pseudoscientific documentation, sym-

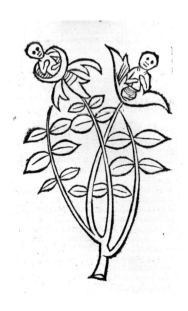

3. ANONYMOUS. *Narcissus*, in *Ortus sanitatis*, 1491. Woodcut, 4⅜ × 2¾ inches (11.1 × 7 cm). British Library, London.

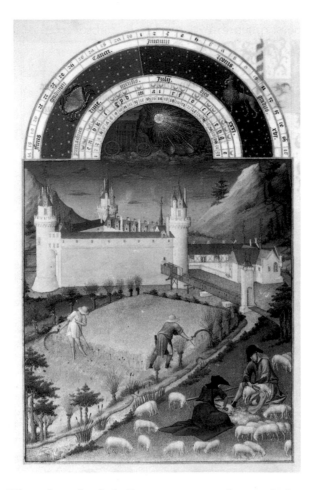

bolism, and decorative whimsy. Therefore, herbal illustrations can be symbolic and fanciful in their imagery as well as charmingly primitive in style, as in the woodcut of the *Narcissus* (daffodil) from the *Ortus sanitatis* (*Garden of Health*) of 1491 (Fig. 3). The artist breathes anthropomorphic life into the blossoms by making them sprout small human forms, probably a reference to the classical legend of Narcissus, who fell in love with the reflection of his own image.

Naturalism in the pictorial description of plants and flowers reentered Western imagery in the Renaissance, not through botany but through art. Artists of the earlier fifteenth century had begun to depict the plant world with increasing realism for naturalistic, decorative, and symbolic purposes. Closely observed and vividly colored flowers—poppies and cornflowers in a field of grain—dot the calendar landscape for July in the *Très Riches Heures* manuscript illuminated by Pol de Limbourg (Fig. 4).[7] The same concern for organic landscape details is evident in the artist's careful rendering of the new shoots sprouting from the gnarled trunks of aging trees along the banks of the stream. Two generations later, Botticelli lavished similar attention on floral detail in his *Primavera* (Fig. 5).[8] The nearly full-scale classical deities are disposed in a verdant landscape setting—an earthy platform of meadow flowers and, as a backdrop, an orange grove in full fruit. On the right, the floating garment of Flora, the

4. POL DE LIMBOURG. *Très Riches Heures of the Duke of Berry. July.* Paint and ink with gold leaf on vellum, 11 7/16 × 8 5/16 inches (29.1 × 21.1 cm). Musée Condé, Chantilly, France.

5. SANDRO BOTTICELLI. *Primavera,* c. 1478. Tempera on wood, 79 7/8 × 123 5/8 inches (202.9 × 314 cm). Galleria degli Uffizi, Florence.

personification of spring, is embroidered with stylized but recognizable roses, carnations, and fringed blue cornflowers.

An extraordinary culmination of naturalism and vitality in floral imagery appears in the work of two Renaissance artists from the north and south of Europe—Albrecht Dürer and Leonardo da Vinci. Two such lively and sensitive renderings of flora as Dürer's *Great Piece of Turf* (Fig. 6) and Leonardo's *A Star of Bethlehem and Other Plants* (Fig. 7) depend largely upon the careful study of live specimens and the inspiration of artistic genius.[9] Leonardo studied the human body intensely, but also held plants, as well as other natural phenomena, to be equally valuable for an understanding of the universe. The observation and description of plant life preoccupied him throughout his career. His list of the studies he produced during his youth records "molti fiori ritratti di naturale,"[10] and his notebooks are filled with precise observations of the intricate structural properties of plants and their organic life. Some of the botanical phenomena which Leonardo describes, such as phyllotaxy (the arrangement of leaves on a stem), heliotropism, geotropism, and, most important, sexual differ-

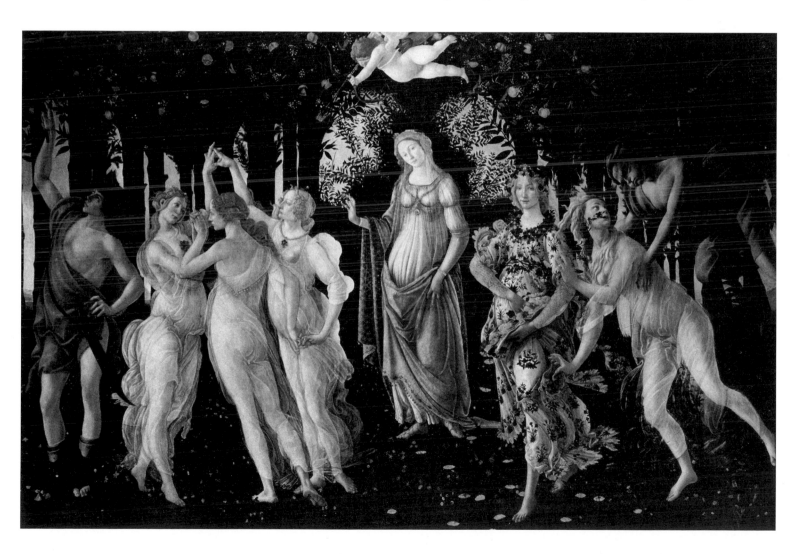

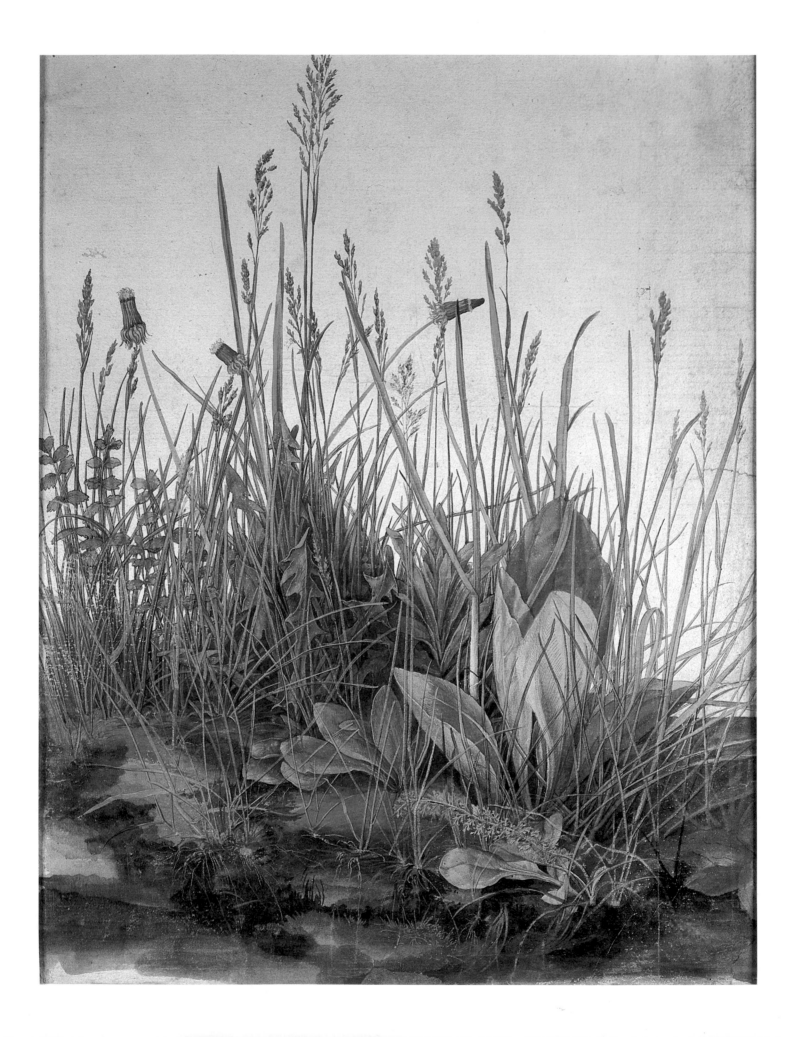

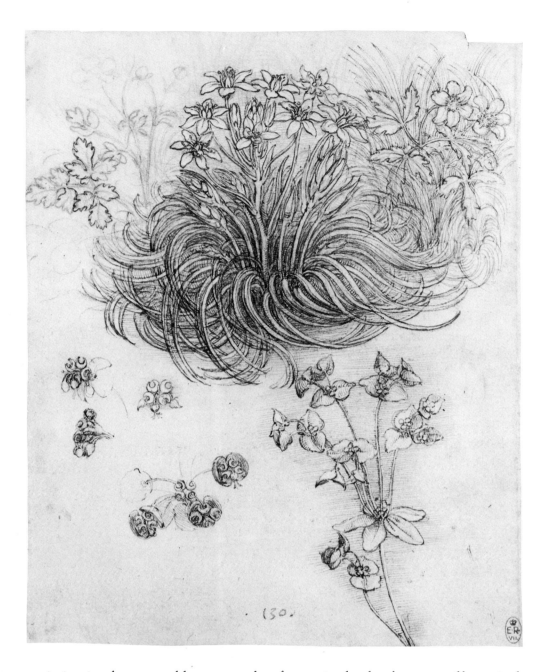

6. ALBRECHT DÜRER. *The Great Piece of Turf*, 1503. Watercolor on paper, 16⅛ × 12½ inches (41 × 31.8 cm). Graphische Sammlung, Albertina, Vienna.

7. LEONARDO DA VINCI. A *Star of Bethlehem and Other Plants*, c. 1506. Ink over red chalk on paper, 7¹³⁄₁₆ × 6⁵⁄₁₆ inches (19.8 × 16 cm). Royal Library, Windsor Castle.

entiation in plants, would emerge as key factors in the development of botanical science in later centuries.[11] It is not surprising that Leonardo would want to pass along to other painters his conviction about the importance of nature to art. Addressing them in his *Treatise on Painting*, he warned: "Therefore, painter . . . to avoid the condemnation of those who know these matters, be prepared to represent everything from nature. . . ."[12] Only such intense conviction could have inspired a drawing like Leonardo's *Star of Bethlehem* (Fig. 7). With its energetic, ribbony leaves and its fully modeled floral blossom, this image conveys a vivid portrait of both the physical character and organic vitality of the plant.

Something of the same rapport with nature emerges in Albrecht Dürer's *Great Piece of Turf* (Fig. 6). In this representation of an ordinary clod of earth, the artist seems to accept nature's compelling invitation, as Henry David Thoreau would later conceive it, "to lay our eye level with the smallest leaf, and take an insect view of its plain."[13] Dürer's drawing resulted from one of the artist's convalescent outings in the Jura Mountains near Nuremberg. His wondrous assembly of plant life clearly goes beyond documentary accuracy to describe a very personal experience of nature. Having been limited to drawing models brought to his bedside during an illness, Dürer here conveys his exhilaration when the warm summer weather permitted him to go outdoors.[14] While the grasses, dandelions, yarrow, and plantain appear to exist in a kind of natural disarray, they rarely overlap and obscure the fine structural details of one another. Instead, each plant maintains a precise and separate identity; all are green and fresh and stretch to gain a place in the sun. In this clear-eyed vision of flora, Dürer exquisitely bridges the gap between the self and objective experience. He accepts the challenge of painting which, as Leonardo said, requires a virtual loss of self, compelling "the mind of the painter to transform itself into the very mind of nature." In this spirit, Dürer achieves the ultimate artistic role of "interpreter between nature and art."[15]

A remarkable feature of Dürer's *Great Piece of Turf* is its combination of plants which could be seen growing together in a single habitat. Such attention to accurate organic relationships would not become common practice in art until the plein-air landscape and flower paintings of the nineteenth century.

If we turn from the landscape to the still-life genre, we find that the realism of assembly was not an important issue in seventeenth-century Dutch flower pieces. In fact, these paintings, which are valued for their botanical accuracy as well as for their aesthetic quality, rarely included floral specimens that could logically be grouped together in a single container. The flower pieces of Ambrosius Bosschaert the Elder, who produced some spectacular examples of the genre, combine, in one vase, flowers that blossom at different times of the year. The symmetrically constructed arrangement in his *Large Bouquet in a Wan-Li Vase on a Gilt Metal Base* (Fig. 8), for example, includes the tulip and the *Narcissus tortuosus*, which bloom in April and May; the columbine and carnation, which bloom in midsummer, and the *Polyanthus narcissus*, a typical winter flower.[16] Clearly, each of the flowers has been keenly observed in live form; the artist also knew scientific renderings of flowers in pattern books of botanical prints such as the glorious *Hortus floridus* (Utrecht, 1614; Arnheim, 1616).[17] From an impression of the organic form derived from nature and art, Bosschaert could produce a precise flower portrait. The sketches he made from nature, which unfortunately have not survived, served him as a kind of paper garden, from which he would pluck a perfect specimen to compose his ideal painted bouquets. The correspondence of an eighteenth-century Dutch flower artist, Jan van Huysum, whose work was much admired in mid-nineteenth-century Amer-

8. AMBROSIUS BOSSCHAERT THE ELDER. *Large Bouquet in a Wan-Li Vase on a Gilt Metal Base*, 1609. Oil on mahogany panel, 19¹³/₁₆ × 14 inches (50.3 × 35.6 cm). Kunsthistorisches Museum, Vienna.

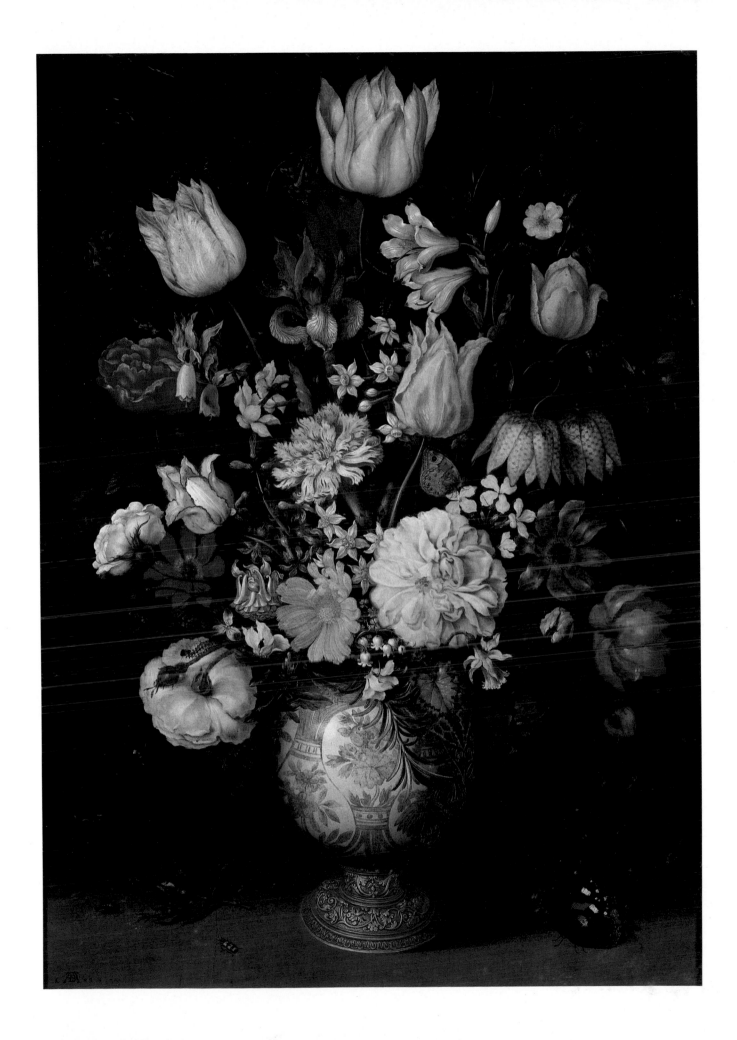

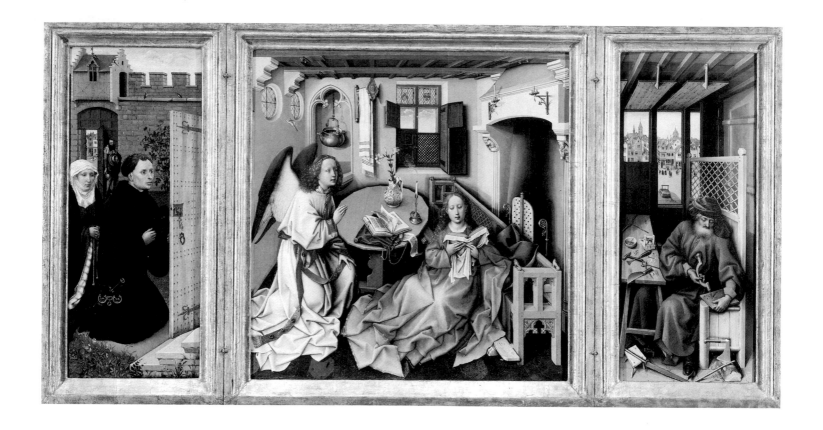

ica, reveals indirectly that he, too, was not working from an assembled group of flowers. In a letter to his patron written in February 1740, van Huysum apologized for the delay in the delivery of a flower painting on which he had been working for almost two years.[18] Since no flowers survive that long, it is apparent that the artist was working from studies.

It seems curious, at first, that a painter like van Huysum, dedicated to the realistic reproduction of a live flower in full bloom, should create artificial arrangements. After all, part of the stimulus for the development of the Dutch genre was the widespread interest in gardening and the cultivation of exotic flowers brought back to Holland from around the world by Dutch trading ships. The city of Leiden, in fact, could boast one of the greatest botanical gardens in the world in the seventeenth century. But it is precisely within this cultural, nationalistic sphere that we find an explanation for the artists' artificial arrangements.

Just before 1600, Flemish and Dutch artists produced the earliest examples of easel paintings which represented large bouquets of flowers arranged in vases. And it was particularly in Holland that the flower piece received its fullest expression. In 1581, the northern provinces of the Low Countries, adhering to the Calvinist faith, gained independence from their Spanish Catholic rulers. The Calvinist religion and the economic prosperity of seventeenth-century Holland are two factors which have an important bearing on the kind of imagery

9. ROBERT CAMPIN. *Mérode Altarpiece*, c. 1425. Oil on wood: center panel, 25³⁄₁₆ × 24⁷⁄₈ inches (64 × 63.2 cm); left panel, 25³⁄₈ × 10³⁄₄ inches (64.5 × 27.3 cm); right panel, 25³⁄₈ × 10¹⁵⁄₁₆ inches (64.5 × 27.8 cm). The Metropolitan Museum of Art, New York; The Cloisters Collection, Purchase.

that we find in Dutch flower painting.[19] After the split with Catholic Flanders, Dutch artists could no longer depend on church sponsorship of their profession. The Calvinist church banned devotional imagery, an iconoclastic attitude that forced Dutch artists to turn to new secular subjects and a new secular source of patronage: the prosperous middle class of merchants and traders in the economically successful new country. In this milieu, "realistic" flower pieces—full bouquets of gloriously colored and unblemished blossoms—clearly reflect Holland's positive national feelings and pride in its new state of economic well-being.

Bosschaert's *Large Bouquet* (Fig. 8) makes an alluring visual offering to his flower-loving and art-buying public. Each flower maintains an unobscured profile to highlight the elegant perfection of the petals' textures and contours. In an effort to appeal to the Dutch spirit, he emphasized the elusive beauty of each flower over the organic consistency of his grouping.

Individual flowers, too, carried a wealth of associations. The inclusion in Bosschaert's painting (and in so many other seventeenth-century Dutch paintings) of a tulip is especially revealing of Dutch cultural concerns. Specimens of these flowers, which we now associate with the Low Countries, were first imported from the Near East into Holland in the late sixteenth century. The tulip became so popular in Dutch horticultural circles that speculation in the bulbs reached a frenzy and price unprecedented in the history of gardening. So absurd were the proportions of this "tulipomania" that farmers are known to have exchanged an entire farm for a single bulb.[20] It is no wonder, then, that the tulip holds such a prominent place in Dutch painted bouquets.

The striped tulip in Bosschaert's painting may have a moral as well as an economic reference. The use of flowers for symbolic purposes had become prominent in fifteenth-century religious art of the Netherlands. The central panel of Robert Campin's *Mérode Altarpiece* (Fig. 9) represents, on the one hand, a trend toward increasing naturalism. Campin placed the Annunciate Virgin in an early fifteenth-century bourgeois living room, which includes a simple table supporting a candlestick and a blue-and-white majolica vase resplendent with a sprig of blossoming lilies. But the lilies, like other domestic accoutrements in the work, serve as symbolic reinforcements—"disguised symbolism"—of the central religious theme.[21] In Christian iconography the lily, because of its white color, came to represent the Virgin's purity, and hence her worthiness to bear Christ.

Such Catholic theological symbolism would not be appropriate in a Dutch flower painting like Bosschaert's *Large Bouquet*. In accordance with Calvinist principles, the symbolism in this painting relates more to human conduct, to lessons about moral behavior. The Dutch version of "disguised symbolism" is often explained in contemporary emblem books—books of symbolic pictures with explanatory texts. In Roemer Visscher's 1614 publication entitled *Sinnepoppen*, we can find a clue to the striped tulip in Bosschaert's image. Visscher's

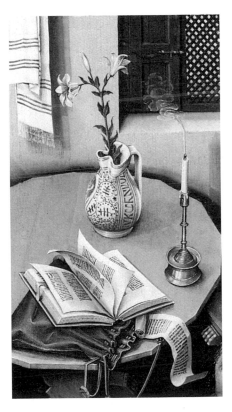

Detail (see Fig. 9).

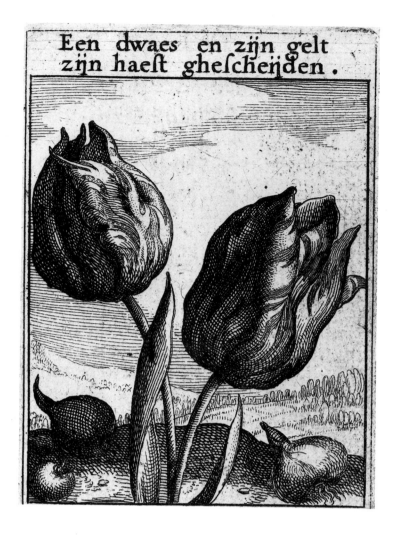

Een dwaes en zijn gelt
zijn haest gheschenden.

emblem of tulips (Fig. 10) depicts two large blossoms of the rare striped variety looming in large, almost ominous, scale over a landscape setting. The inscription crowning the engraving warns the viewer that "a fool and his money are soon parted." In other words, the emblem reminds Dutch flower lovers of the hazards of greed.[22] The passion for transient beauty and financial gain that marked Dutch tulip cultivation could have serious moral consequences. The economic market would soon corroborate the moral lesson of Bosschaert's image, with a sharp drop in the value of tulip bulbs.

These Dutch floral still lifes and their eighteenth- and nineteenth-century descendants would have some influence on the emergence of the flower piece in mid-nineteenth-century American painting (Figs. 27, 81–83). By that time, however, realistic representations of flowers had been produced on this side of the Atlantic for practical and aesthetic purposes, in a sense rehearsing the history of their European predecessors. The discovery of nature in America passed from the hand of the botanical explorer to the hand of the landscape artist. Through the filter of American culture, these artists sought to illuminate the physical appearance of the garden of the New World.

10. ROEMER VISSCHER. *Striped Tulips* ("A fool and his money are soon parted"), in *Sinnepoppen*, 1614. Engraving, 3¾ × 2¼ inches (9.5 × 5.7 cm). Newberry Library, Chicago.

THE ORIGINS OF
AMERICAN FLOWER IMAGERY

The earliest written reports and visual descriptions of American flora were made by artist-naturalists who accompanied exploratory expeditions to America. Hopes ran high in the minds of the European sponsors and of the artists about what they might find on this side of the Atlantic. The expansive unexplored terrain held promise of numerous treasures, both practical and philosophical, for the hearty explorer. Interests ranged from documenting the natural resources to acquiring unimaginable riches. The more lofty souls aspired to extract truths of a cosmic nature from the secretive terrain; perhaps the undiscovered natural specimens of the New World could reveal the design of the scientific system of nature mapped out by God at the moment of creation.

The notion of the American landscape as a repository of fact and truth grew out of the European perception of the New World. It is given a lively visual expression in two paintings by the Flemish artist Jan van Kessel the Elder. His images of *Europe* and *America* (Figs. 11, 12) form part of a series of four allegorical paintings representing the continents, each with a central panel surrounded by sixteen small landscapes. The panels of *Europe* and *America*, despite their similar compositional formats, present very different human figures and objects. The female personification of *Europe*, seated to the left, is dressed in elaborate courtly fashion and surrounds herself with an array of valuable, mostly man-made objects. In fact, the setting appears as kind of a Baroque *Wunderkammer*, a collection of the wonders of the natural world and the cultural achievements of man. This is an image of civilization: Europe sponsors religion (the Bible), art (the palette in the foreground), and science (the globe at the right).

If Europe was the repository of developed culture, America, at least in van Kessel's view, was an untouched treasure-house of nature just waiting to be tapped and documented. Portrayed as a primeval goddess, bare-breasted America lounges casually on the floor of a curiously decorated room. She seems almost oblivious to the extraordinarily fanciful assortment of objects surrounding her. Symbols of the Old World's dreams of the New World's mineral riches encircle her in the form of gold weights of increasing size and value, and there are urns so full of precious jewels and coins that one of them seems to have fallen over from the sheer weight of its contents. America, however, represents more than a figure of economic lust. She is also the female personification of a land filled with an unimaginable variety of creatures—reptile, fish, fowl, and vegetable—that excited the intellectual curiosity as well as the collecting instincts of the European explorer.[23] The physical forms and habits of these New World

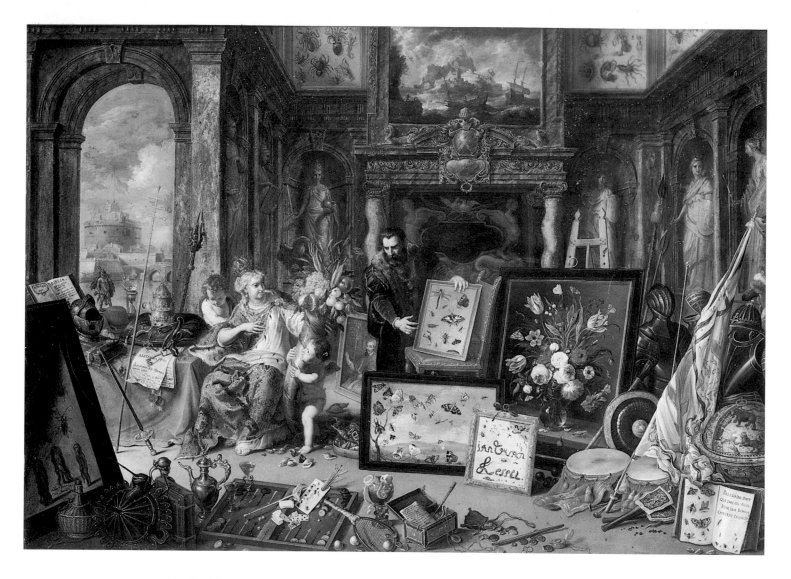

occupants, strewn in a kind of haphazard disarray on the floor in front of America, captivated the imagination of the civilized world. This view of the American landscape as a repository of beneficence—including practical, scientific, and symbolic truths, which could be revealed through an exploration of its natural specimens—would color the approach to nature in America into the twentieth century.

Most of the early travelers who had the opportunity to get a firsthand look at the New World were not disappointed. Confronted with the "fresh green breast" of the eastern shores of Virginia or Maryland, the explorer Verrazzano enthusiastically described the sylvan land in 1524 as "Arcadia." His first sight of "the many vines of natural growth, which, rising, entwine themselves around the trees," conjured up for him the bouquet of the excellent wines they could produce under proper cultivation. It was not practical considerations, however, but the sheer beauty and exotic quality of the wild flowers which caught his eye. "We found wild roses, violets, and lilies, and many kinds of herbs and fragrant

11. JAN VAN KESSEL THE ELDER. *Europe* (detail), 1664. Oil on copper, 19⅛ × 26⅝ inches (48.6 × 67.6 cm). Alte Pinakothek, Munich.

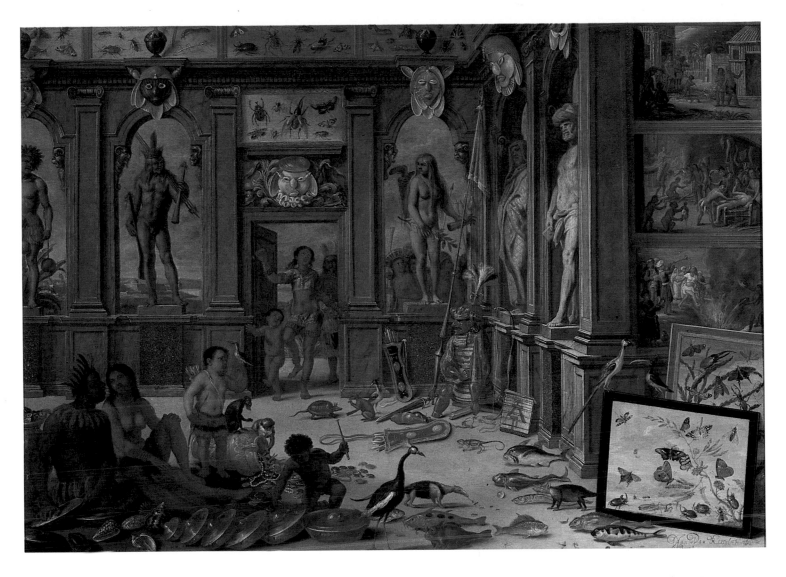

12. JAN VAN KESSEL THE ELDER.
America (detail), 1666. Oil on copper,
19⅛ × 26⅝ inches (48.6 × 67.6 cm).
Alte Pinakothek, Munich.

flowers," Verrazzano remarked with pleasure, and noted further that these natural gems were so "different from ours."[24]

Words alone could not satisfy the aesthetic and scientific curiosity about the flora of America. Artists soon joined the ranks of the exploratory voyagers to breathe visual life into the records of these ventures. While many of the early drawings have been lost or destroyed, a few remarkable ones survive. A gifted French plant draftsman, Jacques Le Moyne de Morgues, accompanied a Huguenot expedition to Florida in 1564. Unfortunately, none of the individual studies of Florida plants which the artist must have produced during his yearlong stay have been found, but his elegant watercolor drawing of *A Young Daughter of the Picts*, made about twenty years later, reflects his American experience (Fig. 13). The figure personifies the glorious physical beauty of northern Britain's ancient inhabitants. An engraved impression of the drawing was included in Theodor de Bry's volume *America* (1590) to show that British ancestors were once as savage as the Indians of Virginia.[25] Clothed in a diaphanous robe embroidered

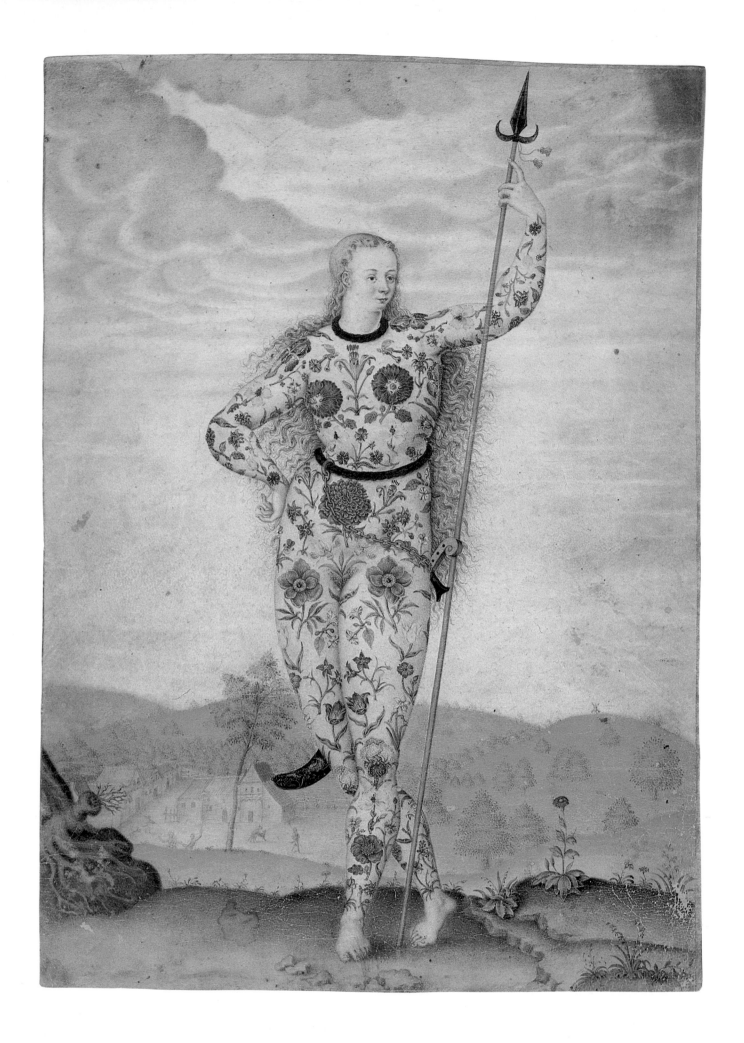

with an exquisite assortment of flowers, the Pict woman strikes an elegant pose as the goddess Flora dominating a landscape vista. A knowledgeable botanical glance at her costume reveals in its fabric a kind of sartorial inventory of flowers recently introduced into western Europe. Among them are specimens from America, such as the vividly colored, funnel-shaped marvel-of-Peru.[26]

In drawing the figure of Flora, Jacques Le Moyne may have engaged the help of a younger British artist, John White. As artist and cartographer to Sir Walter Raleigh's 1585–86 expedition to "Virginia" (now parts of North Carolina and Virginia), White claims remembrance as the first traveler to depict the scenery, the natives, the animals, and the plants of the southern coast of North America. His volume of drawings, now in the British Museum, bears an autograph title page which may represent the first use of the word "truth" in connection with the depiction of nature in America: "THE pictures of sondry things collected and counterfeited according to the truth in the voyage made by Sr. Walter Raleigh knight, for the discouery of La Virginea. In the 27th yeare of the most happie reigne of our Soueraigne lady Queene Elizabeth. And in the yeare of or Lorde God. 1585."[27]

What does a scientific draftsman like John White mean by "truth"? We can examine his watercolor *Sabatia stellaris* (rosegentian), possibly the first plant of temperate North America to be drawn (Fig. 14), in searching for the answer. First, the concept of truth here indicates that John White did not copy his flower from an image in an earlier published source, which continued to be a customary and acceptable practice in the sixteenth century.[28] Instead, the drawing asserts that he observed the live specimen in the field and made sketches of it. "Truth" in this context, however, does not imply that the *finished* drawing was made directly from nature. It surely was not. It is a finished version completed after his return to England (there were probably several replicas), based on quick sketches produced on the spot.

White's intention to render a precise and accurate image of the *Sabatia stellaris* also influences the clear and readable presentation of the specimen on the page. He displays an erect single stem of the plant with roots attached, three wide-open flowers, and a few buds. With deft and careful hand, he also describes the flower's yellowish-green lanceolate leaves.

White's *Sabatia stellaris* is a truthful image of the plant within the framework of contemporary scientific knowledge. It is a drawing in step with the empirical state of science in the sixteenth century, and with the age's penchant for documentary clarity. White approached his specimen the way a portrait painter confronts his human model—not the way a portrait photographer may try to capture the dynamics of a momentary gesture, focusing on a flattering angle, or highlighting an individual trait. The floral sitter is expected to remain still to effect an image that presents its structural form in lucid detail.

13. JACQUES LE MOYNE DE MORGUES. *A Young Daughter of the Picts*, c. 1585. Watercolor and gouache on vellum, 10⅛ × 7¼ inches (25.7 × 18.4 cm). Yale Center for British Art, New Haven, Connecticut; Paul Mellon Collection.

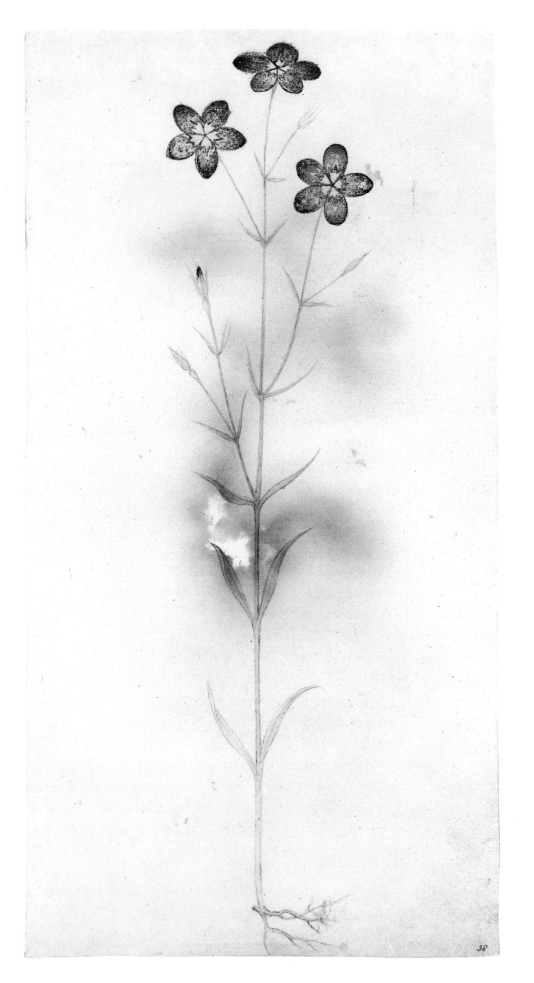

38

14. JOHN WHITE. *Sabatia stellaris* (rosegentian), c. 1586–90. Body color and watercolor touched with white (oxidized) over black lead outlines on paper, 13¾ × 7 inches (34.9 × 17.8 cm). The Trustees of the British Museum, London.

15. MARK CATESBY. *The Mock-bird*, in *The Natural History of Carolina, Florida and the Bahama Islands*, 1731–43. Hand-colored engraving: image, 13½ × 10⅛ inches (34.3 × 25.7 cm); page, 22 × 15¼ inches (55.9 × 38.7 cm). Department of Library Services, The American Museum of Natural History, New York.

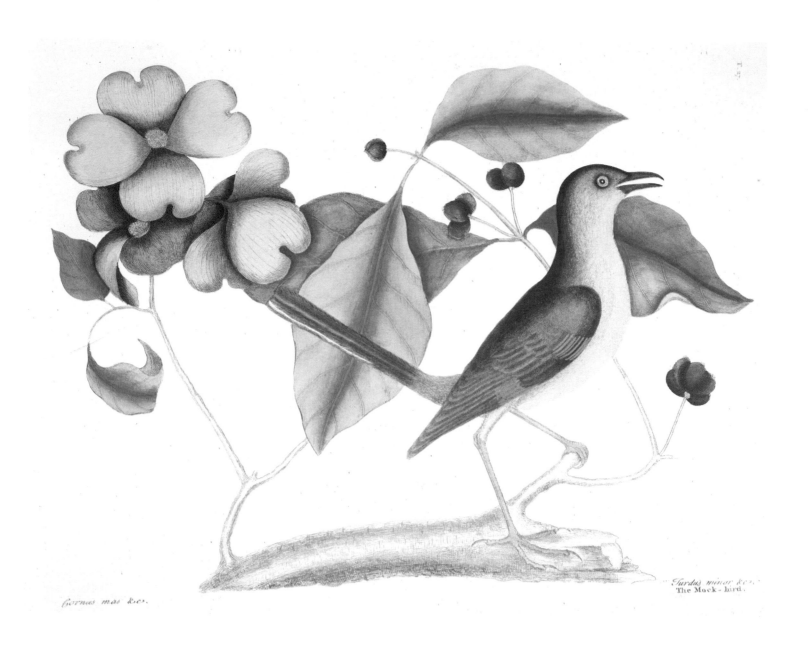

Cornus mas &c.

Turdus minor &c.
The Mock-bird.

White's drawings served as unacknowledged models for the self-taught Eng-lish artist Mark Catesby, who was responsible for the magnificent illustrations of New World flora and fauna in the two-volume *Natural History of Carolina, Flor-ida and the Bahama Islands*, first published in 1731–43.[29] The drawings were produced during Catesby's two visits to this continent. He spent the years 1712 to 1719 with relatives in Virginia, and from 1722 to 1726 traveled through the Carolinas, Georgia, and Florida, with a stop in the Bahamas, before returning to England. Catesby's remarkable nature studies sometimes expand the mode of his predecessor by placing native flora and fauna in their natural habitat. "In designing the Plants, I always did them while fresh and just gather'd," he wrote in his preface, "and where it could be admitted, I have adapted the Birds to those Plants on which they fed, or have any relation to."[30] *The Mock-bird* (Fig. 15) shows the bird poised in graceful profile on the branch of a flowering dogwood, creating an elegant image of relationships in nature (both bird and tree are native to the American Southeast) without obscuring the documentary clarity of either the flower or the bird. However, in the text accompanying this plate, Catesby tells us that the image of the Virginia dogwood represents the tree not as a live specimen observed by the artist at a single time and place, but as a kind of compendium of its seasonal aspects—"As the flowers are a great ornament to the Woods in Summer, so are the berries in Winter."[31] It is as if Catesby were answering Pliny's complaint about the inadequacy of depicting a plant "at one period only of its life." Yet the result is an image which, in its conjunction of flowers and berries, seems untrue to nature. But we must remember that Catesby's idea of truth demanded the presentation of all the facts.

The style of Catesby's drawings also accords with his intention to achieve factual clarity. The second volume of the *Natural History* contains magnificent plant drawings unaccompanied by other specimens. In the beautiful pale flowers of *The Balsam-Tree* (Fig. 16), the fine linear quality derives from his effort to create a readable image. To Catesby, shading and perspective were artful devices that compromised the intelligibility of a nature study: "Things done in a Flat, tho' exact manner, may serve the Purpose of Natural History, better in some Measure, than in a more bold and Painter-like Way."[32] As a result of this "flat, tho' exact manner," Catesby's plant drawings, while they lack many of the structural parts necessary to later systems of classification, can be easily identified by modern botanists.

Catesby's drawing of *Magnolia Buds* (Fig. 71) indicates the procedure he carefully followed to achieve an accurate and graceful finished composition. He began with minute investigations of the plant, then went through many stages of elaboration and compositional refinement. The *Magnolia Buds* may have been based upon specimens sent to England by John Bartram, the first native American botanist.[33] Catesby obviously preferred to rely on his own observations, but he counted on Bartram's descriptions and specimens to fill in the gaps. This connection is important for the history of the flower genre in America, for it shows how the passion of European explorers like Catesby and their patrons encouraged the colonists of the New World to study and draw the natural phenomena around them.

John Bartram, a Pennsylvania farmer, was a self-taught botanist who became an active and respected member of the international community of scientists in the eighteenth century. He served as host to the botanical explorer Peter Kalm, one of the favored students of Carl Linnaeus.[34] Through his acquaintance with Kalm, Bartram entered into direct correspondence with Linnaeus, the Swedish scientist whose sexual system of plant taxonomy revolutionized eighteenth-century botany.

16. MARK CATESBY. *The Balsam-Tree,* in *The Natural History of Carolina, Florida and the Bahama Islands,* 1731–43. Hand-colored engraving: image, 13½ × 10⅛ inches (34.3 × 25.7 cm); page, 22 × 15¼ inches (55.9 × 38.7 cm). Department of Library Services, The American Museum of Natural History, New York.

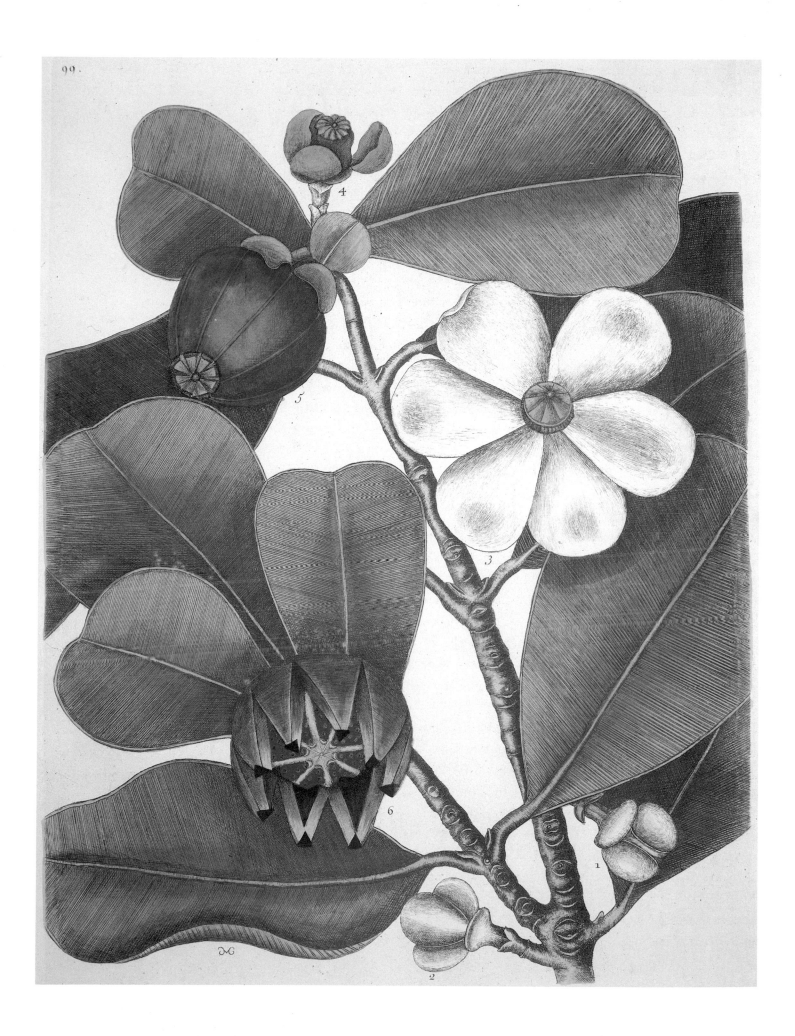

Bartram received an annual stipend from an ardent English horticulturist, Peter Collinson, to observe, write descriptions, and ship specimens of interesting New World plants, many of which were plucked from Bartram's own garden (Fig. 17). Collinson was quick to note the inadequacy of verbal descriptions and even dried cuttings in conveying the lifelike quality of a flower. Catesby would try to make drawings from the specimens and color notes that Bartram sent to Collinson; but problems of fading color and the distorted shape of the dried plant soon frustrated both artist and patron. On one occasion, Collinson wrote to Bartram: "Catesby has a mind to figure the Laurel, or Chamaerhododendron, and by the fine specimens thee has sent, is pretty able to do it; but we are at a loss for the exact figure and shape of the flowers. Thee says it is of a pale red, or blush colour; but in thy last letter thee says they are studded with green spots. Now here we are at a loss again, so if thee can help us, pray do. Thee tells me that thee has a mind to draw or paint it, pray try. One single flower is sufficient, and some marks where the spots are. . . ."[35]

It was not John Bartram but his son William who had the inclination and the talent to fill the need for a colonial botanical artist. William Bartram, therefore, should be considered the first American flower painter. His achievements as a scientific draftsman and man of letters were recognized by the artist Charles Willson Peale. The distinguished Philadelphian painted Bartram's likeness in 1808 to add to the Peale portrait gallery of persons accomplished in public life, the arts, and science (Fig. 18). Bartram, the kindly and learned gentleman, poses with a sprig of white flowers (perhaps a *Jasminum officinale*, a southern vine) tucked inside his jacket.[36] Such a sprig, Peale recognized, would be the proper attribute for a botanist.

William Bartram always aspired to make "accurate drawings [of flowers] from living flourishing subjects." His patron Collinson could have been describing Bartram's magnificent watercolor drawing of the *Franklinia alatamaha* (Fig. 19) when he wrote to Bartram with admiration: "When art is arrived to such perfection to copy close after nature, who can describe the pleasure, but them that feel it. . . ."[37]

The ambition to create a truthful copy after nature, as well as an image of graceful design, clearly inspires the *Franklinia* (a species discovered in the New World by Bartram himself). Unlike Catesby, Bartram included detailed studies of the reproductive organs of the plant, made visible by a direct frontal view. At the bottom of the page, enlarged illustrations of these sexual parts flank the stem. Bartram rendered the leaves to reveal their intricate patterns of venation, including those on the undersides. It is with drawings such as the *Franklinia* that Linnaean botanical theory makes its first appearance in the New World.

Linnaeus believed that "the foundation of botany consists of the division of plants and systematic name-giving,"[38] and he devised a method of taxonomy

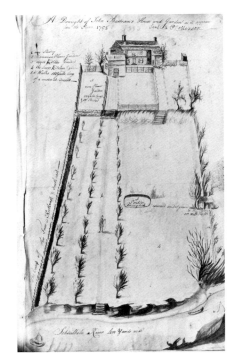

17. JOHN OR WILLIAM BARTRAM. *A Draught of John Bartram's House and Garden as It Appears from the River,* 1758. Ink and pencil on paper, 16½ × 10¼ inches (41.9 × 26 cm). Library of the Earl of Derby's Estate, Prescot, Lancashire, England; Peter Collinson Collection.

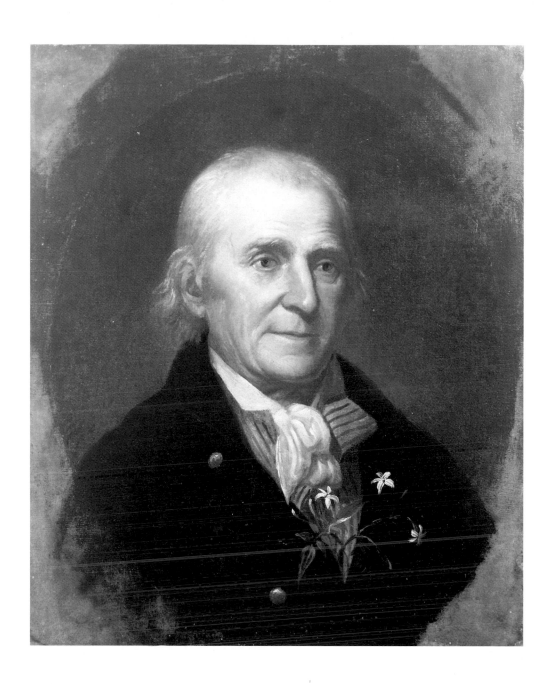

18. Charles Willson Peale.
William Bartram, 1808. Oil on paper,
23¼ × 19¼ inches (59.1 × 48.9 cm).
Independence National Historical Park
Collection, Philadelphia.

called the "sexual system" to establish such a foundation. He designated the reproductive organs of the plant as the essential parts for classification purposes, with leaf veining one of the secondary characteristics. The small scale of these parts required an artist like Bartram not only to work with a "living flourishing" specimen but also to make a close-up study of its structure.

The Linnaean system of plant classification promoted an intimate approach to the vegetable kingdom which imbued flower drawings with a new naturalism. In Bartram's *Franklinia*, the leaves curve gracefully as if bending in response to some gentle wind, and the jagged contour of the cut stem records the plucking of the specimen from its support. William Bartram saw the flowering franklinia tree for the first time in 1765 on an exploratory trip with his father through

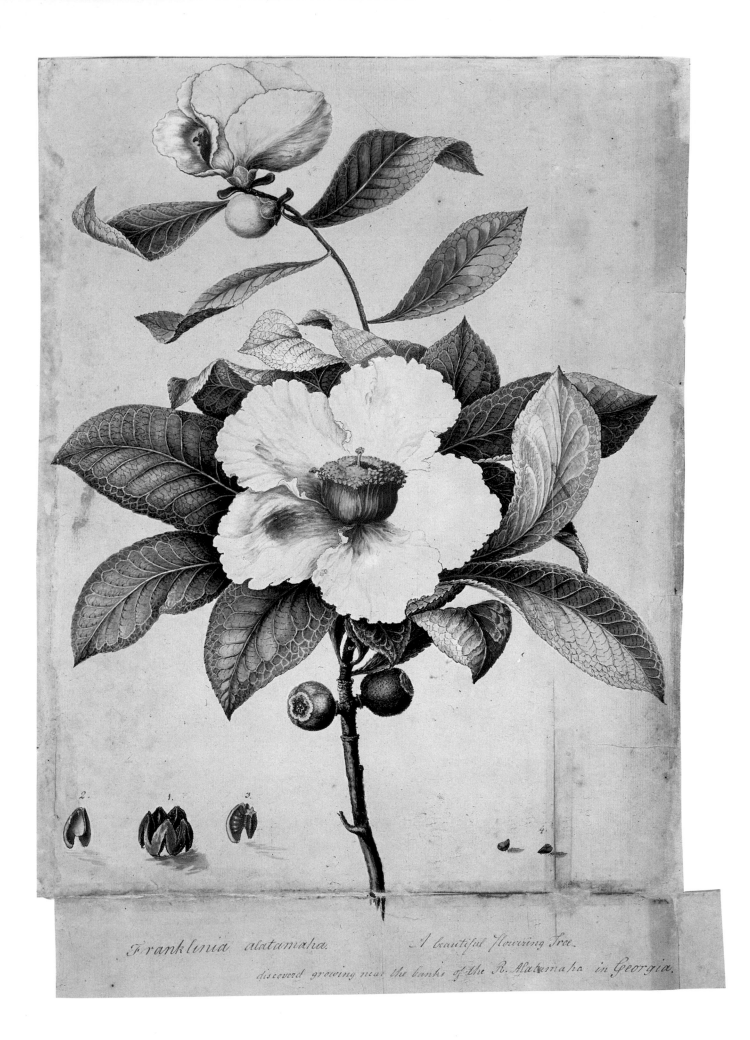

Franklinia alatamaha.   *A beautiful flowering Tree.*

discovered growing near the banks of the R. Alatamaha in Georgia.

Georgia, and he described his thrill at the discovery of "two beautiful shrubs in all their blooming graces." From the seeds and cuttings collected on this trip, the Bartrams were able to bring the franklinia into cultivation in their Philadelphia garden several years later.[39]

While having a specimen of the franklinia at his doorstep offered William Bartram the opportunity for close taxonomic scrutiny, the informal lifelike rendering of his drawing reflects the botanical artist's belief in the vitality of the plant world. For him plants were not just inanimate objects suitable for documentary record, but "vegetable beings endued [sic] with sensible faculties." Hence his *Franklinia alatamaha* is no longer a still-life portrait of a plant in an erect, fixed posture, like John White's *Sabatia stellaris*, but, as Bartram described all plants, the representation of an "organical, living, and self-moving body."

Another remarkable drawing from the portfolio of William Bartram confirms the artist's exceptionally naturalistic approach to the plant world within the scientific view of his day. A *Drawing of the Round Leafed Nymphaea as Flowering. Colocasia* (Fig. 20) displays the graceful forms of the American lotus plant in company with other specimens of flora and fauna in an aquatic setting. Bartram's sense of the energetic movement of natural forms emerges in the bending contours of the lotus leaves and in the position of the bird at the lower left, his leg poised in readiness for the next step forward.

A closer look at Bartram's *Nymphaea* reveals that the presentation of this image conforms to a Linnaean attitude toward nature well known to the American botanist.[40] The flowers and leaves of the American lotus that Bartram identified as a nymphaea dominate the composition. They are depicted from different vantage points and in various stages of maturity—a visual summary of the plant's form and development. But the lower-left corner of the drawing contains a small vignette set against the fanlike contours of a lotus leaf. The bird (probably a great blue heron), Venus's-flytrap, and wild sunflower in this section are disproportionately small in relation to the looming forms of the lotus plants. This sharp shift in scale visually dissociates the vignette from the rest of the picture. Indeed, these specimens were not found in precisely the same locale as the nymphaea, but they are shown together as representative samples of the flora and fauna of the southeastern states, where Bartram traveled on a documentary tour.[41] Such an unnatural juxtaposition of species was not, as in seventeenth-century Dutch flower pieces, a symbolic offering of national abundance, nor simply an effort to convey information no matter how disparate. Rather, Bartram's presentation accords, on a philosophical level, with the Linnaean view of nature.

Linnaeus perceived nature as a static and perfect organization of separate facts, conceived by God at Creation and continuing without change into eter-

19. WILLIAM BARTRAM. *Franklinia alatamaha*, 1788. Watercolor on paper, 14⅜ × 11 inches (36.5 × 27.9 cm). The Trustees of the British Museum (Natural History), London; Fothergill Album.

Tab. I.

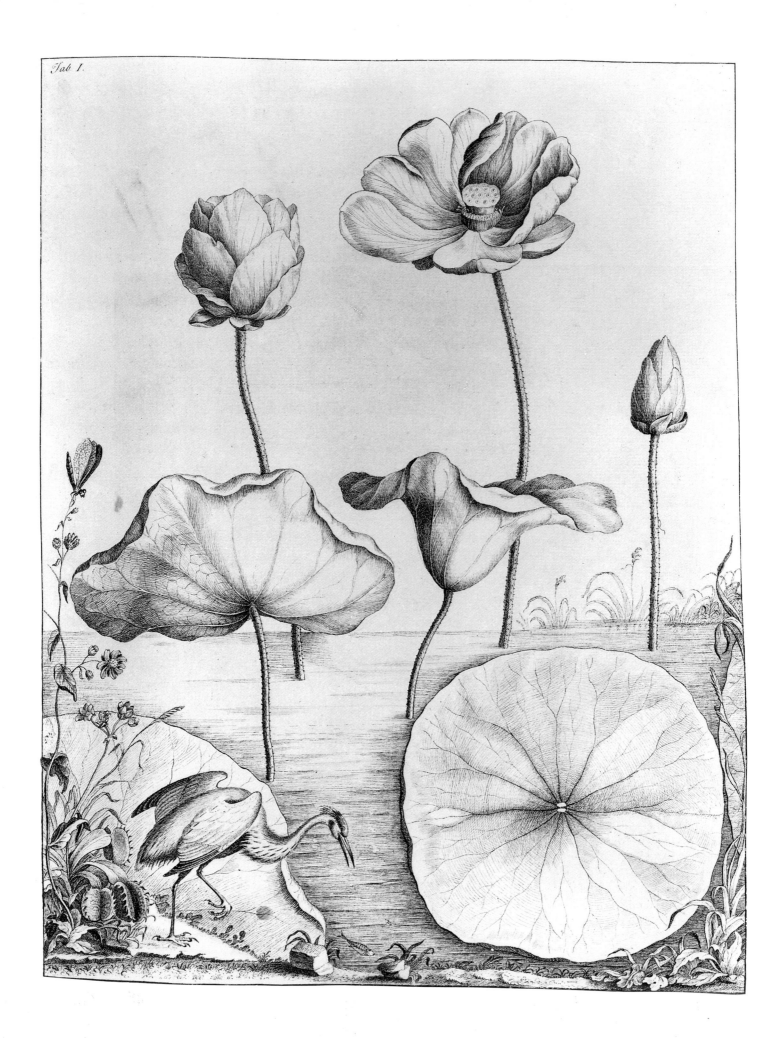

nity. Each natural form was a module of divine creation through its projection of individual beauty and perfection. The world was divided into fixed categories—the mineral, vegetable, and animal kingdoms—whose diverse members were also unchanging. The Linnaean practice of botany, therefore, depended upon observing plants closely in order to distinguish the essential structural parts—that is, the reproductive organs and leaf venations—which related similar plants and divided dissimilar ones.

It was the diversity of nature and the immutable perfection of its parts that revealed God's presence. In this perception of the world order, organic relationships among specimens were immaterial; thus Bartram was free to join the lotus and Venus's-flytrap in a single setting. Each flower, its stamens and pistils clearly visible, is a beautifully fashioned representative of its separate species, of the divine and absolute organization of the kingdoms of nature. Peter Collinson had no difficulty praising Bartram for achieving "such perfection" in his ability "to copy close after nature."[42]

NINETEENTH-CENTURY IMAGES AND ATTITUDES

The static Linnaean world view would continue to dominate the scientific and philosophical approach to nature—and to the flower genre—until after the mid-nineteenth century. But in the meantime the American victory in the Revolutionary War brought a new impetus to the pursuit of flower painting. Americans began to study natural history with enthusiasm, as the rich landscape of the United States became a source of pride to the newly independent nation. Thomas Jefferson articulated the potential of natural history for fostering a confident national self-image. "What a field have we at our doors to signalize ourselves in. The botany of America is far from being exhausted, its mineralogy is untouched, and its Natural History or zoölogy totally mistaken and misrepresented," he exclaimed in 1789 to Dr. Joseph Willard, president of Harvard College. "It is for such institutions as that over which you preside so worthily, sir, to do justice to our country, its productions, and its genius."[43] Once again, as in seventeenth-century Holland, flora were destined to serve a national purpose. Artist-naturalists such as John James Audubon, George Catlin, Titian Ramsay Peale, and Isaac Sprague (Figs. 77–80) would respond with eagerness and talent to the echoes of Jefferson's call.

By the early nineteenth century, professional artists were entering the domain of flower painting, so that the genre was no longer restricted to botanical studies. But the influence of science had taken hold in the realm of art, even in the genres of portraiture and still life, where flowers had traditionally appeared as accessories or decorative elements.

20. WILLIAM BARTRAM. *A Drawing of the Round Leafed Nymphaea as Flowering.* Colocasia (American lotus), 1761–62. Pencil on paper, 15¼ × 9⅝ inches (38.7 × 24.4 cm). The Trustees of the British Museum (Natural History), London; Fothergill Album.

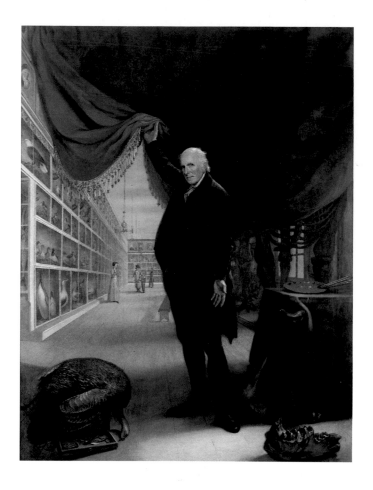

It is not surprising to find such a confluence of science and art in the artistic production of Charles Willson Peale's sons. Their father, after all, had opened a museum in Philadelphia in 1784 to exhibit the wonders of nature and of art. A visitor to Peale's Museum would be invited by his entrance ticket to study and enjoy its collections, "containing the Wonderful Works of Nature and Curious Works of Art."[44] Charles Willson Peale extends the same invitation to the viewer in his self-portrait of 1822 entitled *The Artist in His Museum* (Fig. 21). He lifts the curtain to expose his theater of nature, with its cast of reconstructed skeletal discoveries of extinct species, as well as stuffed birds, and animals performing in wall cabinets with painted backdrops; surmounting these displays is his collection of portraits of distinguished Americans, the leading actors of the animal species.

Two of Charles Willson Peale's sons, Rembrandt and Rubens Peale, learned their lessons particularly well. Rembrandt Peale painted a remarkable portrait of his brother, *Rubens Peale with a Geranium* (Fig. 22), in 1801, just before they went together to Europe to exhibit their father's recent scientific discoveries. Rubens poses with a geranium plant, although the relationship might well be stated the other way around. The geranium is not a conventional accessory in this portrait; it commands an equal, if not dominant, status in the composition.

21. Charles Willson Peale. The Artist in His Museum, 1822. Oil on canvas, 103½ × 80 inches (262.9 × 203.2 cm). Pennsylvania Academy of the Fine Arts, Philadelphia; Joseph and Sarah Harrison Collection.

22. Rembrandt Peale. Rubens Peale with a Geranium, 1801. Oil on canvas, 28 × 24 inches (71.1 × 61 cm). Private collection.

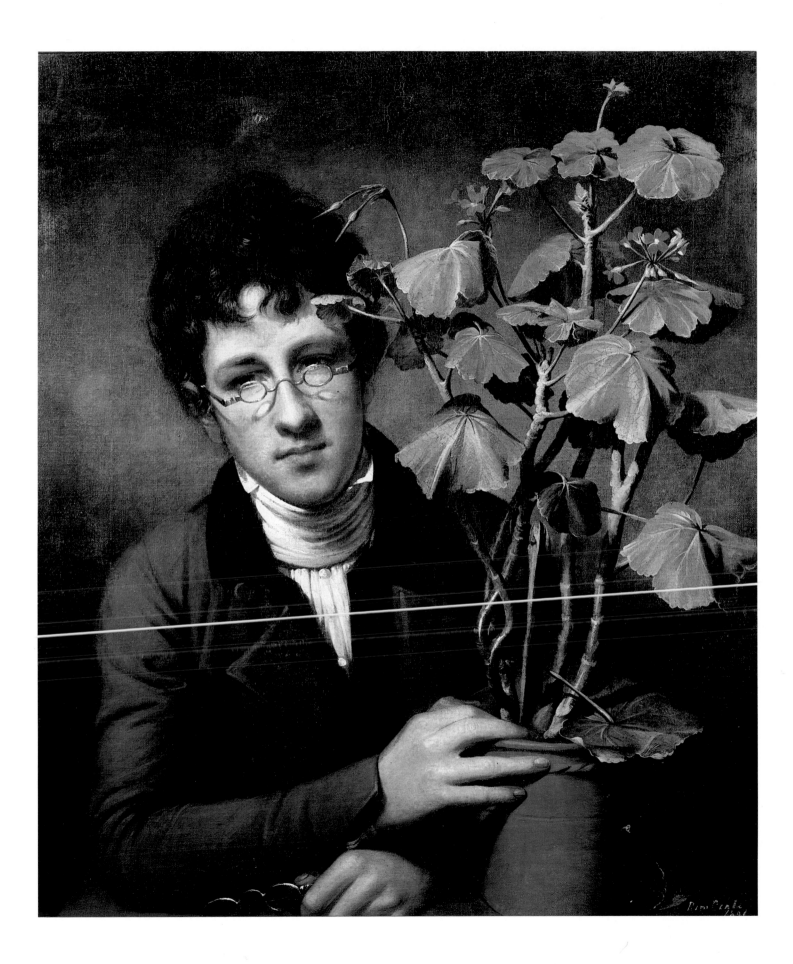

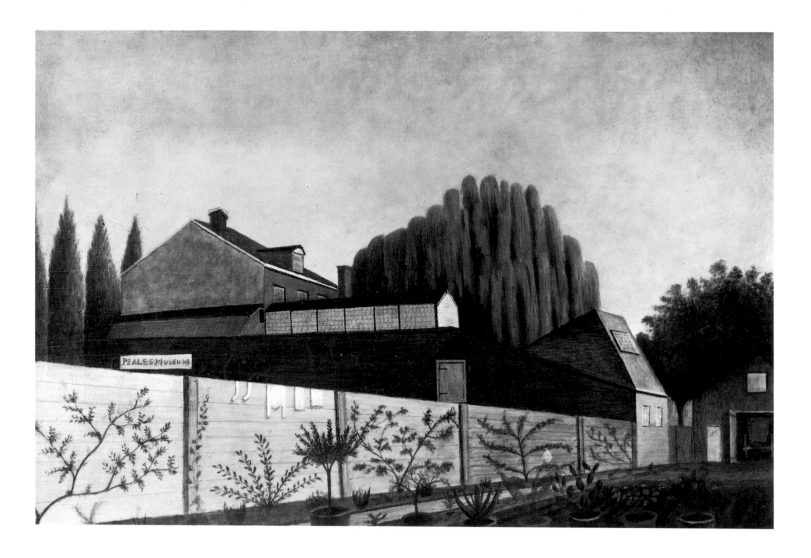

Rubens, who was handicapped by his weak eyes, as his two pairs of spectacles indicate, was the botanist in the family. He cultivated a small garden of exotic plants, mostly seeded with specimens sent from distant lands to Peale's Museum. Some of these decorative botanical wonders grace the wall of *The Old Museum* (Fig. 23). In Rembrandt's portrait, Rubens clearly displays his plant with pride and affection, allowing its umbrella-like leaves to brush across his forehead and placing a firm hand on the pot as he presents its best aspect to the viewer. The now ubiquitous geranium, a species native to South Africa, was considered something of a rarity in Peale's time (Jefferson had it on his list of desired specimens in 1786).[45] This multiblossomed specimen with verdant unmottled leaves and thick waxy stems is a healthy testimony to Rubens Peale's green thumb. (Later nineteenth-century American artists such as Maria Oakey Dewing and George Cochran Lambdin would represent whole gardens; in part, this was out of pride in their own horticultural success [Fig. 45].) Moreover, the close-up view of the leaves, their varied dispositions, and the revelation of all the flower's parts places this still-life composition firmly within the Linnaean concept of nature. The plant may serve as an attribute, but the rendering of its structural and textural peculiarities enables it to be fixed into its species according to the sexual system.

Nineteenth-century artists and critics frequently regarded art as the handmaiden of science in the revelation of both the factual and spiritual truths of nature.[46] They believed that a profound knowledge of the precise and measurable facts of the external world and their accurate depiction could illuminate the secretive truths of the natural world. "Material objects fashioned by the artist's hand," wrote the critic James Jackson Jarves, "become eloquent only as the feeling which dictated them is found to be impregnated with, and expressive of, the truths of science."[47] Jarves published these ideas in 1864 but he spoke, in a sense, for the whole nineteenth century. He warned artists not to indulge too much in flights of creative fancy because they risked self-indulgent falsehood by deviating too far from the truth of nature. Acknowledging that "art should partake of the character of inspiration, free, earnest, and high-toned," Jarves nonetheless felt that it should never neglect "a scientific correctness in every particular," by which it could, "as a unity, be expressive of the general principle at its centre of being."[48]

Throughout the first half of the nineteenth century, the scientific principle of nature which art revealed remained that perceived by Linnaeus. Flower painters, botanists, and artist-naturalists continued to depict nature according to his system of classification, believing that the system expressed a divinely created structure, a manifestation of God's presence. In the writings of nineteenth-century American writers and philosophers, we find literary equivalents to Linnaeus' scientific-spiritual approach to nature. The importance of documenting the specific in search of a universal divine plan nourished Ralph Waldo Emerson's transcendentalist philosophy. He warned against dismissing facts as "dull, strange, despised things," as people were so often wont to do. Remember, he said, that such seemingly limited facts can be transformed into transcendent vehicles, if we could only recognize that "the day of facts is a rock of diamonds; that a fact is an Epiphany of God."[49] "Nature is the symbol of spirit," Emerson concluded, and therefore the painter of flowers, whether in the still-life or landscape genre, took on a reverential as well as documentary task in selecting these "gems of Nature" as subjects for his art.[50]

In the development of nineteenth-century aesthetics, attitudes such as Emerson's came under the heading "truth to nature," a concept more than a term, expressed in a variety of ways in the critical literature of the period. The concept implied more than just an accurate portrait of the physical properties of the flower or landscape setting. It suggested that carefully observed physical phenomena, filtered through the moral and aesthetic mesh of artistic judgment, could reveal fundamental truths. In the attempt to illuminate the natural uni-

23. RUBENS PEALE. *The Old Museum*, c. 1858–60. Oil on tin, 15 × 21 inches (38.1 × 53.3 cm). Pennsylvania Academy of the Fine Arts, Philadelphia; Bequest of Charles Coleman Sellers.

verse through an image of flowers that was "true to nature," the flower painter was guided, sometimes unconsciously, by contemporary scientific attitudes about the character and function of nature.

The notion of flowers as both physical and spiritual facts surfaces frequently in the popular literature of nineteenth-century America. *Godey's Lady's Book* often included illustrations of stylish mid-nineteenth-century bouquets (Fig. 24).[51] The January 1850 issue featured an article entitled "Flowers" by the art critic Henry T. Tuckerman in which he described a simple momentary experience that led him to profound considerations. After spying a vase of flowers decorating a communion table during a church service, Tuckerman began to muse about these natural wonders, which "spoke of nature, of beauty, of truth, more eloquently than the service." "In observing the relation of flower to life and character," he continued, "I have often been tempted to believe . . . that inscriptions of wisdom covered their leaves, and that each petal, stamen, and leaf, was the divining rod or scroll that held an invisible truth."[52] Tuckerman perceived flowers in two ways: first, as facts of nature, to be analyzed according to their position in the scientific classification of nature; and second, as symbolic carriers of human sentiment. It was a source of regret for him that flowers were generally perceived either "through the microscopic lens of mere curiosity, or according to the fanciful and hackneyed alphabet [of] Floral Dictionaries." He felt that more profound truths could be gained from the contemplation of flowers.

Since flowers were seen to have a dual nature, the natural scientist who sought to understand their physical structure and the artist who endeavored to capture their symbolic beauty were joined in a single goal: the spiritual comprehension of natural perfection. In their unchanging perfection of design and God-given beauty, flowers were facts of nature that held out moral and spiritual rewards to those who sought to understand and display them.[53]

Some important aesthetic and scientific attitudes toward floral grouping emerge in a small flower piece by the little-known artist John E. Hollen (Fig. 25). Hollen's *Bouquet in Vase* was not copied from nature but from an earlier published engraving of a *Bouquet of Flowers in a Vase* (Fig. 26) by the French artist Jean-Louis Prévost. Hollen relied on the French engraving for the selection and arrangement of flowers, the design of the vase, and the stemmed glass to the left of its base. However, he made certain additions and substitutions, which give his work a stamp of originality and associate it with naturalist and scientific trends.

Hollen added a number of flowers to Prévost's bouquet: some delicate long-stemmed specimens with light pastel blossoms, including sprigs of cornflowers, pinks, and red clover.[54] Significantly, Hollen plucked mostly common wild flowers, whereas the Prévost bouquet highlights the cultivated glories of hothouse lilies, roses, and possibly an anemone. Hollen's inclusion of ordinary field flowers

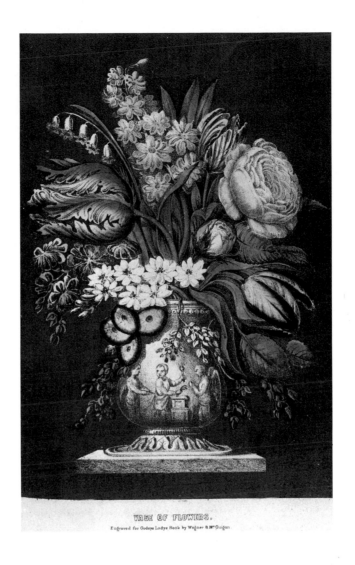

VASE OF FLOWERS.

Engraved for Godeys Ladys Book by Wagner & Mc Guigan

reflects a more personal and informal approach to nature that would become typical of flower painting in the middle and latter part of the nineteenth century. Ruskin despised cultivated flowers (see p. 48), and just as Henry David Thoreau could find meaning in the common surroundings of Walden Pond, so could Hollen find dignity in the wild flower.

Other substitutions in Hollen's composition indicate that scientific concerns often accompanied aesthetic ones in nineteenth-century flower painting. On the table support, Hollen replaced Prévost's jewelry and precious objects with shells and an insect. Most important, he added a book, complete with bookmark and an engraved title on the spine that reads: "Linne's Botanik." Presumably Hollen's grouping of shell, insect, and floral life celebrates the immutable, divinely created designs which characterize Linnaeus' kingdoms of the natural world.

A similar confluence of art and science can be found in the flower pieces of the German immigrant artist Severin Roesen.[55] Working, like Hollen, in the floral still-life format, Roesen relied upon those European compositional models

24. ANONYMOUS. Frontispiece to *Godey's Lady's Book*, 41 (November 1850). Hand-colored lithograph: image, 7¹⁵/₁₆ × 5½ inches (20.2 × 14 cm); page, 9⅞ × 5¾ inches (25.1 × 14.6 cm). The New-York Historical Society.

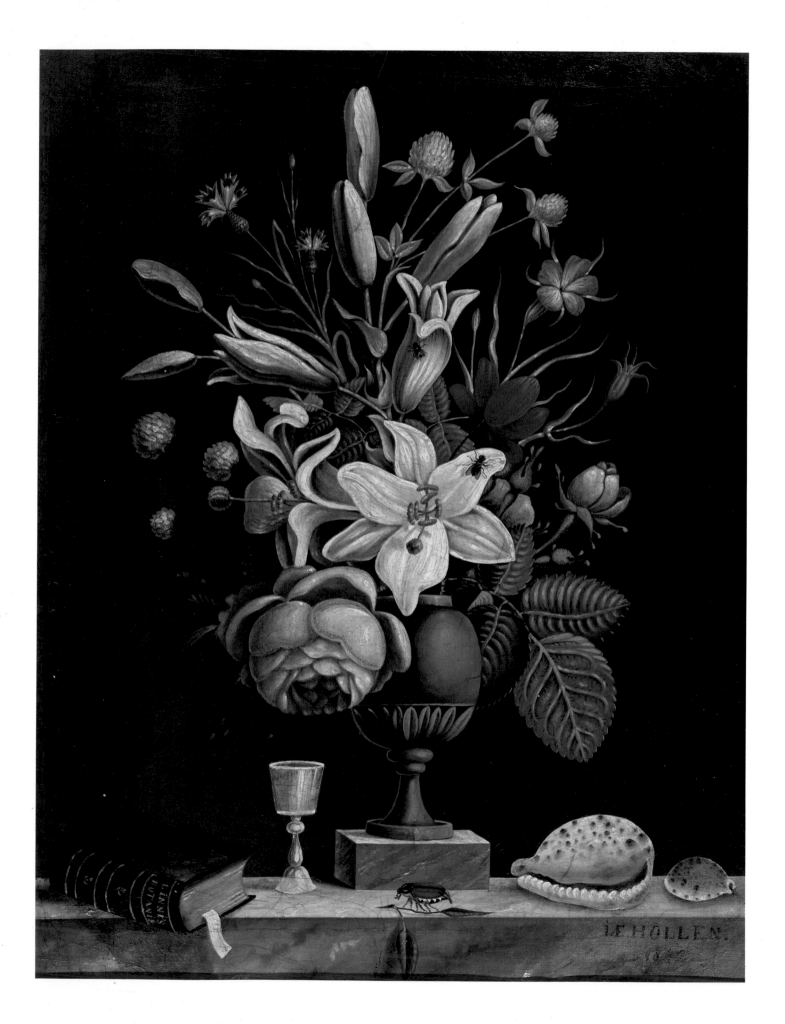

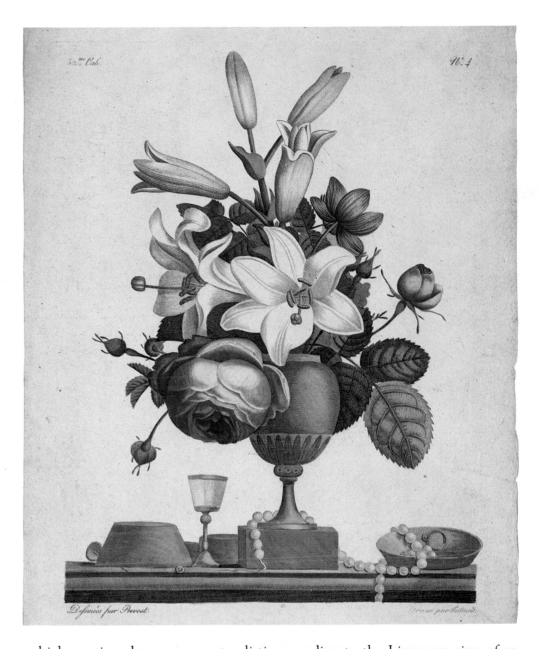

Desinées par Prevost.

Gravé par Teillard.

25. JOHN E. HOLLEN. *Bouquet in Vase*, c. 1842. Oil on canvas, 16½ × 12½ inches (41.9 × 31.8 cm). Hunt Institute for Botanical Documentation, Carnegie-Mellon University, Pittsburgh.

26. JEAN-LOUIS PRÉVOST. *Bouquet of Flowers in a Vase*, c. 1804. Hand-colored stipple engraving, 14⅛ × 9⅝ inches (35.9 × 24.4 cm). Hunt Institute for Botanical Documentation, Carnegie-Mellon University, Pittsburgh.

which continued to appear naturalistic according to the Linnaean view of organic life. The compositions that Roesen produced in America, such as *Victorian Bouquet* (Fig. 27), depend upon the seventeenth-century Dutch tradition of still-life painting and its nineteenth-century Düsseldorf School descendants.[56] The floral combinations in Roesen's *Victorian Bouquet*, as well as the compositional format, are clearly based on the example of earlier Dutch works like Paul Theodor van Brussel's *A Vase of Flowers* (Fig. 28). Both present bouquets that culminate at the top with brilliant red examples of a precious flower called crown imperial. The flowers shown together in Roesen's *Victorian Bouquet* did not bloom at the same time; they could never have been naturally assembled in one vase. The crown imperial blossoms in early spring, while the carnation and the dahlia do not come into flower until midsummer.[57] Nonetheless, con-

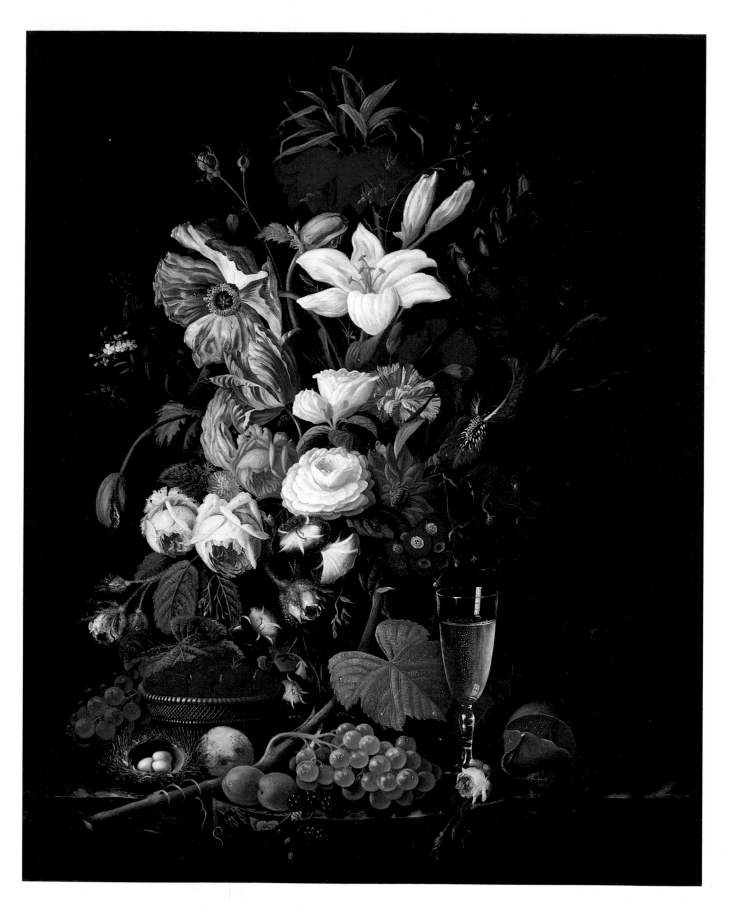

27. SEVERIN ROESEN. *Victorian Bouquet*, c. 1850–55. Oil on canvas, 36½ × 29 inches (92.7 × 73.7 cm). The Museum of Fine Arts, Houston; Museum Purchase, Agnes Cullen Arnold Endowment Fund.

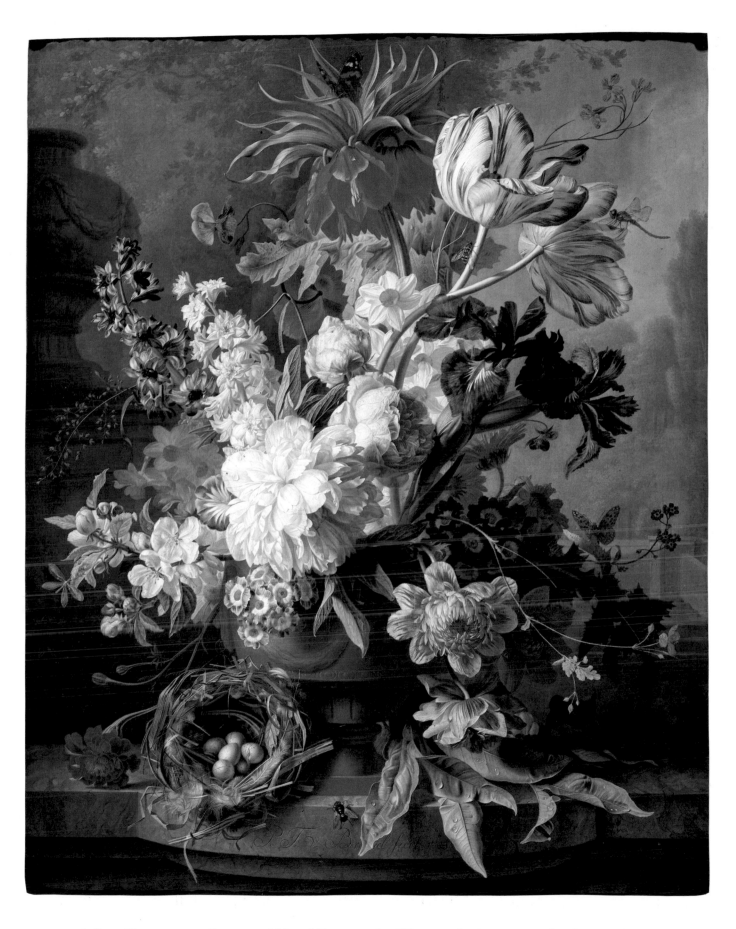

28. Paul Theodor van Brussel. *A Vase of Flowers*, 1783. Oil on panel, 28¼ × 22¼ inches (71.8 × 56.5 cm).
The Syndics of the Fitzwilliam Museum, Cambridge, England.

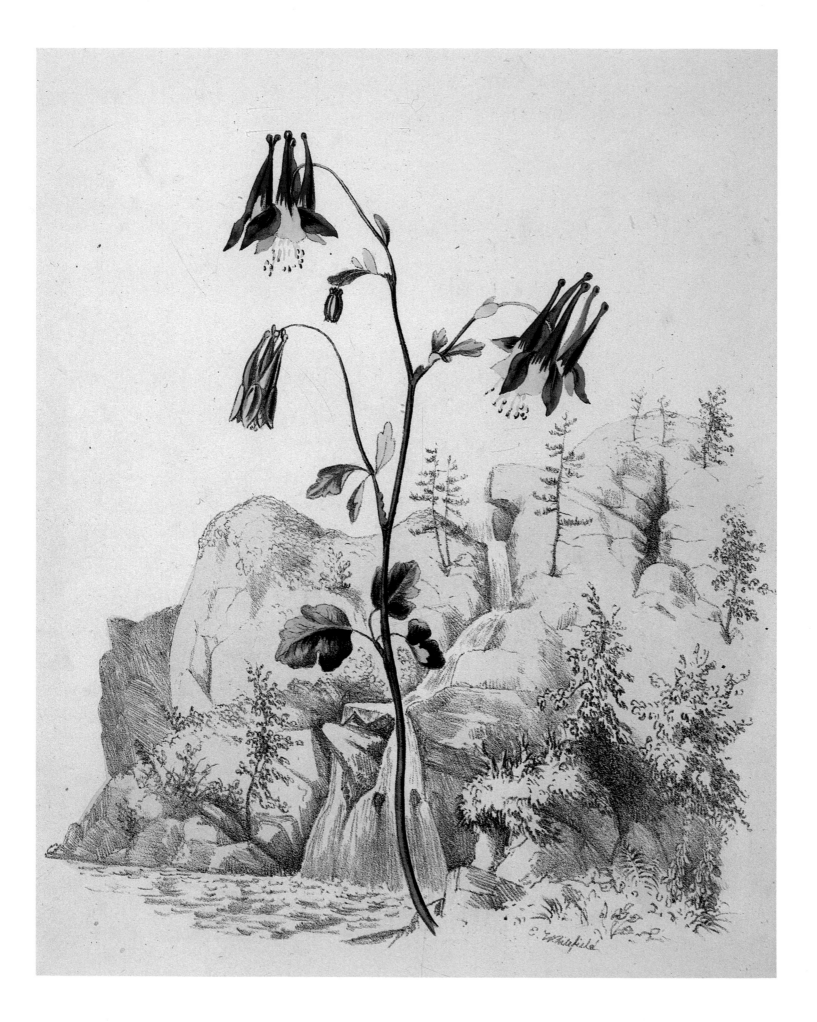

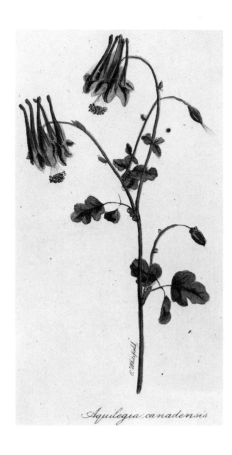

Aquilegia canadensis

temporaries admired these paintings because of what was discerned as their truth to nature. True to the Linnaean concept of universal order, they displayed specimens of divinely created species which were fixed from the moment of their design and remained unmodified by their environment.

Botanical illustrations in the popular literature of mid-nineteenth-century America project a similar view of nature as a composite of perfect but separate truths. Even in a botanical guidebook such as Emma Embury's *American Wild Flowers in Their Native Haunts* (1845), which included illustrations of flowers in landscape scenes, the Linnaean perspective remains dominant. An integrated view of nature as an environment for dynamic organic interaction was not the focus of pre-Darwinian America. Instead, the artist gave visual life to the individual splendors of nature. Emma Embury described wild flowers such as those Hollen included in his still-life bouquet as "the gems which God's own hand has scattered abroad in the wilderness." They should be studied with care and reverence, she said, for they embraced divine truths capable of bringing "to our souls those surprises of sudden joy which keep the heart forever awake to a blessedness like that of innocent childhood."[58]

Edwin Whitefield was responsible for the hand-colored lithographs which accompanied Embury's sentimental poems and prose pieces. Whitefield, an ardent collector of wild flowers, an accomplished gardener, and an award-winning painter, was well qualified for the project. His goal as a flower artist was to project a truthful image of each specimen and its habitat. The descriptive statement on the title page of *American Wild Flowers* notes that the illustrations were "carefully colored after nature and [rendered] from drawings [made] on the spot."[59]

In one of his drawings, *Wild Columbine—View of Matanga Fall* (Fig. 29), Whitefield features a sprig of columbine unnaturally looming over a scenic Pennsylvania waterfall. In addition to the odd juxtaposition of scale, the columbine is further dislocated from its setting by its vivid color, which stands in contrast to the pale blue wash that barely tints the black-and-white background. Whitefield made another drawing of a columbine for a medical text on botany (Fig. 30) and we can see that it is virtually the same image of the flower. Clearly, Whitefield worked from a set of accurate sketches of flowers, each carefully copied from a live specimen, and inserted them in various compositions with little modification. Even when he grafted them onto topographical landscape views, like Matanga Fall, he saw no more reason to integrate the components than had William Bartram almost a century earlier (Fig. 20).[60]

29. EDWIN WHITEFIELD. *Wild Columbine—View of Matanga Fall*, 1845, in Emma Embury, *American Wild Flowers in Their Native Haunts*, 1845. Hand-colored lithograph, 9½ × 7¼ inches (24.1 × 18.4 cm). The New York Public Library, Astor, Lenox and Tilden Foundations.

30. EDWIN WHITEFIELD. *Aquilegia canadensis* (columbine), 1846, in Asa B. Strong, *The American Flora; or, History of Plants and Wild Flowers*, 1846–50. Hand-colored lithograph, 9½ × 6⅝ inches (24.1 × 16.8 cm). The New York Public Library, Astor, Lenox and Tilden Foundations.

WHAT ENGAGED ARTISTS from about 1850 on was the representation of flowers, often wild flowers, in naturalistic outdoor environments. In this pursuit, Amer-

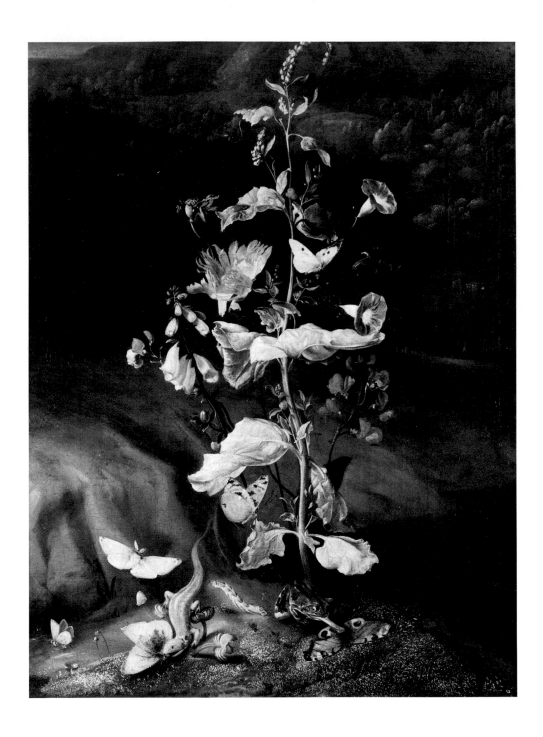

ican artists departed significantly from their European predecessors, who, as early as the seventeenth century, had been painting flowers in outdoor settings.

The Dutch artist Otto Marseus van Schriek, for example, produced a remarkable group of outdoor compositions. In *Still Life with Flowers* (Fig. 31), he depicts a flowering marsh plant growing from a mossy ground beside a low bank with a background view of trees. The plant is entwined with poppies, convolvulus, and foxglove; lizards, toads, and moths converge on it. Van Schriek had a garden of botanical specimens and was an avid collector of live reptiles, but

31. Otto Marseus van Schriek. *Still Life with Flowers*, n.d. Oil on canvas, 27⅛ × 21 inches (18.9 × 53.3 cm). Collection of the Honourable Henry Rogers Broughton, Fitzwilliam Museum, Cambridge, England.

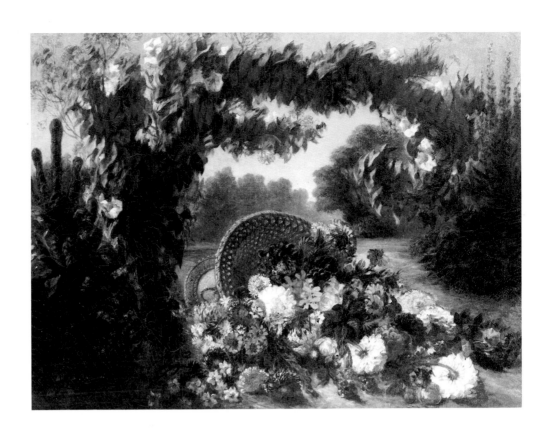

these apparently scientific images of nature contain hidden symbolic associations.[61] More decorative images of flowers in a landscape setting can be found in the painting of a *Basket of Flowers Overturned in a Park* (Fig. 32) by Eugène Delacroix. A rich bouquet of flowers spills from an overturned basket toward the viewer at center stage of a verdant landscape. A tree in the left foreground of the composition, and its overhanging branches, frame a view into the distant landscape on the right, creating an elegant and artful view of nature. Delacroix's letters confirm that his dominant concern in paintings like *Basket of Flowers* was formal arrangement rather than natural veracity: "I have subordinated the details to the ensemble as much as possible," he wrote; and, "I have tried to do some pieces of nature as they appear in gardens, only bringing together within the same frame and in a somewhat plausible manner the greatest possible variety of flowers."[62]

In contrast to van Schriek's symbolic presentation or Delacroix's cultivated formalism, American artists after mid-century began to display their flowers in natural settings. Moreover, they took a special interest in wild flowers. To Emma Embury, wild flowers had been "the gems [of] God's own hand"; but her illustrator, Edwin Whitefield, set them against artificially scaled and colored backgrounds (Fig. 29). Not so in the later watercolors of John William Hill and Henry Roderick Newman, where the contrivances of Whitefield's compositions disappear in favor of close-up, naturally integrated views (Figs. 33, 34). In *Bird's Nest and Dogroses* and *Wild Flowers*, the artists seem to delight in, if not revere,

32. EUGÈNE DELACROIX. *Basket of Flowers Overturned in a Park*, c. 1848–49. Oil on canvas, 41¼ × 56 inches (104.8 × 142.2 cm). The Metropolitan Museum of Art, New York; Bequest of Miss Adelaide Milton de Groot.

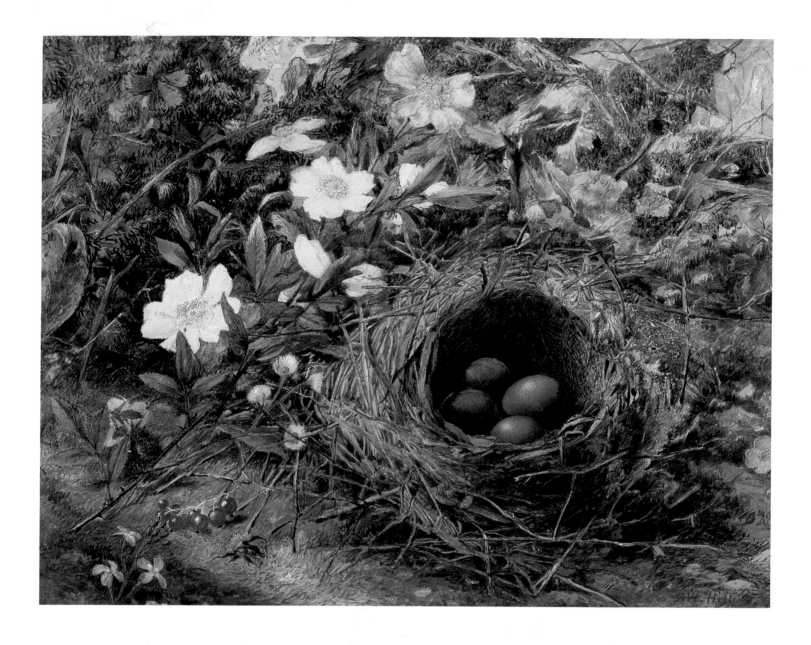

nature's small but exquisite floral gems. They may have found encouragement for their myopic perspectives in the writings of Thoreau, who asserted that nature, being perfect in its smallest details, "will bear the closest inspection." Such images of wild flowers in outdoor settings also reflect the aesthetic treatises of John Ruskin, which were widely available on this side of the Atlantic, and between 1855 and 1865 were enthusiastically promoted in two periodicals, *The Crayon* and *The New Path*.[63]

Ruskin was an ardent advocate of nature study, although he was fully aware of the difficulty of the task. He directed young artists to approach nature with an open heart, "rejecting nothing, selecting nothing, and scorning nothing."[64] With such freedom of spirit, the artist could discover the inherent aesthetic

33. JOHN WILLIAM HILL. *Bird's Nest and Dogroses,* 1867. Watercolor on paper, 10¾ × 13⅞ inches (27.3 × 35.2 cm). The New-York Historical Society.

34. HENRY RODERICK NEWMAN. *Wild Flowers,* 1885. Watercolor on paper, 15 × 10 inches (38.1 × 25.4 cm). Museum of Fine Arts, Boston; Ross Collection.

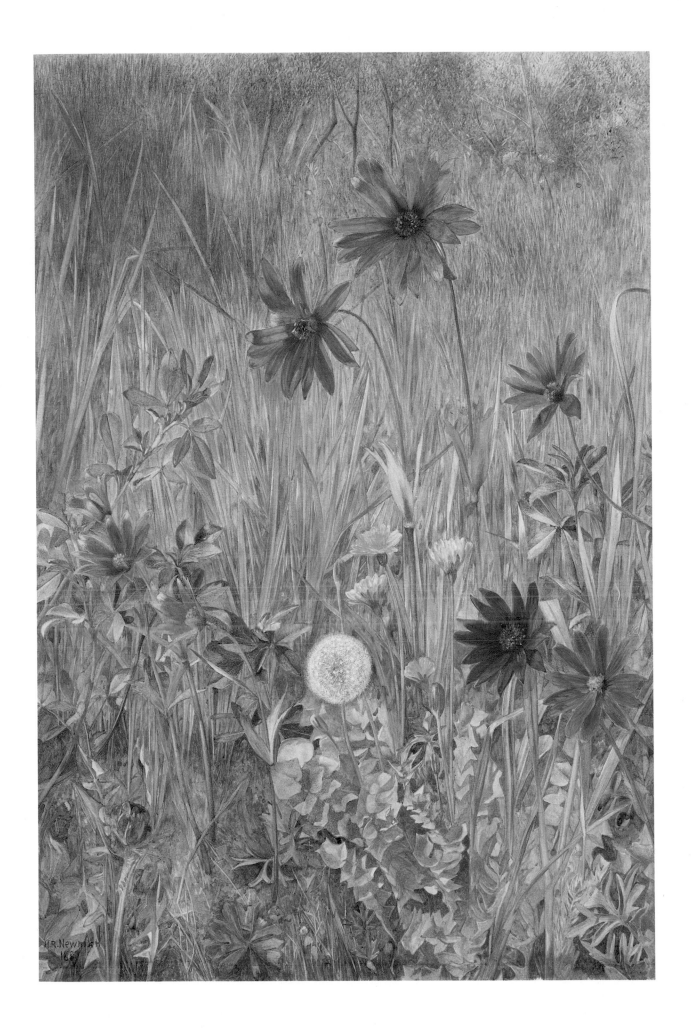

order of nature in her least conspicuous details. For Ruskin, truth to nature could be found much more readily in wild flowers than in cultivated specimens. The wild flower retained a truth, a purity, and an innocence because it had not been spoiled by human interference.[65] To cultivated flowers, Ruskin gave the derogatory title "florist's flowers." He detested them not only as subjects for art but as varieties to be included in gardens. "A flower-garden is an ugly thing, even when best managed," he wrote. "It is an assembly of unfortunate beings, pampered and bloated above their natural size, stewed and heated into diseased growth; corrupted by evil communication into speckled and inharmonious colours; torn from the soil which they loved, and of which they were the spirit and the glory, to glare away their term of tormented life among the mixed and incongruous essences of each other, in earth that they know not, and in air that is poison to them."[66]

Ruskin encouraged artists to capture his beloved wild flowers in their proper natural settings: "A flower is to be watched as it grows, in its association with the earth, the air, and the dew," he declared. "Its leaves are to be seen as they expand in the sunshine; its colours, as they embroider the field, or illumine the forest."[67]

That John William Hill was strongly influenced by the Ruskinian point of view is evident in *Bird's Nest and Dogroses* (Fig. 33), both in the selection of floral specimens and in their arrangement. The painting presents a close-up, informal assembly of wild flowers, including the very uncommon beauty of the common wild rose, of daisies, and yellow buttercups. Followers of Ruskin's aesthetic, however, were not always rigorous in their representation of flowers actually *growing* outdoors. In Hill's painting, the roses and the daisies are plucked specimens—as is apparent from their broken stems—which the artist has placed in a carefully "casual" arrangement around the bird's nest.

Images of flowers against background settings also appear in the sketches of nineteenth-century landscape artists. Frederic E. Church, for example, traveled great distances to gather visual bouquets of extraordinary floral specimens.[68] He produced some of his most exquisite plant drawings, such as *Cardamun* (wild ginger; Fig. 35), on a trip to Jamaica in 1865. Church shows the voluptuous lavender blossom of this exotic flower firmly rooted in the deep green foliage of its native tropical setting. The vitality of the flower strongly suggests that the *Cardamun* was meticulously copied from a live specimen in its natural surroundings.

In his own day Church was praised for his attention to the small wonders of nature and for capturing their lifelike forms with such precision. After all, in 1865 very few Americans had the opportunity to travel to the Caribbean, and Church's realism had welcome documentary value. It pleased Henry Tuckerman that Church not only chose to study "the general features of nature," such as

35. FREDERIC E. CHURCH. *Cardamun* (wild ginger), 1865. Oil and pencil on cardboard, 11 × 8½ inches (27.9 × 21.6 cm). Cooper-Hewitt Museum, The Smithsonian Institution's National Museum of Design, New York.

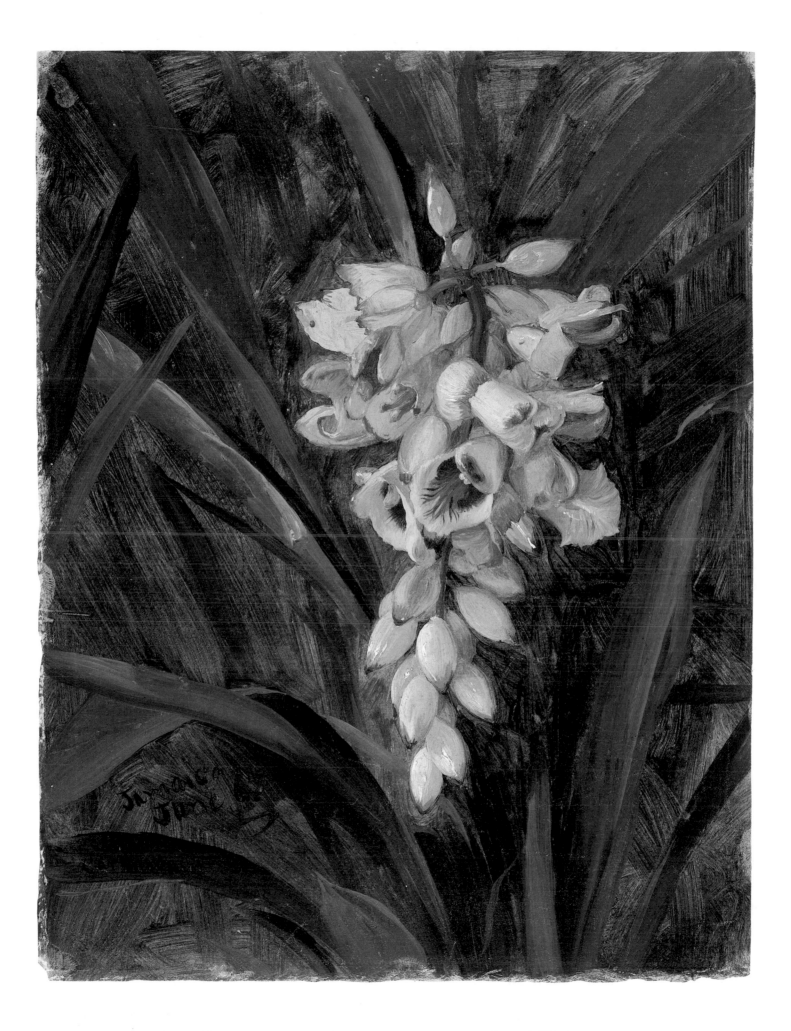

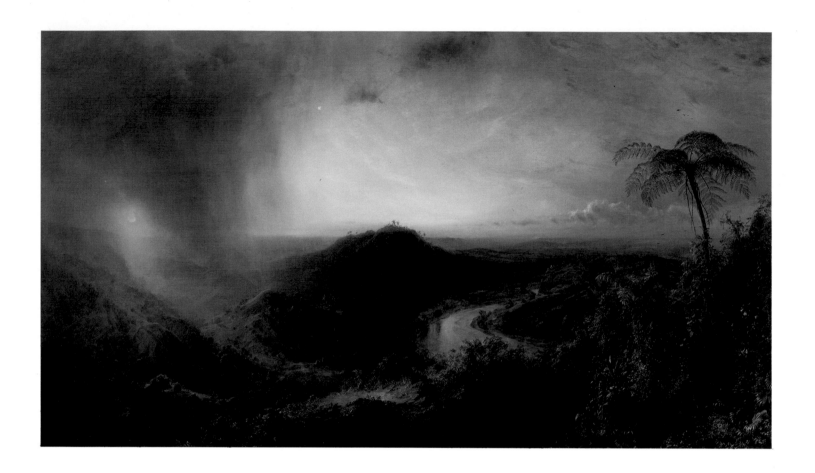

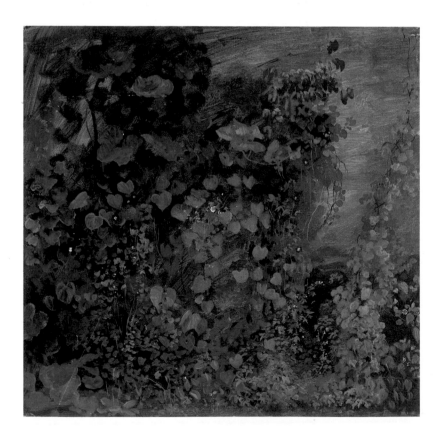

36. Frederic E. Church. *The Vale of St. Thomas, Jamaica*, 1867. Oil on canvas, 48 × 55 inches (121.9 × 139.7 cm). Wadsworth Atheneum, Hartford.

37. Frederic E. Church. *Philodendron Vines, Jamaica*, 1865. Oil on paperboard, 11⅞ × 12¼ inches (30.2 × 31.1 cm). Cooper-Hewitt Museum, The Smithsonian Institution's National Museum of Design, New York.

panoramic sunsets, mountain contours, and coastlines, but that he cared to delineate "minute and elaborate studies of vegetation—the palms, ferns, cane-brakes, flowers, grasses, and lizards; in a word, all the materials of a tropical insular landscape, with every local trait carefully noted." However, for all his admiration, Tuckerman saw the oil sketches merely as source "material" for works of art. "It is when comparing these materials with their combined result in a grand scenic composition that we realize that the fame and faculty of Church are the legitimate fruits of rare and individual endowments conscientiously exercised."[69]

One of these "combined results" is Church's large canvas *The Vale of St. Thomas, Jamaica* (Fig. 36). In the lower right foreground of the painting, Church has planted a microcosmic garden of tropical flora. Among the plant specimens are some blooming vines that closely resemble those recorded in his oil sketch *Philodendron Vines, Jamaica* (Fig. 37). The landscape composition was completed in 1867, less than two years after the sketch, and therefore it may have been the work to which Tuckerman referred when he wrote that Church "has already elaborated one landscape from his Jamaica studies—highly finished in details of vegetation, and full of character."[70]

Although studied from nature and executed in loving and exquisite detail, the tropical flora in Church's finished works ultimately appear as small foreground details dwarfed by the grandeur of the artist's large-scale landscape scenes. It remained for Martin Johnson Heade, who followed his friend Church's itinerary through the tropics, to cast flowers in the leading role on the landscape stage.

DARWINIAN CORRESPONDENCES

While some of the impetus for Martin Johnson Heade's flower imagery can be found in contemporary aesthetic developments, there is an originality to his flower painting, in both his choice of subject and his manner of presenting it, which indicates a source of influence outside art. His paintings of exotic tropical flowers and hummingbirds display strong correspondences to the new evolutionary view of nature proposed by Charles Darwin.

To understand how this relationship evolved in Heade's work, it is instructive to look at one of the artist's early, more conventional still lifes with flowers. By 1860, Heade was already recognized as a distinguished painter of flowers. In that year, an issue of *The Crayon* reported that "Mr. Heade, of Providence, gives us occasional glimpses of flowers and trailing vines—such exquisite groups—that we are almost tempted to wish that he were less successful as a landscapist."[71] In Heade's earliest known flower piece, *A Vase of Corn Lilies and Heli-*

otrope (Fig. 38), he achieves the effect of casual naturalism. We sense that Heade worked up his composition in front of an arrangement of live flowers, since the blossoms are shown in precise detail and fit comfortably into their container. The voluminous bouquets of earlier Dutch compositions often included many more flowers than could ever possibly be squeezed into a single vase (Figs. 8, 28). Stylization and overcrowding also characterized the work of nineteenth-century imitators such as Severin Roesen (Figs. 27, 81, 82). By contrast, Heade seems to have plucked his live specimens and reordered them in a vase set before his easel, since heliotropes and corn lilies grow wild (and can be cultivated) in the northeastern United States and come into bloom during the same season, from May to August.[72]

Just as Heade's flower piece suggests a move away from the still-life representation of accurate but organically unrelated specimens of the natural world, so do his more mature flower paintings represent a further development toward a dynamic and integrated view of nature. Most of these compositions incorporate tropical flora, typically orchids and passionflowers, within a dense, humid tropical landscape setting, and include the subject of the artist's keen and well-informed interest—the hummingbird (Figs. 39, 41, 42).[73] A brilliant mature work like *Hummingbird with a White Orchid*, executed in the 1870s (Fig. 39), introduces the flower in large scale, with its elegantly contoured white petals, sepals, and brilliant amethyst lip, growing in the center of a tropical landscape. There is no doubt that this orchid is the crowning glory as well as the central subject of the painting and that the artist is intent upon expressing the organic vitality of the plant.

Like most artists before him, Heade produced his compositions in the studio, relying upon sketches of landscape and floral details recorded *in situ*.[74] (He made three trips to South America—in 1863, 1866, and 1870—sparked by his interest in natural history and his desire to find exotic subjects for his paintings.) Within the portfolio of dazzling flower sketches Heade has left us, the model for the orchid in *Hummingbird with a White Orchid*, plucked fresh from nature by the artist's hand, can be identified in his *Study of "Lealia Purpurata" and Another Orchid* (Fig. 40).[75] The finished work projects a more complete portrait of the orchid, with an additional unopened blossom, and includes the plant's waxy leaves, winding stems, and pseudobulbs. Although the central orchid flower takes on a more substantial opaque appearance in the painting, none of the vital energy of the sketched version has been lost in the translation.

In both subject and composition, Heade's images of passionflowers and orchids are highly innovative: the flowers grow in an environmentally appropriate outdoor setting, and the format intensifies their compelling expressive quality (Figs. 39, 41, 42).[76] He positions the orchid and passionflower blossoms very close to the picture plane, and angles them so that they appear to grow out

38. MARTIN JOHNSON HEADE. *A Vase of Corn Lilies and Heliotrope,* 1863. Oil on canvas, 16⅜ × 12⅜ inches (41.6 × 31.4 cm). The St. Louis Art Museum.

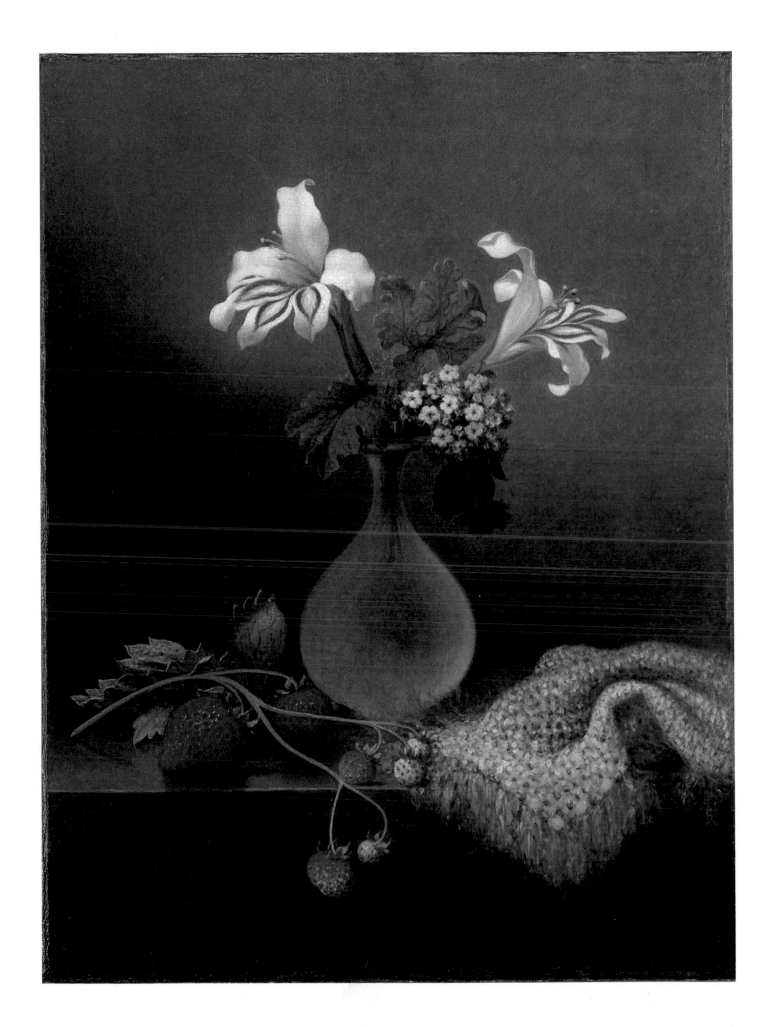

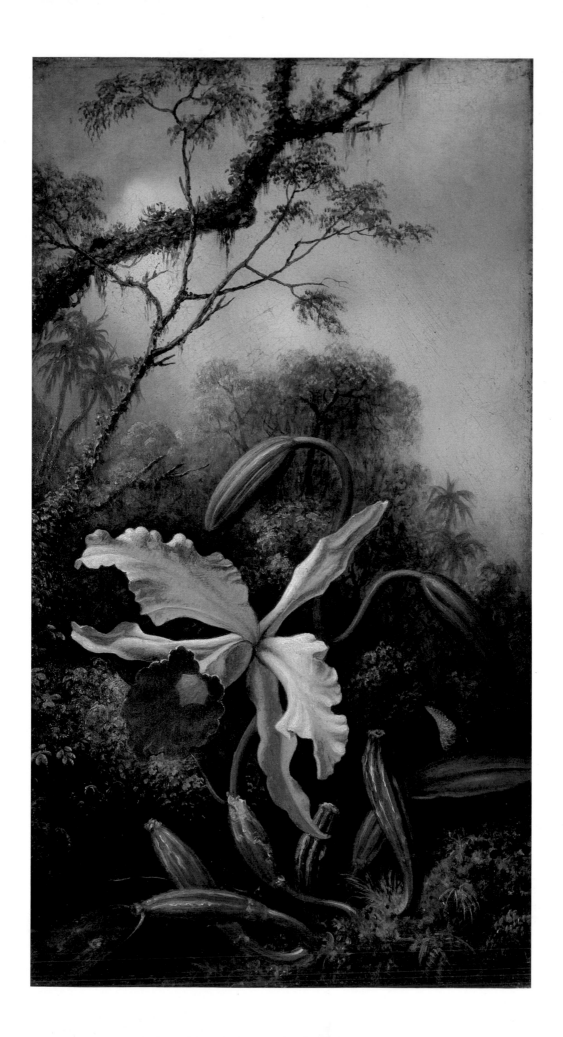

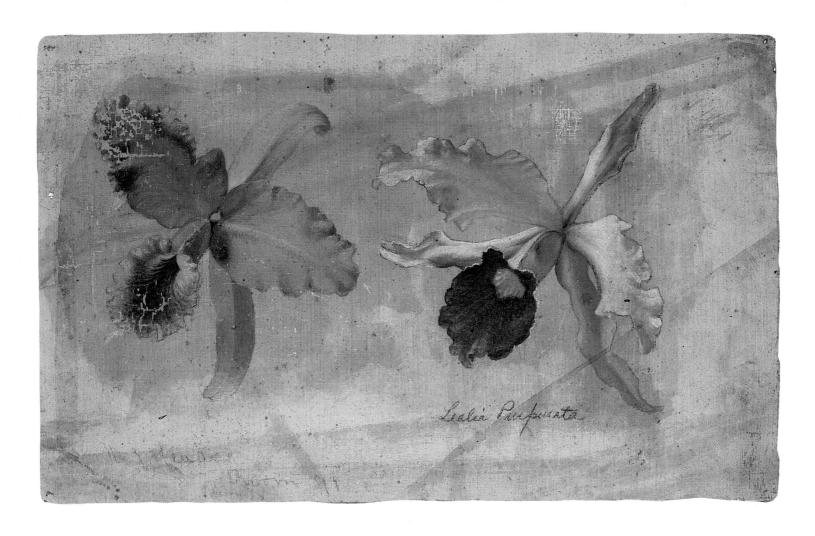

39. MARTIN JOHNSON HEADE.
Hummingbird with a White Orchid,
1870s. Oil on canvas, 20 × 10½ inches
(50.8 × 26.7 cm). Shelburne Museum,
Vermont.

40. MARTIN JOHNSON HEADE. *Study
of "Lealia Purpurata" and Another Orchid,* 1865–75. Oil on canvas, 8½ × 13
inches (21.6 × 33 cm). St. Augustine
Historical Society, Florida.

toward the viewer. The tough but sensuous texture of the stems is emphasized
and the artist threads these securely around their supports; the flowers are firmly
rooted, vigorously growing in their natural habitat, accompanied by brilliant
specimens of hummingbirds.

Heade's unprecedented images invite comparison with a contemporary, and
revolutionary, scientific view of the natural world. In 1859, Charles Darwin
published *On the Origin of Species by Means of Natural Selection; or, The Preservation of Favoured Races in the Struggle for Life.* There is strong evidence to
suggest that Heade, an ardent devotee of natural history who contributed numerous articles to the wildlife- and conservation-oriented periodical *Forest and
Stream,* was well aware of Darwin's theory of evolution.[77] He also undoubtedly
knew of the scientist's subsequent publications on plant life, which appeared
between 1860 and 1880. The titles of some of these books are worth noting,
for they reveal a good deal about Darwin's approach to the plant world: *On the
Various Contrivances by Which British and Foreign Orchids Are Fertilised by Insects* (1862), *The Movements and Habits of Climbing Plants* (1865, 1876), and
The Effects of Cross and Self Fertilisation in the Vegetable Kingdom (1876).

Darwin focused upon two fundamental concerns: the physiology or active life processes of the plant, such as movement and fertilization; and the interaction of the plant with its environment. The orchid was Darwin's principal model for the application of evolution to the plant world because of its "endless diversity of beautiful adaptations" to the environment.[78] It seems more than a mere coincidence that Heade featured orchids in over twenty-five paintings and numerous sketches.

Two Fighting Hummingbirds and Two Orchids (Fig. 41) is one of Heade's most dazzling floral compositions. The pale pink blossoms and their gracefully curving stems serve to focus our attention on the pair of fighting birds in the center foreground. These magnificent creatures, with their iridescent plumage, are silhouetted against the pale gray background of a passing tropical shower. Heade clearly intends to highlight this vignette by placing it at center stage and emphasizing the intricate contours of the colorful birds. Combat in nature is the central drama in this painting; it was also a fundamental component of the Darwinian view.

The struggle for survival formed a basic part of Darwin's scheme, which held that species were formed and continued to be modified through a process of evolution. This was not a new idea, but the mechanism generating the process constituted Darwin's revolutionary contribution. He called the mechanism "natural selection," and it was essentially a two-step process. The first step is the production of variation. In every generation, according to Darwin, an enormous number of variations occurs within each species. The second step is selection through survival in the struggle for existence. In most species of plants and animals, parents produce many more offspring than survive.[79] Because of the tendency of organisms to multiply far beyond the means of subsistence, a ceaseless battle for existence takes place in nature. Those organisms which possess variations that are useful in the struggle survive, reproduce, and thus transmit these variations to the next generation. By this long and gradual process, species slowly evolve in the direction of the variations that are most functional in the battle for life.[80] Therefore, the notion of combat, such as that pictured in *Two Fighting Hummingbirds*, took on critical importance in the Darwinian view of nature. It was not an isolated occurrence, but a fundamental component of nature's life process. And Heade seems to celebrate this concept.

The passionflower was another subject that engaged both Darwin and Heade. Darwin tested the movement of the plant's tendrils for their various responses to changing environmental conditions, such as temperature, light, and touch.[81] He noted that the beaks of hummingbirds were "specially adapted" to fertilize the passionflower.[82] Heade's *Passion Flowers and Hummingbirds* (Fig. 42) offers a striking analogy both to Darwin's particular study of the flower and to his general view of nature. The image places visual emphasis on the plant's

41. MARTIN JOHNSON HEADE. *Two Fighting Hummingbirds and Two Orchids*, 1875. Oil on canvas, 17½ × 27¾ inches (44.5 × 70.5 cm). Whitney Museum of American Art, New York; Gift of Henry Schnakenberg in memory of Juliana Force 67.5.

growth properties and its physical integration and interaction with the environment. Darwin could have been describing this painting when he wrote:

> It is interesting to contemplate an entangled bank, clothed with many plants of many kinds, with birds singing in the bushes, with various insects flitting about, and with worms crawling through the damp earth, and to reflect that these elaborately constructed forms, so different from each other, and dependent on each other in so complex a manner, have all been produced by laws acting around us . . . and that, whilst this planet has gone cycling on according to the fixed law of gravity, from so simple a beginning endless forms most beautiful and most wonderful have been, and are being, evolved.[83]

Heade's paintings signal a revised interpretation of the aesthetic goal of "truth to nature" which corresponds to new patterns in scientific thinking. The works and writings of other American artists of the late nineteenth century share an expression of this new view.

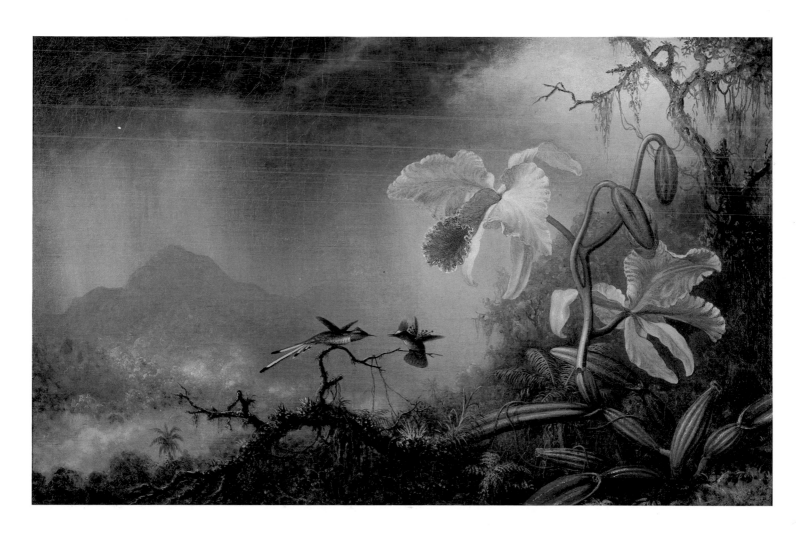

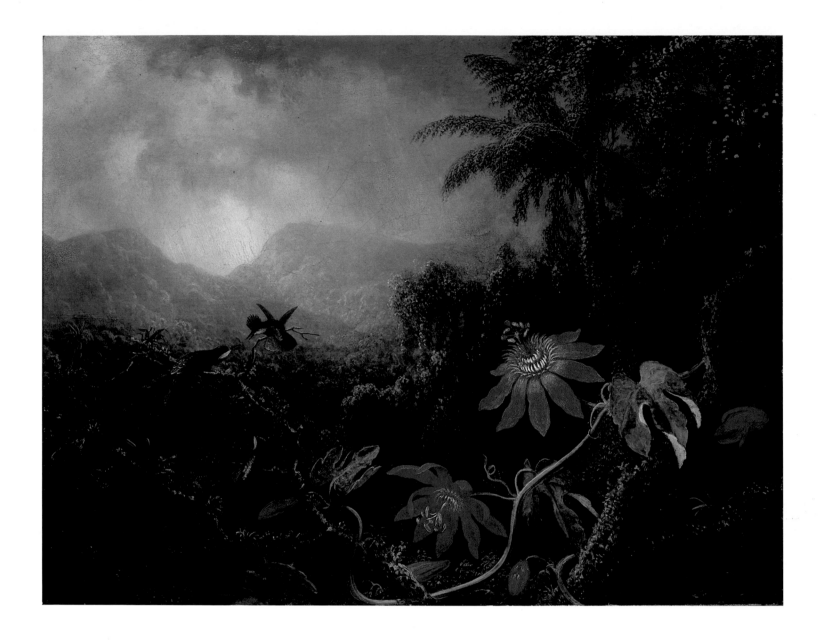

John La Farge, a contemporary of Heade, devoted a significant portion of the work he produced from the 1860s through the 1890s to the subject of flowers.[84] The interests of this cosmopolitan artist were wide-ranging, and new developments in the natural sciences did not escape his notice. When his library was sold at auction in 1881, the catalogue listed Darwin's *The Expression of Emotions in Man and Animals* (1872), in which the evolutionary principles of variation and inheritance were related to the development of emotional expression in man and other animal species.[85] Another collection of scientific volumes in the La Farge library, sold at a later auction, was a complete set of the *Bulletin of the Torrey Botanical Club*, issued from 1870 to 1899.[86]

In reading this journal, the first botanical serial published in America, La Farge would have absorbed direct and indirect expositions of the Darwinian thesis. The first issue encouraged the amateur botanist to become an expert in the flora of his local surroundings. He could contribute significant information to the advancement of science by observing "plants in their native haunts," and by paying particular attention to the development of the "plant from its cradle to its grave . . . its atmospheric and entomological economies . . . its relations to the past, or experiment on its utility to man."[87] With such encouragement, La Farge made frequent visits to a lily pond in Newport, Rhode Island, to study the plants in their natural settings. The visits inspired a number of sensitive aesthetic renderings of the water lily, a plant that held a special fascination for him as well as for many other late nineteenth-century artists. The water lily "always appealed to the sense of something of a meaning," remarked La Farge, and that meaning lurked elusively beyond the realm of symbolic or formal categorization. He could only compare it to "a mysterious appeal such as comes to us from certain arrangements of notes of music."[88] Earlier, Henry David Thoreau had expressed a similar fascination with the water lily. For him, the flower seemed to elude even the closest objective scrutiny and thereby posed a continual challenge to literary expression. "No one," Thoreau remarked, "has ever put into words what the odor of water-lilies expresses."[89]

In his images of water lilies, both in still-life settings and outdoor environments (Figs. 43, 44), La Farge captured a convincing likeness of every part of the plant. The two lilies floating in a white bowl display all their structural components while maintaining the naturalism of live specimens. Such vital representations of floral forms depended upon the artist's close and ongoing study of his live models. La Farge's son tells us that his father considered it essential to "live with" his flowers in order to observe "their buddings, unfoldings, and witherings." According to the artist, the life processes of the plant could, through careful and prolonged observation, become "part of one's life." Through such an intimate acquaintance with the floral subject, La Farge hoped that in his own re-creation of it, "the painting itself might in turn be a living thing."[90]

La Farge does, indeed, create "a living thing" in his small but exquisite painting of *Wild Roses and Water Lily* (Fig. 44). The flowers are securely ensconced in an appropriate aquatic setting. They seem to stretch open their petals to reveal for us their vital, tiny reproductive parts. The saturated color of the blossoms—the vibrant pink rose petals and intense yellow sepals of the lily—juxtaposed with the muted tones of their surroundings, enhances their vigorous presence. Emphatic and active brushwork, which becomes more limpid in the water areas, captures the glittering reflections of sunlight sparkling across the surface of the pond. The flowers, too, are bathed in the glow of this all-encompassing light. La Farge conveys to us, in this small slice of floral life, the much larger organic cosmos of a beautifully dynamic and interactive universe.

Maria Oakey Dewing, a pupil of John La Farge and an accomplished flower

42. MARTIN JOHNSON HEADE. Passion Flowers and Hummingbirds, c. 1875–85. Oil on canvas, 17¼ × 22⅛ inches (43.8 × 56.2 cm). San Antonio Museum Association, Texas; Purchased with funds provided by the Robert J. Kleberg, Jr., and Helen C. Kleberg Foundation.

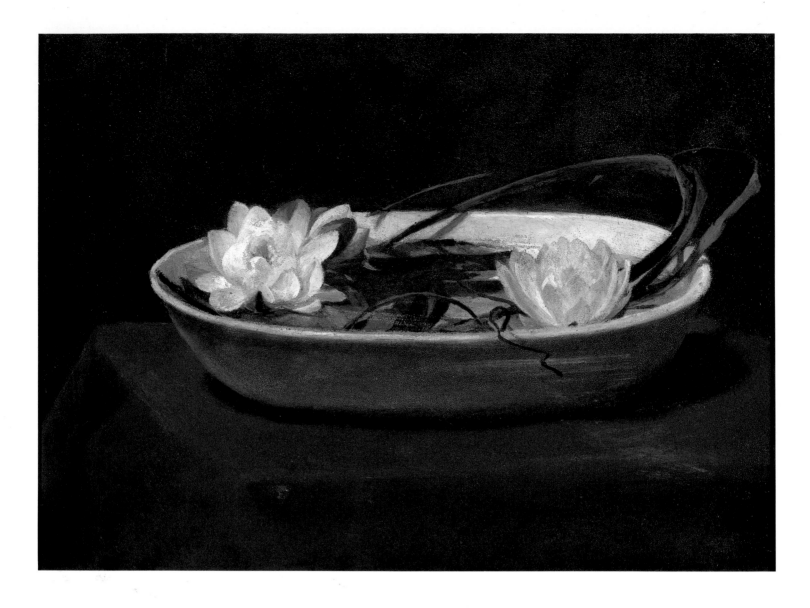

painter, wrote an article in 1915 entitled "Flower Painters and What the Flower Offers to Art."[91] Although she was writing fifteen years into the twentieth century, her attitudes continued to reflect the concerns of a nineteenth-century artist. In her consideration of works produced in many periods and cultures—she included Dutch flower paintings, and those of Henri Fantin-Latour and John La Farge, as well as Japanese screens—she provided a new definition of the concept of "truth to nature" in flower painting. Dewing saw flagrant inaccuracies in the Dutch flower pieces that earlier American critics had praised for their botanical accuracy.[92] What sparked her most ardent objection was the Dutch practice of combining flowers that had no organic relationship to each other. "They are grouped with no idea of truth to nature," wrote Dewing disdainfully. "The tulip . . . placed in a bouquet with a passion flower—the hot-house and the spring garden mixed."[93] For her, a truly naturalistic depiction of flowers required loyalty to relationships that could be found in nature. Dewing—like

43. JOHN LA FARGE. *Water Lilies in a White Bowl*, 1859. Oil on academy board, 9½ × 13 inches (24.1 × 33 cm). Private collection.

44. JOHN LA FARGE. *Wild Roses and Water Lily*, 1882–85. Watercolor on paper, 10⅝ × 8⅞ inches (27 × 22.5 cm). Collection of Mr. and Mrs. Raymond J. Horowitz.

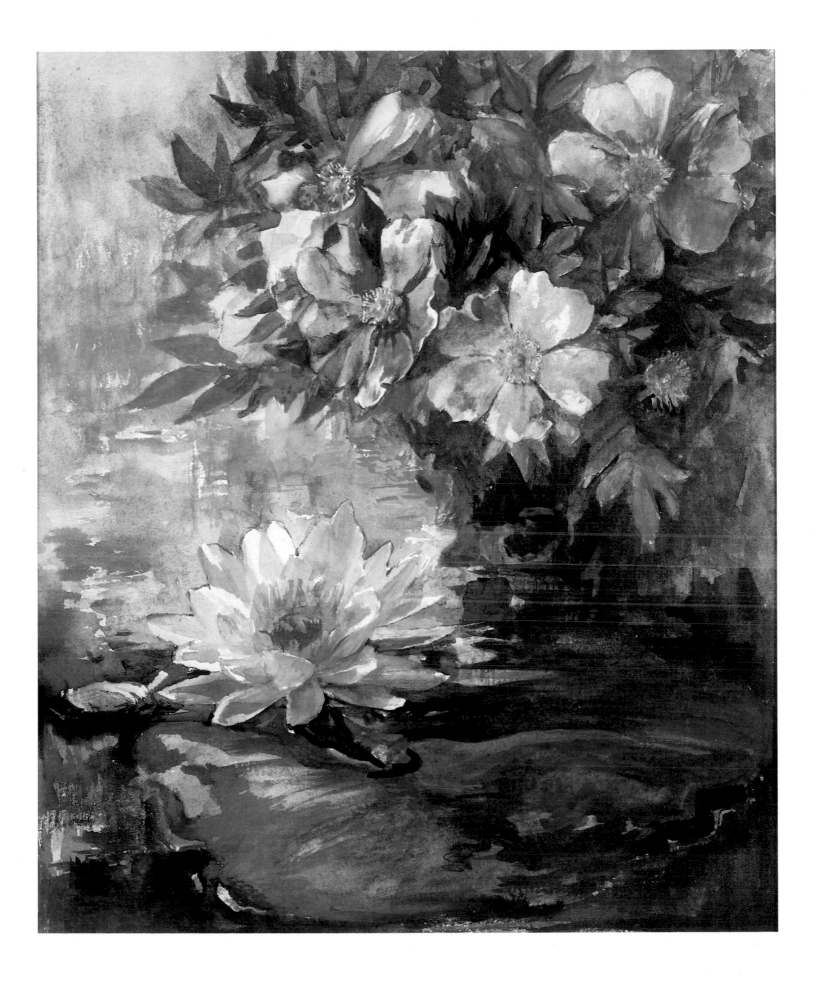

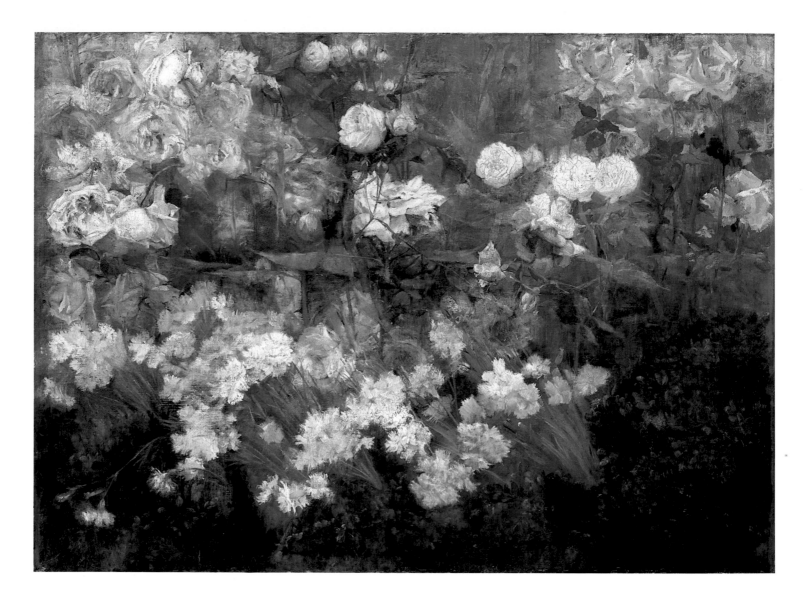

Ruskin and, in a different context, Darwin—emphasized the importance of capturing the flower's "manner of growth" and of creating an integrated image of the object in its natural setting. She herself achieved such a visual projection of the organic life of the floral world in her painting *Garden in May* of 1895 (Fig. 45).[94] A lusty assembly of roses and carnations, seen in close-up view, grows with natural abandon amid dense green foliage. Since the sky is not indicated, we experience the flora from the gardener's perspective, and, indeed, Dewing is representing the garden in her own backyard. She believed that direct experience with floral life was essential training for aspiring flower artists, and she advised them to "bind themselves to a long apprenticeship in a garden."[95]

Many other artists of the late nineteenth century followed similar prescriptions, translating their gardening experience into vivid flower paintings. Both George Cochran Lambdin and John Henry Twachtman recorded some of the prized potted specimens cultivated in their greenhouses (Figs. 94, 95) and created images of flowers growing outdoors (Fig. 115). Despite differences in style—Lambdin was a nineteenth-century realist, Twachtman an Impressionist—they shared a commitment to the direct experience of nature as the source of their artistic projection, and to the depiction of the organic vitality of the plant world derived from that experience.

Even a style as painterly as Impressionism could be made to cohere with the contemporaneous definition of "truth to nature." It encouraged the artist to enter into a direct relationship with nature in order to capture its changing aspects under varying light conditions. Color was an important issue in this plein-air aesthetic, and the flower, especially in gardens and fields, offered an ideal subject for experimentation. Floral themes allowed Renoir to concentrate on formal issues; for this reason, he approached flower pieces and garden images with a freedom of spirit. "I just let my brain rest when I paint flowers," he noted. "I establish the tones, I study the values carefully, without worrying about losing the picture."[96]

Experimentation with formal issues certainly influenced the brightened palette of Childe Hassam in his *Gathering Flowers in a French Garden* of 1888 (Fig. 46). Dappled sunlight, filtered through overhanging branches of hydrangeas, falls on the garden and intensifies the chroma of the specimens bathed in its reflection. There is a constructive order to this garden painting, produced during Hassam's stay in France, that is less apparent in a later floral image painted on this side of the Atlantic. While Hassam continues to explore the Impressionist formal concern with color and light in his 1892 painting of *Celia Thaxter in Her Garden* (Fig. 47), he eliminates much of the self-conscious, planar ordering that appears in the sharp divisions of color areas (hedge, path, lawn, house) of the earlier work. Hassam's friend, the writer Celia Thaxter, stands comfortably surrounded by the floral specimens that she cultivated and loved so well.[97] Like the structure of the picture, her informal gardening style was far removed from the ordered hedges and vines depicted in Hassam's French garden painting.

A watercolor painting of this same garden on the island of Appledore, off the coast of New Hampshire, shows a further relaxation of Hassam's structure. *The Island Garden* of 1892 (Fig. 48) offers an informal close-up view of a brilliantly colored bed of poppies. While this particular image did not serve as one of Hassam's illustrations for Thaxter's book *An Island Garden* (1894), its glorification of the poppy closely parallels the laudatory description of that flower in her text. Thaxter draws on Ruskin to project a verbal vision of the *Papaver rhoeas*, the same wild variety of the poppy that he so admired in the fifteenth-century herbal drawing of Andrea Amadio (Fig. 1). Ruskin praised the poppy as a kind of quintessential flower, "all silk and flame, a scarlet cup, perfect edged all round, seen among the wild grass . . . or with the light, always it is a flame, and warms the wind like a blown ruby."[98]

Perhaps in response to Ruskin's advice to artists to let nature guide their

45. MARIA OAKEY DEWING. *Garden in May*, 1895. Oil on canvas, 23⅝ × 32½ inches (60 × 82.6 cm). National Museum of American Art, Smithsonian Institution, Washington, D.C.; Gift of John Gellatly.

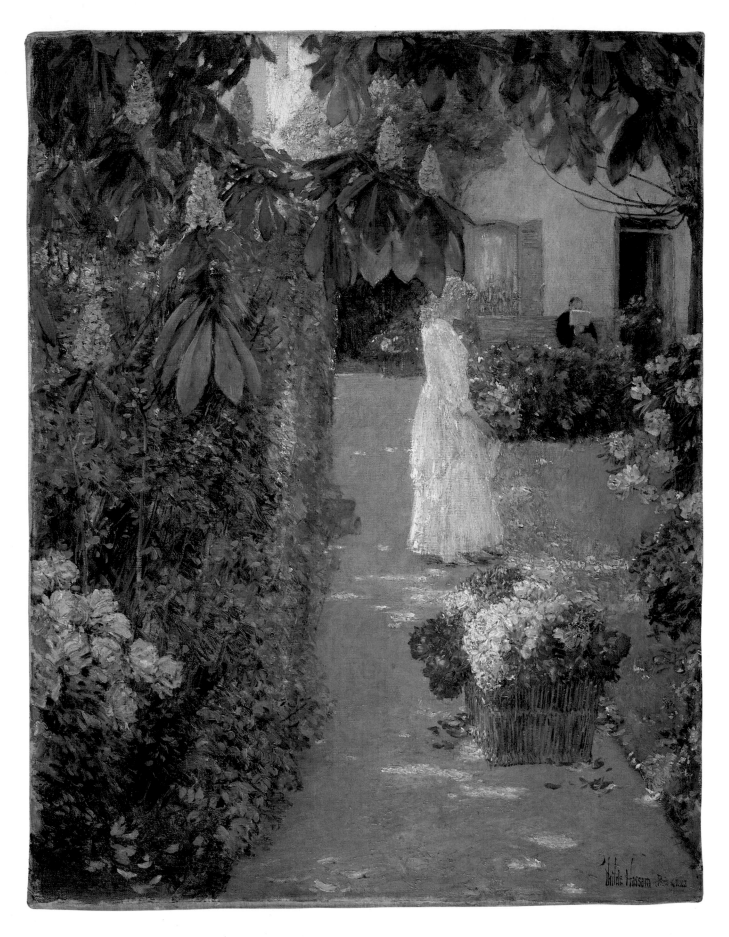

46. FREDERICK CHILDE HASSAM. *Gathering Flowers in a French Garden*, 1888. Oil on canvas, 28 × 21⅝ inches
(71.1 × 54.9 cm). Worcester Art Museum, Massachusetts; Theodore T. and Mary G. Ellis Collection.

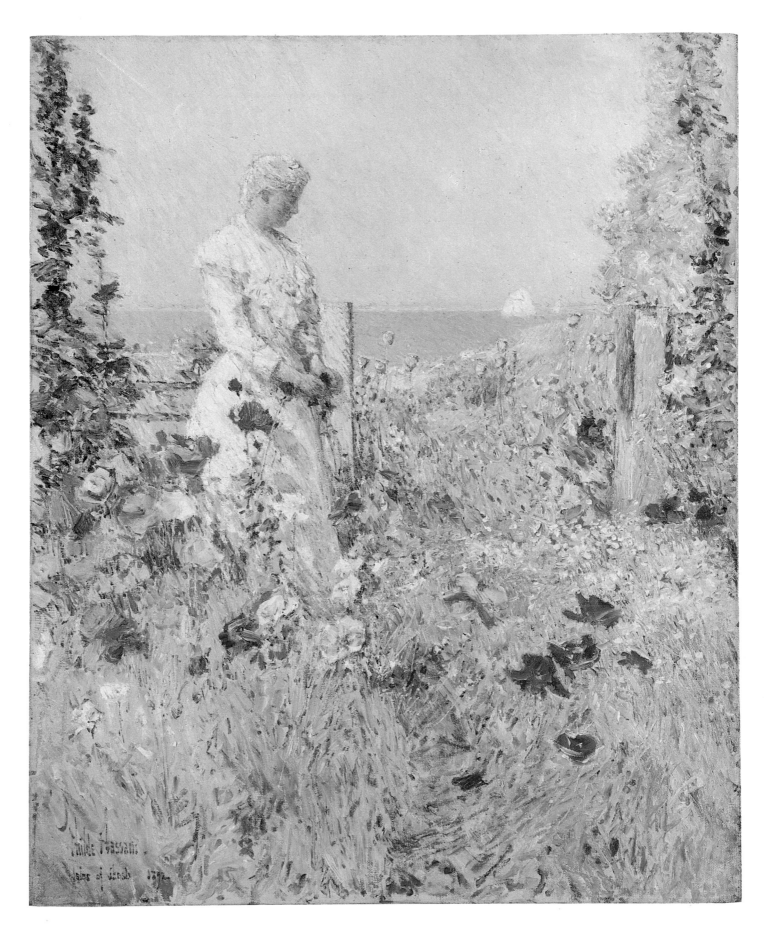

47. FREDERICK CHILDE HASSAM. *Celia Thaxter in Her Garden*, 1892. Oil on canvas, 22⅛ × 18⅛ inches (56.2 × 46 cm). National Museum of American Art, Smithsonian Institution, Washington, D.C.; Gift of John Gellatly.

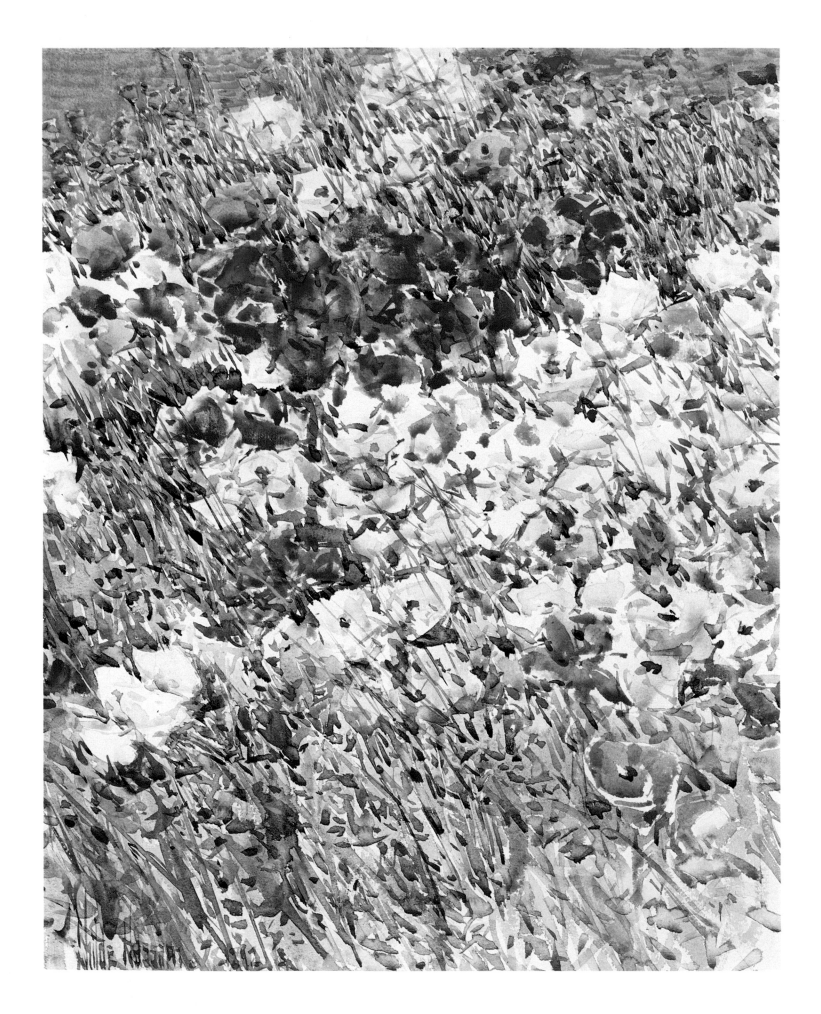

compositions, Hassam allows a lively cluster of wild poppies to fill the surface of this drawing, with only cursory indications of the blue sky or sea behind. It is as if the artist, in the course of a casual walk, has caught sight of an especially appealing group of flowers and sketched it quickly just as he saw it. The poppies in this painting seem to bend more in response to the pressure of a passing breeze than to the firm grip of the artist's hand.

Celia Thaxter often described pleasurable walks through the flower-filled landscape of Appledore. "I'm so struck with the flowers along our way," she remarked in a letter to a friend, that "I am going to set them down . . . as I see them."[99] There follows a random listing of the flowers that captured her attention. An avid horticulturist, well versed in plant identification, Thaxter easily pinpoints not fewer than thirty-five varieties. A direct and accepting view of nature lent a freshness and vitality of vision to the floral imagery of writer and painter alike.

IT WOULD BE impossible to measure the relative impact of stylistic and cultural developments on the emerging naturalism of late nineteenth-century American flower painting. The more direct influence of new aesthetics such as Impressionism are easier to document, especially in the work of an artist like Hassam, who had direct access to the modern style. But any fundamental shift in approach results from a network of interactive changes. Important among these, in nineteenth-century America, was Darwin's theory of evolution, his conception of nature as a dynamic universe. The active physiological life of flora and the relationships of living forms to each other and to their surroundings created a world in continuous process. Flower artists drew inspiration from this exhilarating new view of the natural world, and it supplied the American flower genre with a wealth of imagery and aesthetic accomplishment to match.

TWENTIETH-CENTURY AMERICAN FLOWER IMAGERY

Modern pictures deal with contemporary subject matter in terms of art. The artist does not exercise his freedom in a non-material world. Science has created a new environment, in which new forms, lights, speeds, and spaces are a reality.

—Stuart Davis, 1943[100]

48. FREDERICK CHILDE HASSAM. *The Island Garden*, 1892. Watercolor on paper, 17½ × 14 inches (44.5 × 35.6 cm). National Museum of American Art, Smithsonian Institution, Washington, D.C.; Gift of John Gellatly.

The nineteenth-century consensus about the close relationship of art, science, and nature is not shared by the critics and artists of twentieth-century America. There are critics who claim that art is entirely self-referential and that, therefore, even the notion of a relationship beyond the canvas, stone, or steel is irrelevant, or at least makes for bad art. Following the formalist aesthetic guidelines established early in the twentieth century by Roger Fry, Clement Greenberg defined "the essence of Modernism," in all forms of artistic endeavor, as "the use of the characteristic methods of a discipline to criticize the discipline itself."[101] In his most succinct and precise exposition of this isolationist, or perhaps involuted, view of art, Greenberg said that "Modernism used art to call attention to art." From this perspective, Leonardo's concept of the artist performing the ultimate role of "interpreter between art and nature" would become outmoded.

However, not all critics, even among the champions of abstract art, have found questions of relationship to the natural world inappropriate. While John Graham, for instance, thought that it was not the proper business of art to describe or reproduce the data of nature (he left that role to photography and bookkeeping), he steadfastly asserted that "a legitimate abstract work of art can be produced only on the basis of profound knowledge of nature."[102] Only an artist who thoroughly absorbed a working knowledge of the space and things around him would make a legitimate and meaningful aesthetic transformation of his experience in abstract terms.

Twentieth-century artists have shared with critics a variety of attitudes toward the relationship between art and nature. For some, both figurative and nonfigurative artists, the relationship is subjective and intimate. They view nature less as something to learn about and describe than as an extension of the self. Such artists aim to commune with nature and experience it with such intensity that their creative identities assimilate the spirit of natural phenomena. In one of his characteristically sensitive musings, Arthur Dove wondered whether "maybe the world is a dream and everything in it is your self."[103] Jackson Pollock took a more assertive approach to the same idea when he dismissed all notions of relationship between the artist and nature, including both separation and affinity, with the categorical claim "I am nature."[104] Alternatively, Frank Stella conceived of a work of art as a discrete object, with no humanistic relation to the self and without allusion to the external world. "My painting is based on the fact that only what can be seen there *is* there," he said. "It really is an object." In other words, beware of trying to make connections; be forewarned by the artist's conviction that "what you see is what you see."[105]

It is important to outline the range of attitudes toward the relationship between nature and art because, as we have seen, flower painting in America derived from nature painting. It developed from a documentary approach to the natural wonders of the New World, and some of its later manifestations were closely linked to landscape painting. But the grasp of the twentieth-century artist on the character and functioning of the natural world is necessarily more tenuous. Modern science has removed "truth to nature" to a domain beyond our

49. CHARLES SHEELER. *Flower Forms*, 1917. Oil on canvas, 23¼ × 19⅛ inches (59.1 × 48.6 cm). Private collection.

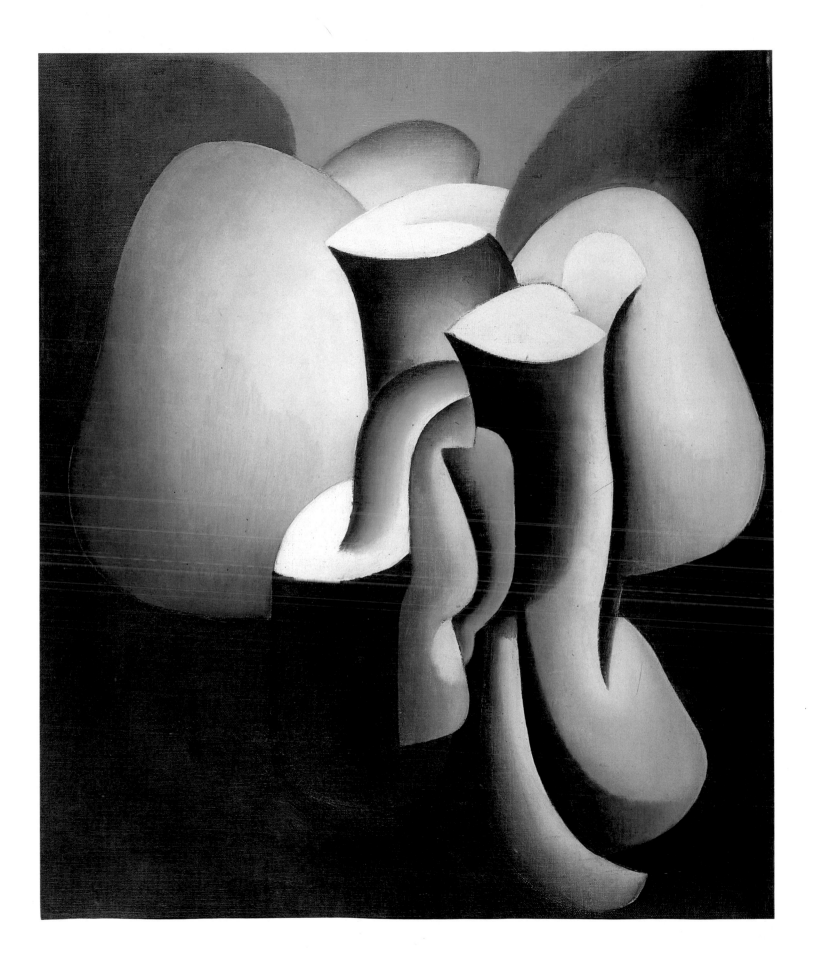

sensory experience, even with the aid of the microscope; its facts have become too far, too big, too small, and certainly too complex to be fully apprehended. [106]

In other words, a descriptive analysis of the physical world around us may not render profound insights into its essential workings. These are to be found on a much grander and more complex scale, only accessible to the trained specialist. As the British physicist Lancelot L. Whyte puts it: "Nature seems to be saying with all possible emphasis . . . [that] the laws of complex systems are not written in terms of quantitative properties of their localized constituents, but in terms of global properties and collective parameters." [107]

The general acknowledgment of an inaccessible framework—beyond sensory grasp—proposed by modern science may account, in part, for the efforts of twentieth-century artists to search out underlying forms. Charles Sheeler believed that a hidden framework exists in the natural world and that art should strive to reveal it. "All nature *has* an underlying abstract structure," Sheeler affirmed, and with typical taciturn conviction he added that "it is within the province of the artist to search for it." [108] His own work—whether it represents natural forms, still-life objects, or architecture—demonstrates a firm commitment to a search for formal designs which synthesize his personal response to objects and his aesthetic conception of abstract structure. Sheeler used the stylistic vocabulary of Cubism, which he assimilated on visits abroad and to the Armory Show in New York, to give formal expression to his artistic goal: "Our chief object is to increase our capacity for perception," he stated unequivocally. "The degree of accomplishment determines the caliber of the artist." [109]

Early in his career, Sheeler's effort to increase his capabilities of visual perception and compositional ordering led him to produce *Flower Forms* (Fig. 49), a semi-abstract image of plant life. His palette, with its restricted range of blue/ green and ochre/brown tones, maintains a consistent allusion to the local colors of nature; and his interlocking tubular shapes, in their modeled convexity and curving contours, retain suggestions of organic form. Within these sectioned tubes, which resemble digestive organs, we can conjure the ebb and flow of the vital juices of vegetable life. What clearly differentiates Sheeler's image from a close-up view of an orchid by Martin Johnson Heade is that the intensity of his perception seems to penetrate the flower to reveal its internal physiology. Sheeler's representation of visceral processes beneath the surface of natural forms bears a general comparison to the study of biochemistry. [110] This twentieth-century development in the life sciences investigates biological processes at the chemical and molecular levels, which lie far beyond the visual range of the naked eye and depend for their perception on advanced technological equipment. In the plant sciences, it followed important late nineteenth-century discoveries in cytology, or cell science, most relevantly the investigation of protoplasm as the basic cell substance of plants and animals. [111] While Charles

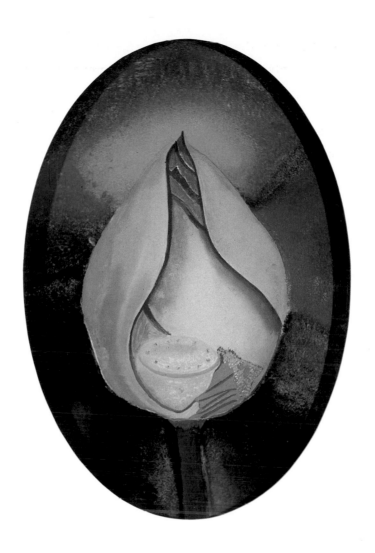

50. Joseph Stella. *Lotus Flower*, 1920. Oil on glass, 11 × 7¼ inches (27.9 × 18.4 cm). Collection of Dr. and Mrs. Martin Weissman.

Sheeler may not have been aware of the specifics of these new developments, his keen interest in probing beneath the surface of things relates in a general way to the direction science was taking. If Sheeler wanted art "to increase our capacity for perception," it is tantalizing to consider that in 1912, just five years before the painter peeled through the plant surface in *Flower Forms*, the scientist Max von Laue had discovered the X-ray—a form of light which profoundly increased our capacity to penetrate solid form.

Sheeler was not alone in his passion to expand his visual powers in search of new aesthetic structure for his art. Many other painters, as well as photographers, were engaged in similar pursuits. In 1920, Joseph Stella produced a small painting of a single lotus blossom set against a deep green ground (Fig. 50). He executed *Lotus Flower* with oil on glass, which gives the sharply focused close-up of the flower a luminous crystalline clarity. What is most compelling about this work is that Stella simultaneously presents an external and internal view of the blossom. The internal seed pod emerges in golden splendor through the layers of pink petals. In effect, Stella offers us a creative X-ray of the plant.

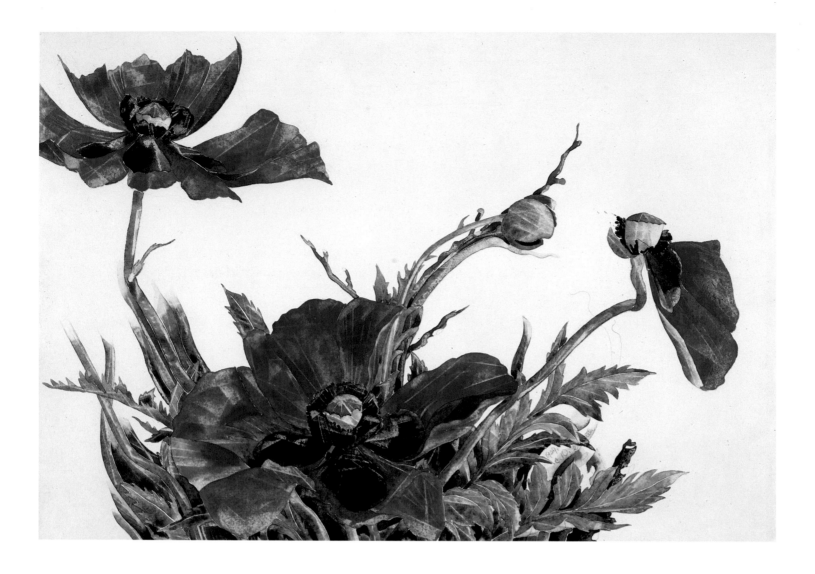

Charles Demuth, an extraordinary twentieth-century painter of flowers, considered the ability to see the essential criterion of communication between the artist and the connoisseur. Demuth talked about an intensity of vision, something beyond the ordinary perception of form, as the critical transmitter of conceptual understanding. For him, paintings were "the n'th whooppee of sight." "Paintings must be looked at and looked at. . . . They must be understood, and that's not the word either, through the eyes."[112]

Demuth, like Maria Oakey Dewing, developed his own intense perception of the floral world through "a long apprenticeship in a garden." Most of his flower paintings were produced at his home in Lancaster, Pennsylvania, in a studio overlooking an exquisite garden. While the Victorian garden was the creation of his mother, Demuth spent a good deal of time on its care, particularly after diabetes began to limit his activities during the 1920s. So thoroughly did Demuth absorb his direct experience with cultivated varieties of flowers that the critic Henry McBride did not think museums could provide an appropriately vital setting for his lifelike images. "The proper place for a Demuth flower, I sometimes think, is in the hands of an educated gardener," wrote McBride, "one who knows what a flower is and what an artist is."[113]

In a mature work by Demuth (Fig. 51), there is something to please the poet as well as the gardener. His image of the graceful poppy presents a distillation of spirit as well as form. What is implied conveys an expression as potent as what is described. The four poppy blossoms, in various stages of organic development, bend and sway in a thoroughly tangible, but unmarked space. While they are surrounded by nothing more than a blank page, their disposition is so powerful that it suggests the nourishing pull of the sun above and the secure footing of the roots below. The poppies could serve as a visual complement to William Carlos Williams' poem "Spring Strains" (1917):

> crowded erect with desire against the sky—
> tense blue-grey twigs
> slenderly anchoring them down, drawing
> them in—[114]

Like the poet, and like the painters of the exquisite birds and flowers of the Sung Dynasty, Demuth draws spatial eloquence from the undescribed context of his floral subjects.

Precision performs as a companion to poetry in the flower paintings of Charles Demuth. He envisions a simple bouquet of gladioli (Fig. 52) with such clarity of focus that his mode of perception allies itself as much with scientific investigation as with Emerson's "transparent eyeball."[115] Demuth endows every stem, leaf, and blossom in *Red and Yellow Gladioli* with equal clarity of contour and saturation of color. Each member of the group is rendered with a precision that invokes the name of science. "Demuth, with the aid of science," commented McBride, "doubtless wraps himself in some sort of transparent cloak and shields himself from contrary winds. . . . Not a ripple from the upper airs is allowed to disturb the intensity of his study."[116]

A close scrutiny of the natural world laid the groundwork for the most impressive floral images of the twentieth century—those produced by Demuth's personal and aesthetic comrade, Georgia O'Keeffe. In recognition of her unrivaled sensitivity to the vegetable kingdom, Demuth painted O'Keeffe's portrait in the guise of an aspidistra plant (Fig. 53).

Like Demuth, O'Keeffe felt that flowers challenged the human ability to see. She sought them out as potential keys to understanding a natural universe whose dimensions escape our grasp. The central concern of her art, said O'Keeffe, was to give form to "the unexplainable thing in nature that makes me feel the world is big far beyond my understanding."[117] Flowers, as microcosms of

51. CHARLES DEMUTH. *Red Poppies*, 1929. Watercolor and pencil on paper, 13⅞ × 19¾ inches (35.2 × 50.2 cm). The Metropolitan Museum of Art, New York; Gift of Mr. and Mrs. Henry A. Loeb.

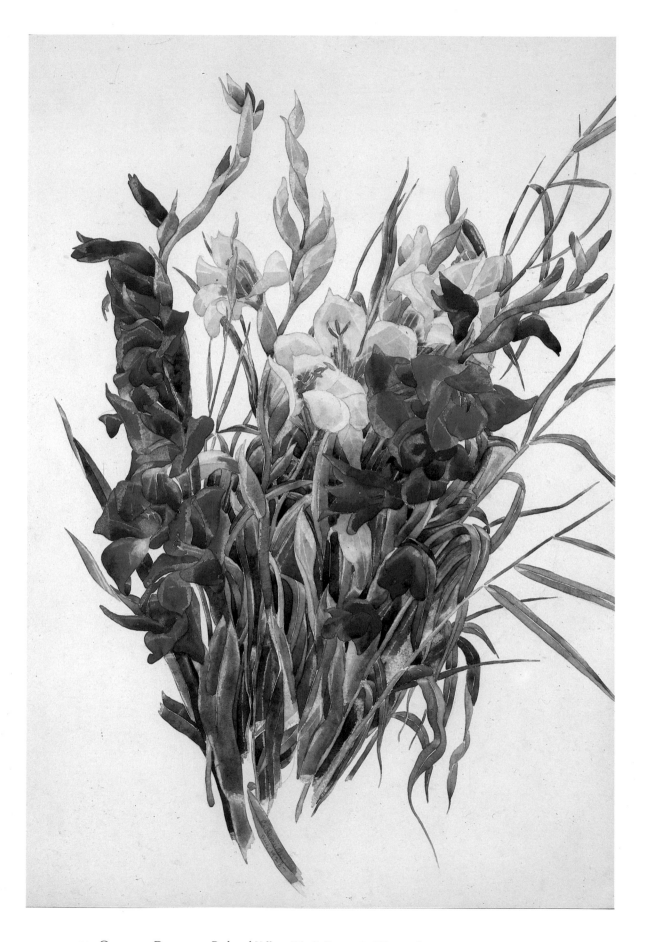

52. CHARLES DEMUTH. *Red and Yellow Gladioli*, 1928. Watercolor on paper, 20 × 14 inches
(50.8 × 35.6 cm). Collection of Alan and Marianne Schwartz.

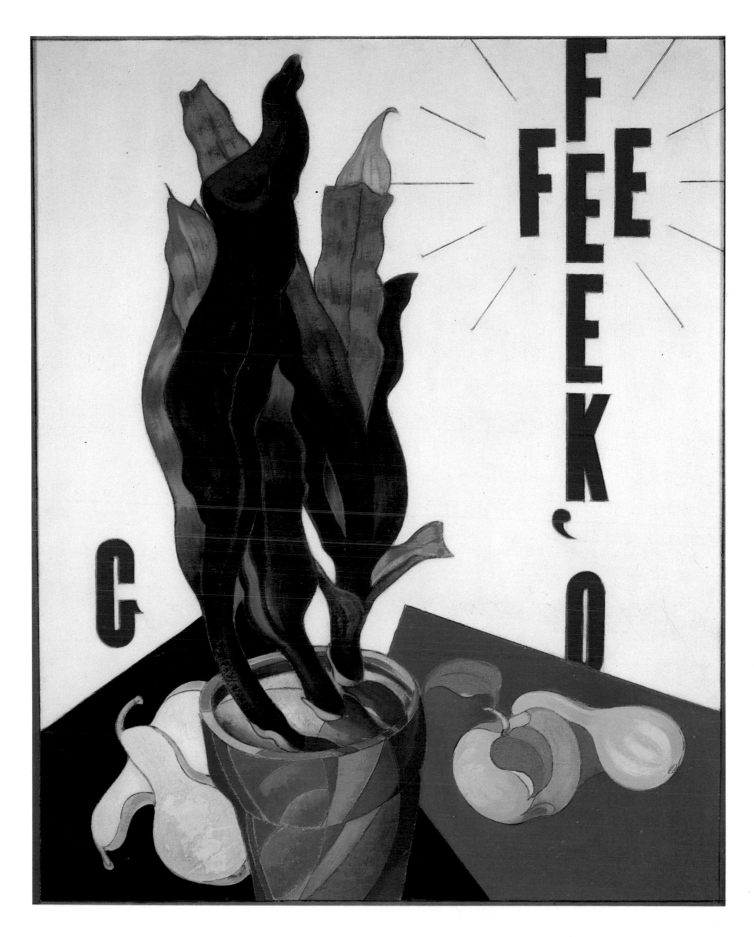

53. CHARLES DEMUTH. *Poster Portrait: Georgia O'Keeffe*, 1924. Oil on board, 20½ × 16½ inches (52.1 × 41.9 cm).
Collection of American Literature, Beinecke Rare Book and Manuscript Library, Yale University, New Haven, Connecticut.

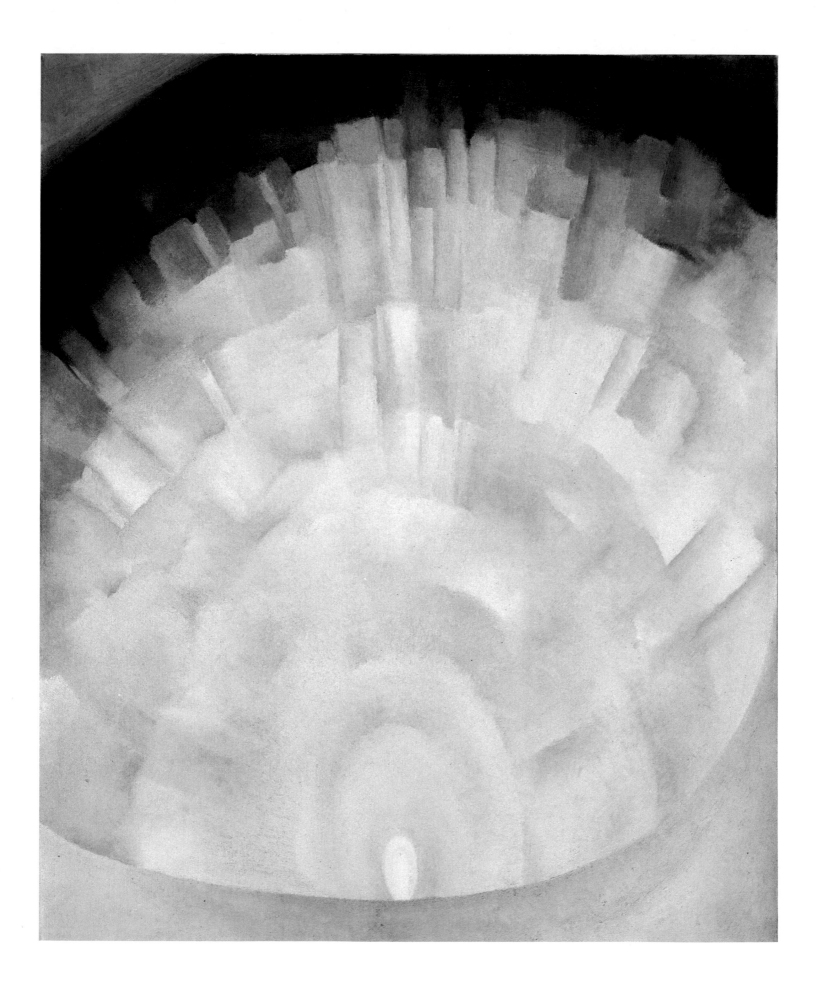

the organic world, embraced explainable truths, if only we could look at them properly.

In the text accompanying a reproduction of her painting *Abstraction—White Rose III* (Fig. 54), O'Keeffe complained that most people do not exercise their powers of perception acutely. They seem merely to pass through nature, failing to see it in any meaningful way. She felt that while we often respond to a flower by smelling it and touching it, we rarely *look* at it. "In a way—nobody sees a flower—really," she said with mild disdain, "it is so small."[118] Because she is a powerful artist, O'Keeffe is able to direct and focus our lines of sight. In *Abstraction—White Rose III*, she created an image which appears to be based upon the experience of placing her own eye just centimeters from the core of the blossom. Such an intense close-up point of view expands the flower to fill the entire range of peripheral vision. O'Keeffe translated this magnified sensory experience into art—a canvas of thirty-six by thirty inches. In the process of creative enlargement, she ignored the surface data of the flower and exposed its structural soul.

A few years after the completion of *Abstraction—White Rose III*, O'Keeffe produced a series of six paintings depicting the jack-in-the-pulpit (Figs. 55–60), a flower that had captured her fancy since childhood. She recalled a classroom experience in which a teacher held up a specimen of the plant for study: "she pointed out the strange shapes and variations in color—from the deep, almost black earthy violet through all the greens, from the pale whitish green in the flower through the heavy green of the leaves. She held up the purplish hood and showed us the Jack inside."[119]

In its shape, the flower is secretive: its trumpet form serves as an envelope to an interior chamber which secures the plant's reproductive organs. To see inside, we must draw very near and look carefully. O'Keeffe had the opportunity to do that later in her life. She found two wild varieties of the flower growing in the woods near her summer home at Lake George. The earlier experience directed her eye to the flowers as a subject for painting. O'Keeffe's memory of the classroom display centered on the experience of looking. The teacher, O'Keeffe remembered, "started me looking at things—looking very carefully at details. It was certainly the first time my attention was called to the outline and color of any growing thing with the idea of drawing or painting it."[120]

In O'Keeffe's *Jack-in-the-Pulpit* series, each successive image draws us closer to the flower without blurring the focus. A smaller portion of the flower is submitted to greater magnification while the scale of the canvases remains the same. Although the flower is seen from a frontal point of view in all of the paintings, there are subtle shifts in the angle of sight. These changes in perspective contribute to a stylistic progression from a realistic representation of the flower to a more abstract rendering.[121]

The *Jack-in-the-Pulpit* paintings force us to wonder about the relationship

54. GEORGIA O'KEEFFE. *Abstraction—White Rose III*, 1927. Oil on canvas, 36 × 30 inches (91.4 × 76.2 cm). Collection of the artist.

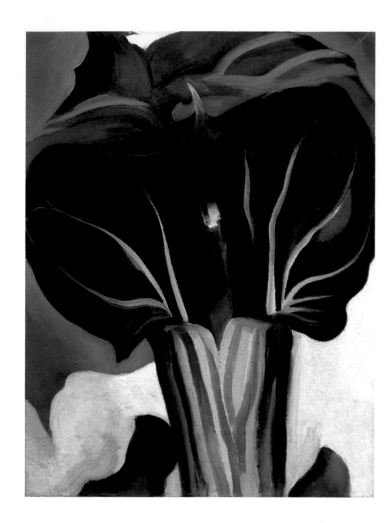

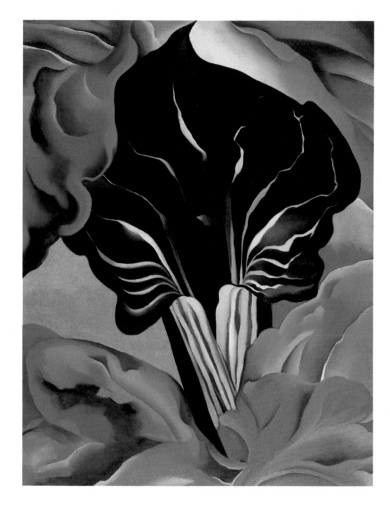

between seeing and knowing. The farther we are from the blossom, the more we know about the details of its structure; the closer we come to it, the less of it we see. But do we understand the jack-in-the-pulpit better from the recognizable depiction of its structural parts in number II (Fig. 56), or from the penetrating view of its pistil projected in number VI (Fig. 60)? The series gives visual form to the enigmatic relationship of art and nature. O'Keeffe confronted a natural universe whose scale and complexity eluded comprehension, so she sought out its smaller components to penetrate their secrets. The closer she drew near to them with her aesthetic eye, the larger they became. With a single flower, she expressed the limits and the possibilities of our capacity to understand the natural universe.

It is not only in the representation of isolated plant forms that twentieth-century artists have tried to penetrate the underpinnings of nature. Floral groupings and images of flowers in nature also convey suspicions about the network supporting the visible forms of nature. In searching for this network, some artists rely upon both their personal identification with the natural world and more objective experience.

55. GEORGIA O'KEEFFE. *Jack-in-the-Pulpit I*, 1930. Oil on canvas, 12 × 9 inches (30.5 × 22.9 cm). Private collection.

56. GEORGIA O'KEEFFE. *Jack-in-the-Pulpit II*, 1930. Oil on canvas, 40 × 30 inches (101.6 × 76.2 cm). Collection of the artist.

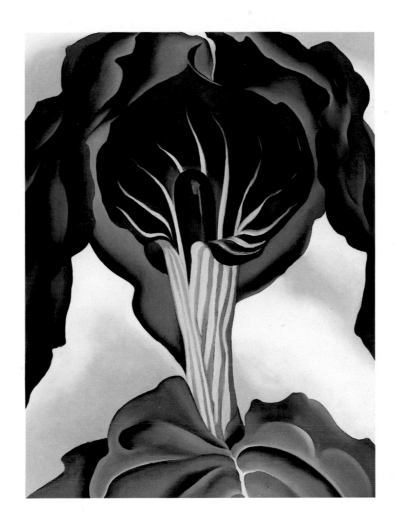

57. GEORGIA O'KEEFFE. *Jack-in-the-Pulpit III*, 1930. Oil on canvas, 40 × 30 inches (101.6 × 76.2 cm). Collection of the artist.

Charles Burchfield, an artist who has been described as "the last pantheist" and whose work projects a sense of formal order, painted a number of striking images of flowers in a natural setting.[122] For him, natural forms in all their diversity offered visual equivalents to the full range of human experience. The delicate blossoms of white violets grimace menacingly in the leafless mineral landscape of *White Violets and Coal Mine* (Fig. 61). They serve as a complement to rather than a relief from this external projection of the artist's melancholy psychic landscape.[123] Other flower-filled landscape scenes could serve as smiling reminders of the life-affirming spirit of integration and renewal in nature. Goldenrod seemed to inspire the kind of positive response that Burchfield experienced when he "stopped a moment in a meadow to savor its rich smells and infinite variety of plant life. . . . All nature seemed to smile on me, every leaf and grass blade full of meaning."[124] The physical and spiritual glow of the sun fairly pulsates through the hazy field of dancing meadow flowers in Burchfield's *Goldenrod in December* (Fig. 62).

However, even for an artist like Burchfield, who experienced nature as an extension of his spiritual self, the facts of the external world would remain of

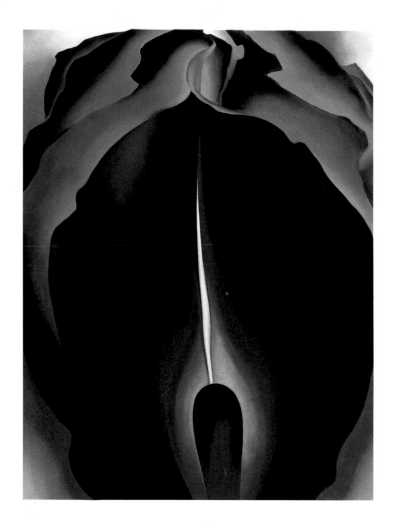

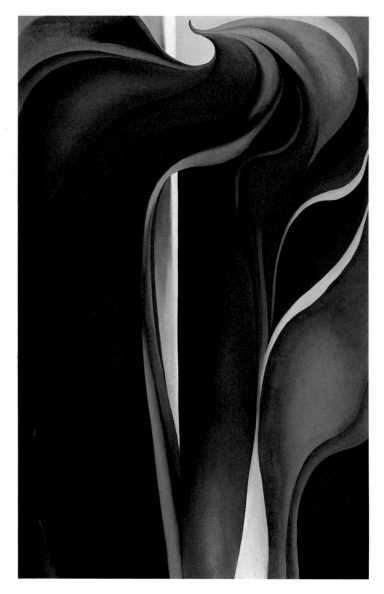

critical importance. With Jeffersonian delight, he kept records in his journal of the working facts of nature, noting the appearance of the first hepatica, the first redbird, the first cicada of every season. He collected specimens for his own wild-flower garden on sketching trips, and, like the Bartrams, dreamed of producing exotic hybrids in his own microcosm of nature.[125]

Burchfield's garden, like that of Demuth, was no more than a glance away from his studio window. He recorded a flourishing bed of brilliant red-orange cannas with the precision of a botanical artist in *Cannas and Studio* (Fig. 63). In fact, throughout his career Burchfield produced numerous studies of flowers and insects based upon direct observation and depicted with unemotional clarity. The propensity to describe the floral world from both an objective and a subjective point of view appears also in the work of Joseph Stella. He painted a

58. GEORGIA O'KEEFFE. *Jack-in-the-Pulpit IV*, 1930. Oil on canvas, 40 × 30 inches (101.6 × 76.2 cm). Collection of the artist.

59. GEORGIA O'KEEFFE. *Jack-in-the-Pulpit V*, 1930. Oil on canvas, 48 × 30 inches (121.9 × 76.2 cm). Collection of the artist.

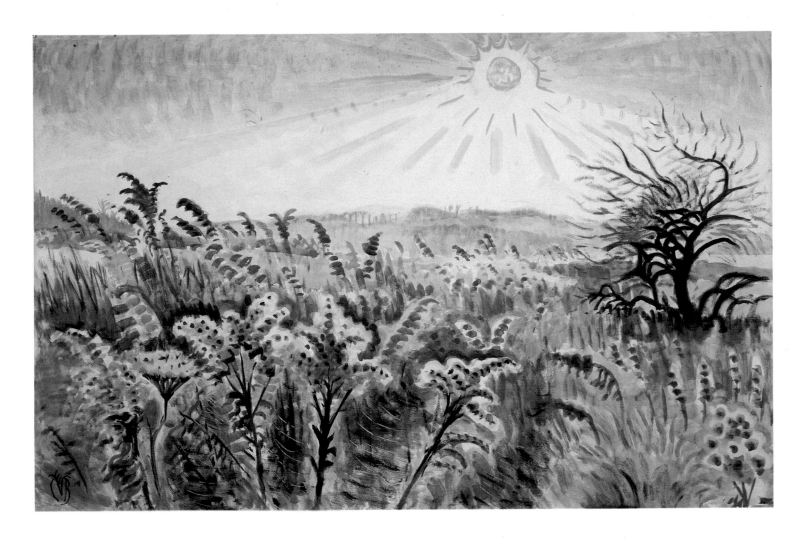

62. CHARLES BURCHFIELD. *Goldenrod in December*, 1948. Watercolor on paper, 26 × 40 inches (66 × 101.6 cm). Whitney Museum of American Art, New York; Gift of Flora Whitney Miller in honor of John I. H. Baur 74.62.

small documentary study of a lupine in the same year as his large symbolic image of plant life, *Tree of My Life* (Fig. 131). Smaller botanical studies often found their way into Stella's larger paintings.

Burchfield felt that it was only through this more objective approach to the natural world that an artist could hope to acquire insight into the patterns of relationship underlying the surface manifestations of nature. For a painting of nature to project meaningful aesthetic form, Burchfield said that its "inner structure must be the result of the close study of nature's laws, and not of human invention. The artist must come to nature, not with a ready-made formula, but in humble reverence to learn. The work of an artist is superior to the surface appearance of nature, but not its basic laws."[126]

Theodoros Stamos, like Burchfield, balances a spiritual response to nature with a strong interest in the patterns of activity inherent in organic life. His abstract rendering of natural forms in *Movement of Plants* (Fig. 64) draws inspiration directly from the dynamic Darwinian view of life. Stamos titled the work after Darwin's 1880 publication, *The Power of Movement in Plants*, one of the many volumes on natural science in the artist's library.[127] The book investigated

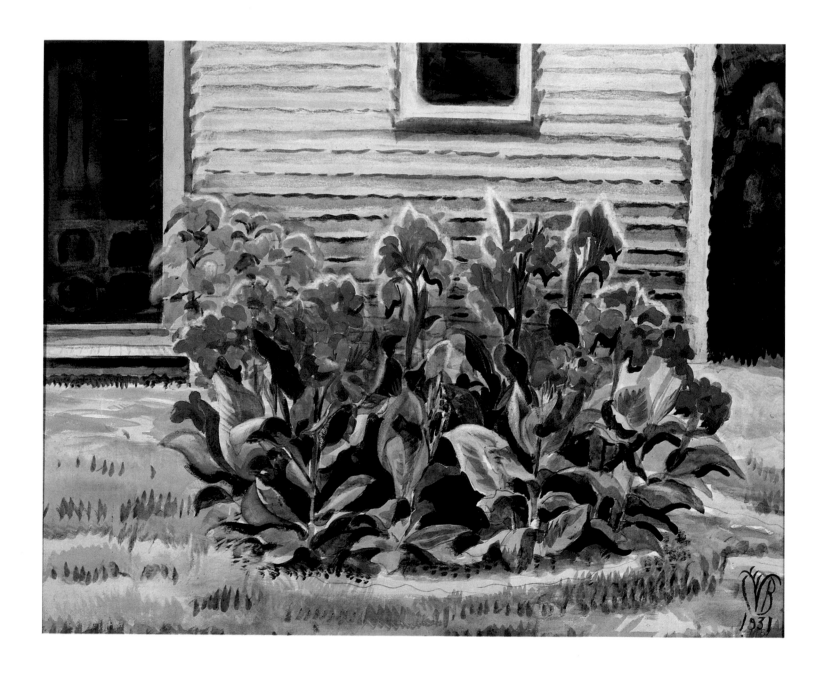

63. CHARLES BURCHFIELD. *Cannas and Studio*, c. 1931. Watercolor on paper, 22 × 28 inches (55.9 × 71.1 cm). Collection of Mrs. William Green.

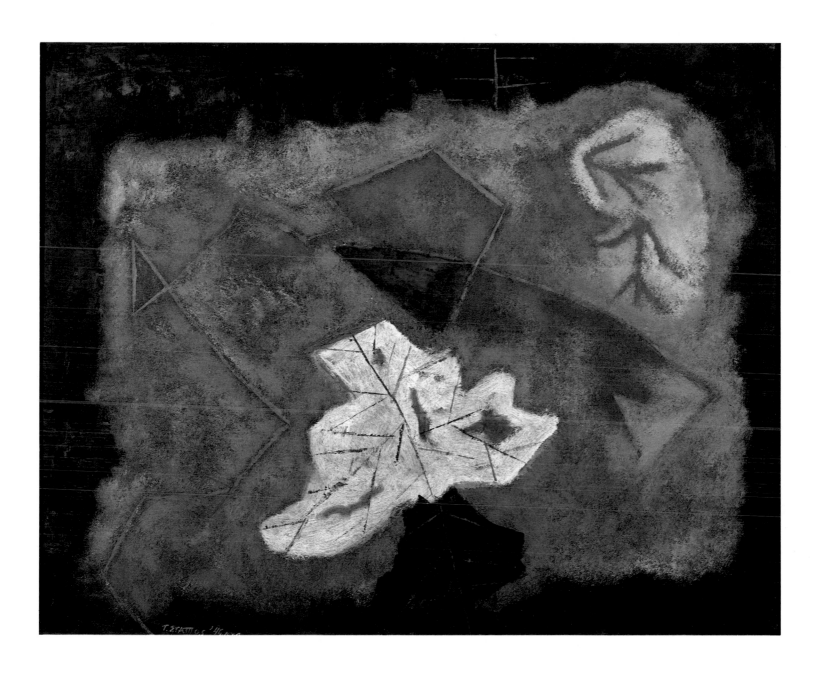

64. THEODOROS STAMOS. *Movement of Plants*, 1945. Oil on masonite, 16 × 20 inches (40.6 × 50.8 cm).
Munson-Williams-Proctor Institute, Utica, New York; Edward W. Root Bequest.

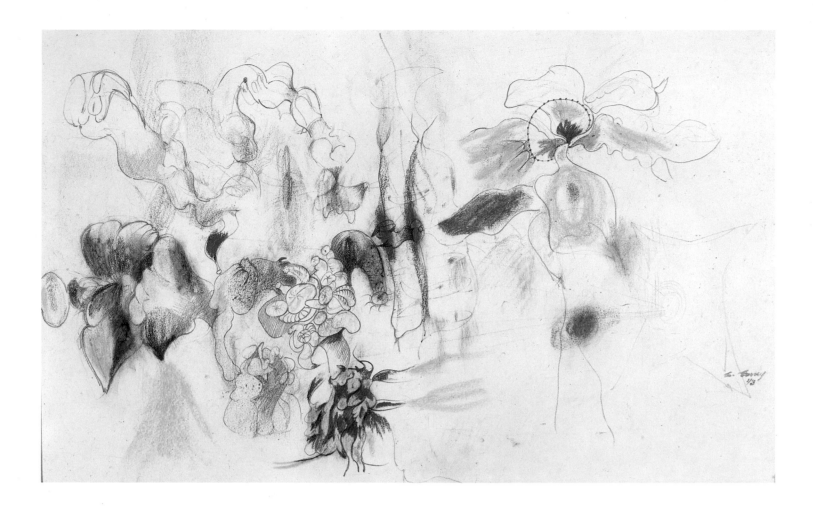

the nature of plant movement in relation to changing environmental conditions such as light, gravity, heat, and insect activity. Darwin showed that the plant is a continuously active organism which moves in response to stimuli, purposely and for its own benefit. One type of movement described by Darwin is characterized by irregular, angular changes of direction in response to light or gravity (heliotropism and geotropism).[128] The blue-green line meandering across the surface of Stamos' *Movement of Plants* may suggest a diagrammatic equivalent of this kind of plant movement. The line describes a path through depictions of leaf and tree forms which turn in various directions. Their positions may indicate the impetus for movement in the vegetable kingdom—to secure the best advantage in relation to the sun or the earth. Darwin viewed the plant world as an active participant in the struggle for life. But we must beware of forcing Stamos' imagery to serve as a scientific illustration of Darwin's theory. While Stamos preferred to work directly from nature, he emphasized that art should not engage in direct transcription of the visible world. "Art is not an adjunct to existence, a reduplication of the actual," he said. "It is a hint and at the same time a promise of the perfect rhythm, the ideal life."[129] His images of the plant world do not describe the organic forms and their settings. Instead, they allude

65. ARSHILE GORKY. *Flowers*, 1943. Graphite and colored wax crayons on paper, 19⅞ × 25⅞ inches (50.5 × 65.7 cm). Fogg Art Museum, Harvard University, Cambridge, Massachusetts; Anonymous loan.

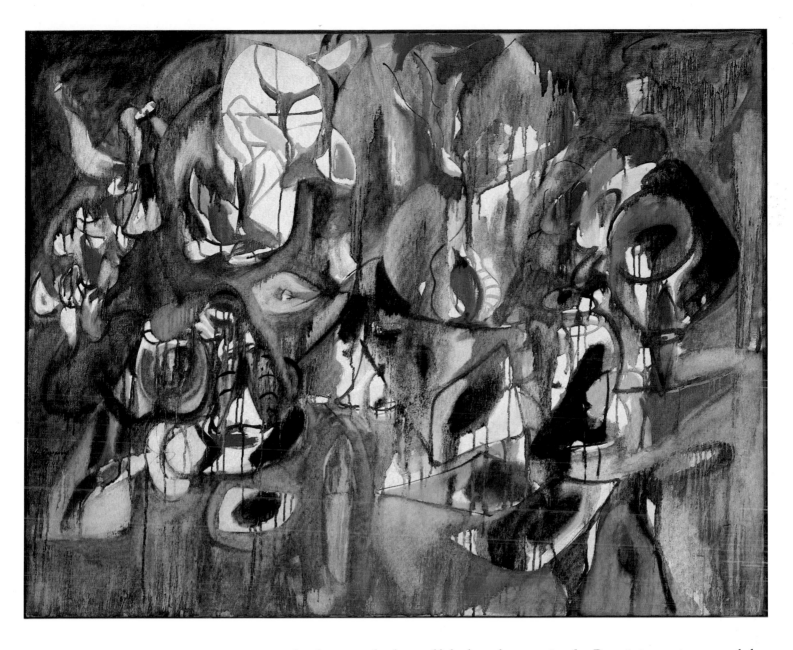

66. ARSHILE GORKY. *One Year the Milkweed*, 1944. Oil on canvas, 37 × 47 inches (94 × 119.4 cm). National Gallery of Art, Washington, D.C.; Ailsa Mellon Bruce Fund.

to the dynamic rhythms of life that characterize the Darwinian universe and the artist's concept of the spiritual fabric of nature.

Arshile Gorky used his intimate, firsthand knowledge of nature to give vital structural expression to his art. As the titles of two of his late works, *Flowers* and *One Year the Milkweed* (Figs. 65, 66), suggest, Gorky drew inspiration from the shapes of the vegetable world as a means of creating spontaneous but ordered compositions in his art. Internal parts of the milkweed flower (*Asclepias*) can be discerned by the tutored botanical eye in *One Year the Milkweed*.[130] It is possible that the artist dissected the milkweed and viewed its parts through a microscope, or perhaps he looked at botanical drawings of the dissected plant.

However, Gorky transforms such shapes by passing them through the filter of his allusive stylistic vocabulary, making it difficult, as in all of his work, to make positive identification of plant parts.[131] In their compositional disposition, Gorky treats these organic references to a kind of musical theme-and-variations development that we can see in *One Year the Milkweed*. The thematic shape is a vaguely geometric enclosure surrounding a lozenge of color. The configuration of the outlines as well as the enclosed forms relate to each other without repeating themselves. These provocative shapes are linked by a thin veil of green paint falling like a spring rain down the surface of the canvas.

Gorky's early love for the gardens and landscape of his native Armenia remained vivid in his memory throughout his life, emerging in his later drawings and oils.[132] Summer visits to the Connecticut and Virginia countryside in the early 1940s renewed his direct communion with nature and sparked a new vocabulary of suggestive abstract forms in his work. Describing some of his crayon sketches (Fig. 65), Gorky pointed out to a friend some specific natural details in the drawings and described how he went about making them. "You see, these are the leaves, this is the grass," he explained. "I got down close to see it. I got them from getting down close to the earth. I could hear it and smell it. Like a little world down there."[133]

Gorky's close inspection of plant life implies a realization that an artist needs to increase his perceptual acuity to draw both structural and expressive power from nature for his art. Gorky used all his five senses and possibly some magnifying apparatus to penetrate the surface of the natural world and extract its aesthetic innards.[134]

André Breton recognized Gorky's creative compulsion to unravel the mysteries of nature, comparing it to the "sublime struggle of flowers growing toward the light of day." Gorky's *Flowers* and works from the pastoral series, Breton wrote, show nature "treated as a cryptogram. . . . The artist has a code by reason of his own sensitive anterior impressions, and can decode nature to reveal the very rhythm of life."[135]

Breaking the "code" of nature poses a compelling challenge to many artists and scientists of the twentieth century. There is a realization that this code lies beyond the grasp of unaided, and even aided, human sensory equipment. It is hidden at the cellular, atomic, subatomic, and finally theoretical levels. The nature artist is often tempted to respond to the verdant pond, the open meadow, or the exotic garden as though they were microcosms of the world. Therefore, new aesthetic formulations have been and will continue to be devised in response to new scientific conceptions of the world around us.

Direct visual experience alone is no longer sufficient for penetrating the truths of nature. Jennifer Bartlett has expressed frustration at the limits of perception even with the apparatus of advanced technology. "There is a point even with the aid of the microscope," she said, "you can't see anymore."[136] She is

67. JENNIFER BARTLETT. *In the Garden #201*, 1983. Oil on canvas; two panels, 84 × 144 inches (213.4 × 365.8 cm) overall. Paula Cooper Gallery, New York.

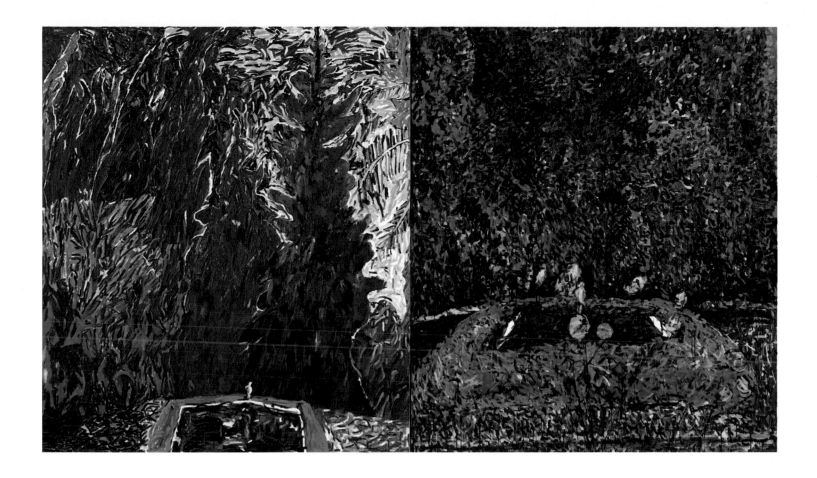

cognizant of the paradox that the closer we get, the less we see. Our diminished understanding of the world is therefore a direct result of new scientific conceptions of the universe. Bartlett called Einstein's theory of relativity "heartbreaking" in its degree of abstraction and immensity of conception: "His ideas? They seem a little sad. Because they're so large."[137]

In her art, however, Bartlett has drawn inspiration from the complexity and scale of the world in which she lives. It was not enough for her to describe a simple garden setting in the south of France in a single painting or even a series of paintings. One hundred and ninety-seven drawings, which involve ten different media, constitute merely the beginning of her ongoing work, *In the Garden*, begun in 1980 (Figs. 145–149). About half the drawings as well as numerous photographs were produced *in situ*, cataloguing the artist's direct response to the setting under varying conditions and from many points of view. At a remove from the location, Bartlett continues to pursue the garden subject, enlarging the scale of her work and increasing the variety of media involved: seven paintings can comprise a single work and can incorporate glass, canvas, and steel plates as supports for paint, paper, and baked enamel. The garden appears in woodcut and silkscreen impressions and in lavishly painted, large-scale oils (Fig. 67). If tallied in parts, Bartlett has devoted close to 250 works to a single garden setting—and she has not yet finished.

This encyclopedic rendering significantly includes countless vantage points: a variety of perspectives on the entire scene, fragments of the scene, and combinations of fragments. *In the Garden* has been aptly described as a crossbreed of "possible ways of seeing . . . with possible ways of setting down what has been seen."[138] Bartlett's multiplicity of approaches suggests an artistic response to a physical universe that escapes our sensory grasp.

STUART DAVIS recognized almost forty years ago that modern science has created a "new environment" for artists. The accelerating speed of scientific advance makes his words even truer today. Contemporary artists, therefore, are challenged to respond to rapidly changing truths of nature. Attempts to create formal aesthetic equivalents to our expanding universe and the covert patterns of life within it have pushed the creative sensors of modern flower artists to their limits and produced some remarkable works of art.

A comparison of three representations of the water lily by American flower artists of the last three centuries demonstrates the abiding search for an aesthetic illumination of the "truth to nature." The plant looms large in its pond setting in William Bartram's *Drawing of the Round Leafed Nymphaea* of 1761–62 (Fig. 20). Just one hundred years later, John La Farge pictured the flower in an intensely verdant environment crowned by a shady branch of linden leaves, in *Water Lily and Linden Leaves* of 1862 (Fig. 68). A penetrating distillation of the plant, which goes so far as to eliminate its exquisite blossom, emerges in Ellsworth Kelly's elegant drawing *Water Lily*, of 1968 (Fig. 69).

All three artists select plant forms to embody their aesthetic insights into the natural relationships in the world around them. Each artist brings to the task his personal vision, his artistic conceptions, and his understanding of the natural world. Either consciously or unconsciously, each is guided in his aesthetic formulations by contemporary cultural attitudes toward nature. As these attitudes develop, artistic reactions to the "truths" of nature begin to appear. Bartram's drawing, as we have seen, is full of Linnaean details in its clearly defined image of the plant's reproductive organs and in its textural rendering of foliate patterns. A sharp shift in scale dislocates the small vignette of bird and flower from the tall aquatic plants on the right. Both nature and art give evidence of the pre-Darwinian concept of earthly design: a static world of separate but perfect parts.

La Farge focuses on a small but vitally interdependent representation of vegetable life in his *Water Lily and Linden Leaves*. The blossom of the water lily is presented in full bloom, slightly off-center, in a fertile environment. Broad washes of transparent yet saturated tones of blue and green lubricate the water

68. JOHN LA FARGE. *Water Lily and Linden Leaves*, 1862. Oil on panel, 12 × 11 inches (30.5 × 27.9 cm). Mead Art Museum, Amherst College, Massachusetts.

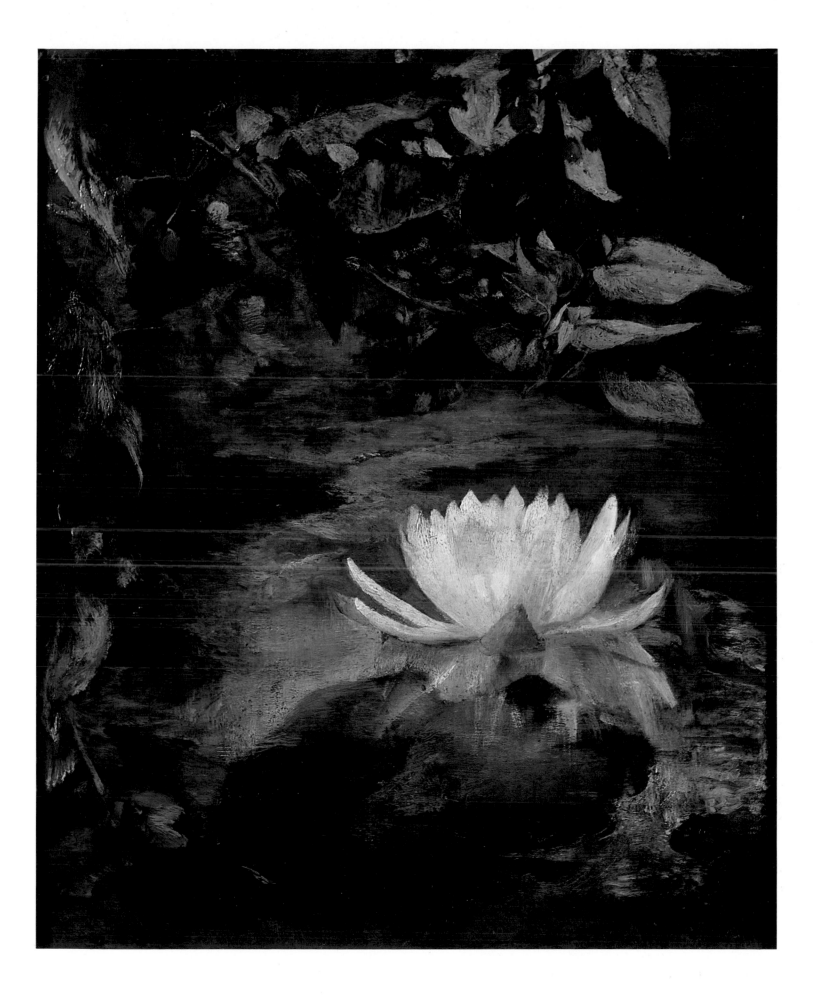

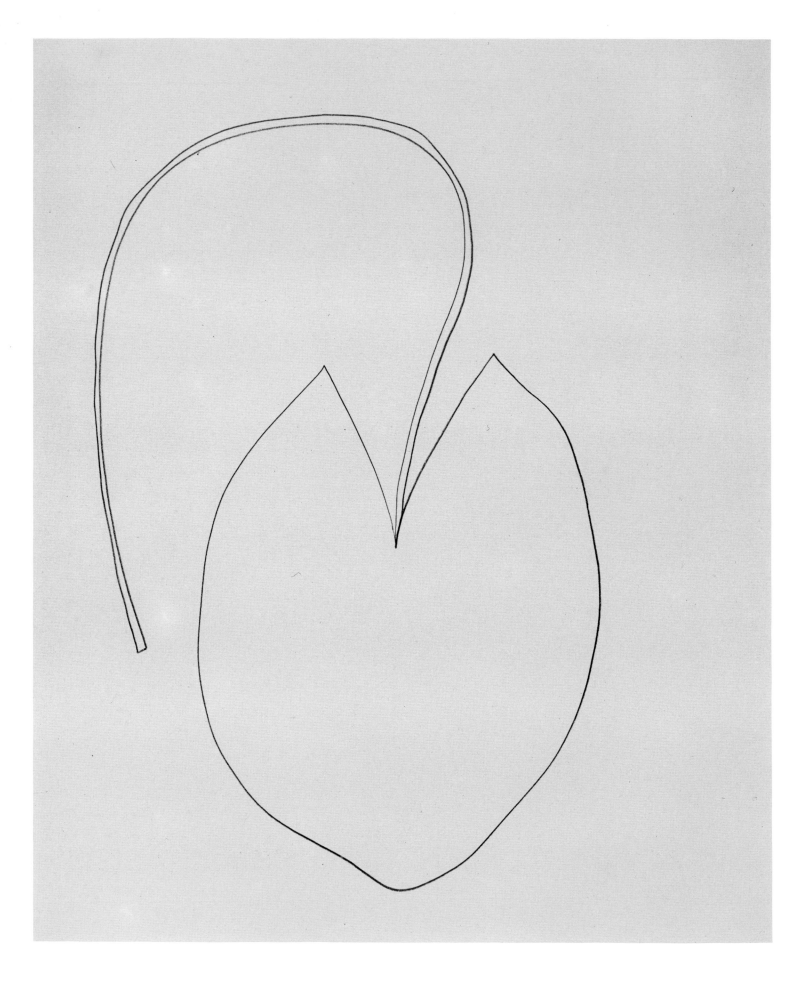

with a reflective, glimmering quality. Vigorous and varied brushwork further heightens the vitality of the foliated pond setting. In the midst of the rich but somber aqueous surroundings, the brilliant white water lily glows with luminous life. La Farge gives visual life to the Darwinian view of nature as an interactive environment. Like the scientists of his period, he knew "that the world *is* in a process of development, and that gradually, as advancing knowledge has enabled us to take a sufficiently wide view of the world, we have come to see that it is so."[139]

Ellsworth Kelly selected an isolated leaf to project the essence of nature in his representation of a water lily (Fig. 69). Like all of his images, the water lily developed from a direct visual experience.[140] He took the plant from its pond setting, placed it in a large bowl so that he could take a long look at its floating form, and made thirteen separate drawings of it in a single session. Kelly said that he felt frustrated most of the time because he "couldn't get the quality of the leaf." Only later, at a remove from the experience, could he acknowledge that he had "finally done it."[141] *Water Lily* was made after that concentrated series of studies. It is a distillation of the plant's contour: the essential line which identifies and gives integrity to the live form. Kelly has removed leaf veining and all surface data from his record of the visual world in his effort to synthesize its essential form. He takes an aesthetic direction in line with the modern scientific perspective on nature: the pursuit of hidden design.

Three artists among many, then, over a span of three centuries, selected flowers as a subject for their art. William Bartram, John La Farge, and Ellsworth Kelly believed that these natural forms could hold within their graceful contours important truths about the character of life. Using what André Breton described as their "sensitive anterior impressions," they explored the vegetable kingdom in pursuit of factual, spiritual, and aesthetic essences. Through their images of flowers, these artists sought to "decode nature to reveal the very rhythm of life." "Lower exercise," Sir Joshua, indeed.

69. ELLSWORTH KELLY. *Water Lily*, 1968. Pencil on paper, 29 × 23 inches (73.7 × 58.4 cm). Private collection.

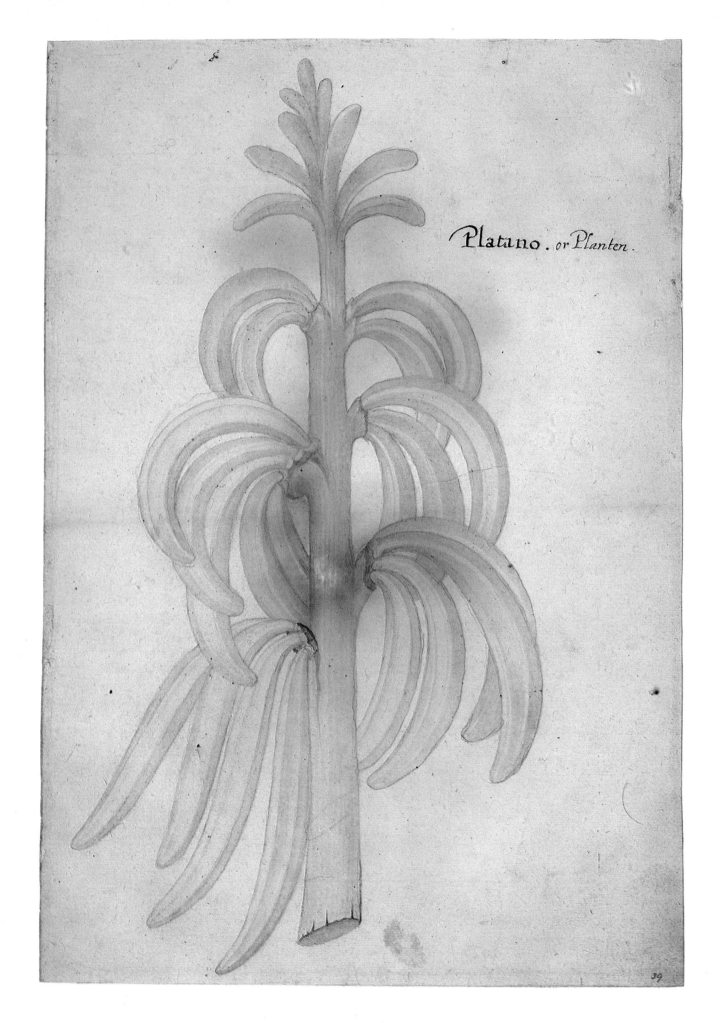

Platano. or Planten.

39

Botanical Drawings

THE EARLIEST IMAGES of American flora were produced by European artist-explorers seeking to document the newly discovered natural products of the New World. Both under commission and in response to personal curiosity, such artists made drawings on location which were often published as engravings after their return home. Some of the original drawings, however, survive, among them John White's *Horn Plantains on the Stalk (Plantano or Planten)* (Fig. 70), an edible fruit introduced into the West Indies by the Spanish, and the purely decorative *Sabatia stellaris* (rosegentian) (Fig. 14), with its colorful tints and graceful contours.

The drawings of John White are simple plant portraits, presenting a single specimen of a flower suspended on a blank page. Usually the flower is represented from a frontal point of view to convey as much information as possible about its structure. From colonial times to the present, American artists produced this kind of documentary drawing. The Philadelphian William Bartram, the first American botanical artist, discovered the *Franklinia alatamaha* (Fig. 19), a magnificent flowering tree, on an exploratory trip through Georgia. His lively drawing reflects his delight in spotting "two beautiful shrubs in all their blooming graces."[1] Bartram's drawing remains the only accurate record of this tree growing in its native habitat. Every specimen of the franklinia known in this country is descended from the seeds he procured on his Georgian expedition.[2]

Botanical artists, however, did not always stick to the facts in their representations of plants. William Young, another Philadelphian, produced a sprightly watercolor drawing of a palm tree, *Palmata digitalis*, and assorted flowers (Fig. 74), which, although documentary in purpose, defies identification. The artist applied so much imagination and decorative whimsy to his drawing that an effort to identify the species of the palm has been compared to the futility of naming a breed of dog with horns.[3]

The art of accurate botanical drawing in the form of plant portraits sur-

70. JOHN WHITE. *Horn Plantains on the Stalk (Platano or Planten)*, c. 1586. Watercolor over black lead outlines on paper, 12¾ × 8¾ inches (32.4 × 22.2 cm). The Trustees of the British Museum, London.

vived in the work of the nineteenth-century artist Isaac Sprague. Sprague accompanied John James Audubon on one of his Missouri excursions and later illustrated numerous botanical texts, including some by Asa Gray.[4] The *Magnolia auriculata* (Fig. 80) was one of a series of drawings prepared between 1849 and 1859 to illustrate Gray's report on the forest trees of North America.[5] The magnolia in its many varieties is one of the spectacles of American flora. It had already captured the attention of the eighteenth-century English artist-explorer Mark Catesby, who made a detailed drawing of its internal parts (Fig. 71).

It was not only botanical illustrators who produced documentary plant portraits. Professional artists such as Jasper Cropsey, Samuel Colman, and Martin Johnson Heade (Figs. 99, 101, 104) made accurate representations of individual flowers to serve as studies for finished still-life and landscape compositions. Heade, for example, also responded to the allure of the magnolia with numerous sketches and finished paintings of the flower (Figs. 105, 108). Even among twentieth-century artists, we find examples of documentary drawings of plants. The practiced eye can readily identify a floating bladderwort in company with Joseph Stella's *Lupine* (Fig. 130) as well as the ragweed in Charles Burchfield's *Wild Flower Study* (Fig. 133). Nevertheless, the creative use of artistic license in these drawings makes them unacceptable images for a botanical textbook.

Plant portraits also appear in more elaborate botanical drawings, studies that include multiple specimens and landscape settings. Flowers and birds together are depicted in many of Mark Catesby's nature compositions (Fig. 15). Complex and artful arrangements of plant and bird specimens with landscape backgrounds characterize illustrations for John James Audubon's *Birds of America* (Figs. 77, 78). In fact, the distinction between nature study and landscape painting is obscured in the work of many American artists. Early on, William Bartram had included environments for his flora and fauna. Martin Johnson Heade later produced many compositions with both birds and plants situated in tropical settings. Hummingbirds and passionflowers populate the landscape in two works: *Tropical Landscape with Ten Hummingbirds* (Fig. 106) and *Passion Flowers and Hummingbirds* (Fig. 42). It is only the arrangement of the subjects and the number of specimens depicted that make the *Tropical Landscape* seem more of a nature study than a landscape composition, although no less magnificent.[6] The relationship of floral subject to its setting can be explored further in the still-life compositions featuring flowers and in flower drawings made by landscape artists.

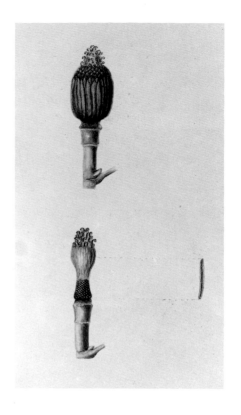

71. MARK CATESBY. *Magnolia Buds*, c. 1726. Gouache and pencil on paper, 14¾ × 10½ inches (37.5 × 26.7 cm). The Pierpont Morgan Library, New York; Gift of Henry S. Morgan.

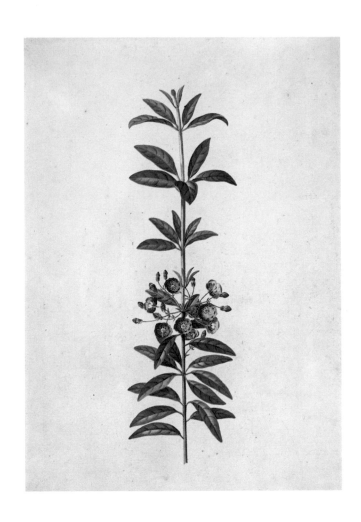

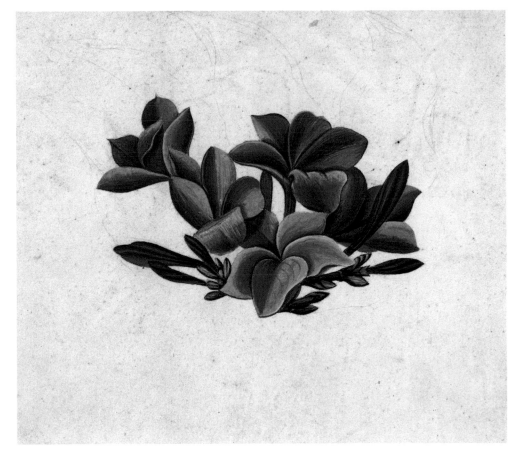

72. MARK CATESBY. *Kalmia*, c. 1726. Gouache on paper, 15 × 11 ¼ inches (38.1 × 28.6 cm). The Pierpont Morgan Library, New York; Gift of Henry S. Morgan.

73. MARK CATESBY. *Plumeria flore rosea*, c. 1726. Gouache and pencil on vellum mounted on backing, 14 × 9 inches (35.6 × 22.9 cm). The Pierpont Morgan Library, New York; Gift of Henry S. Morgan.

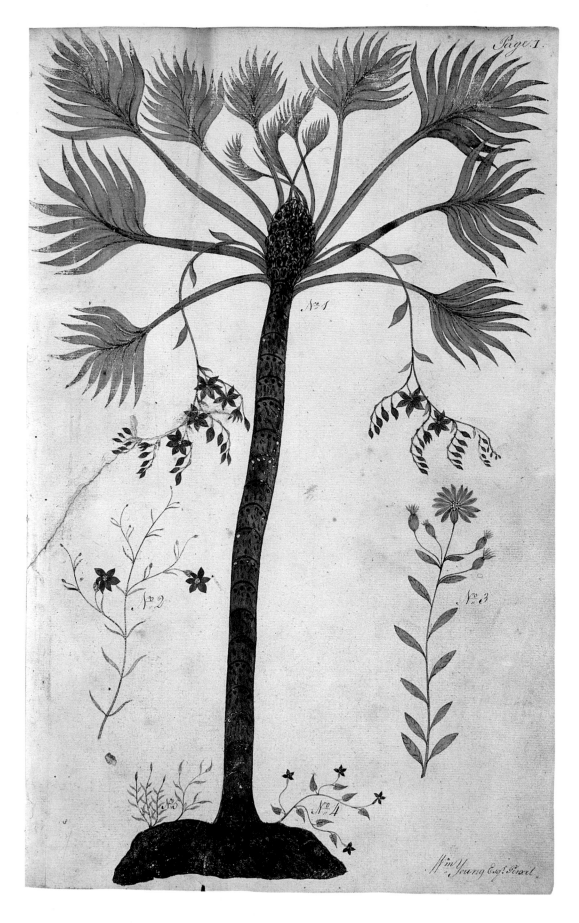

74. WILLIAM YOUNG. *Palmata digitalis, Aster, Tetandria Moss*, 1766–67. Watercolor on paper, 15 × 8½ inches (38.1 × 21.6 cm). The Trustees of the British Museum (Natural History), London.

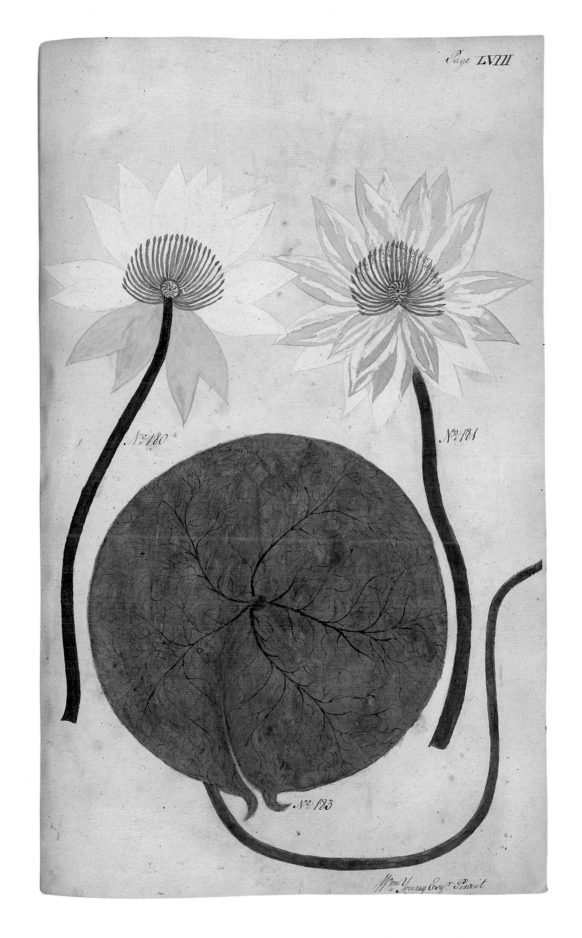

75. WILLIAM YOUNG. *Nymphaea, Nymphaea, Nymphaea Leaf*, 1766–67. Watercolor on
paper, 15 × 8½ inches (38.1 × 21.6 cm). The Trustees of the British Museum (Natural
History), London.

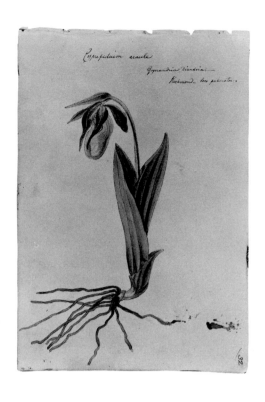

76. BENJAMIN H. LATROBE. *Cyprepedium acaule*, c. 1798. Ink, pencil, and water-color on paper, 7 × 10¼ inches (17.8 × 26 cm). Benjamin Latrobe Papers, Museum and Library of Maryland History, Maryland Historical Society, Baltimore.

77. JOHN JAMES AUDUBON. *Key West Quail Dove*, 1832. Watercolor and cutouts on paper, 24 × 19 inches (61 × 48.3 cm). The New-York Historical Society.

78. JOHN JAMES AUDUBON. *Ruby-throated Hummingbirds*, c. 1825. Watercolor on paper, 24 × 19 inches (61 × 48.3 cm). The New-York Historical Society.

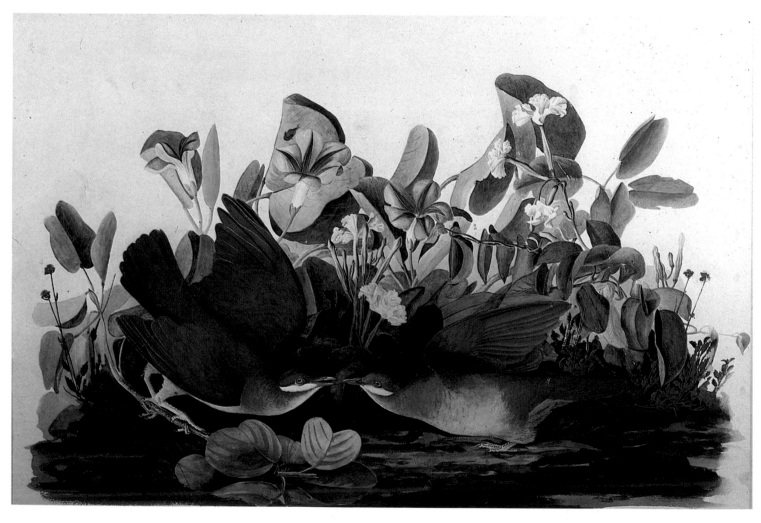

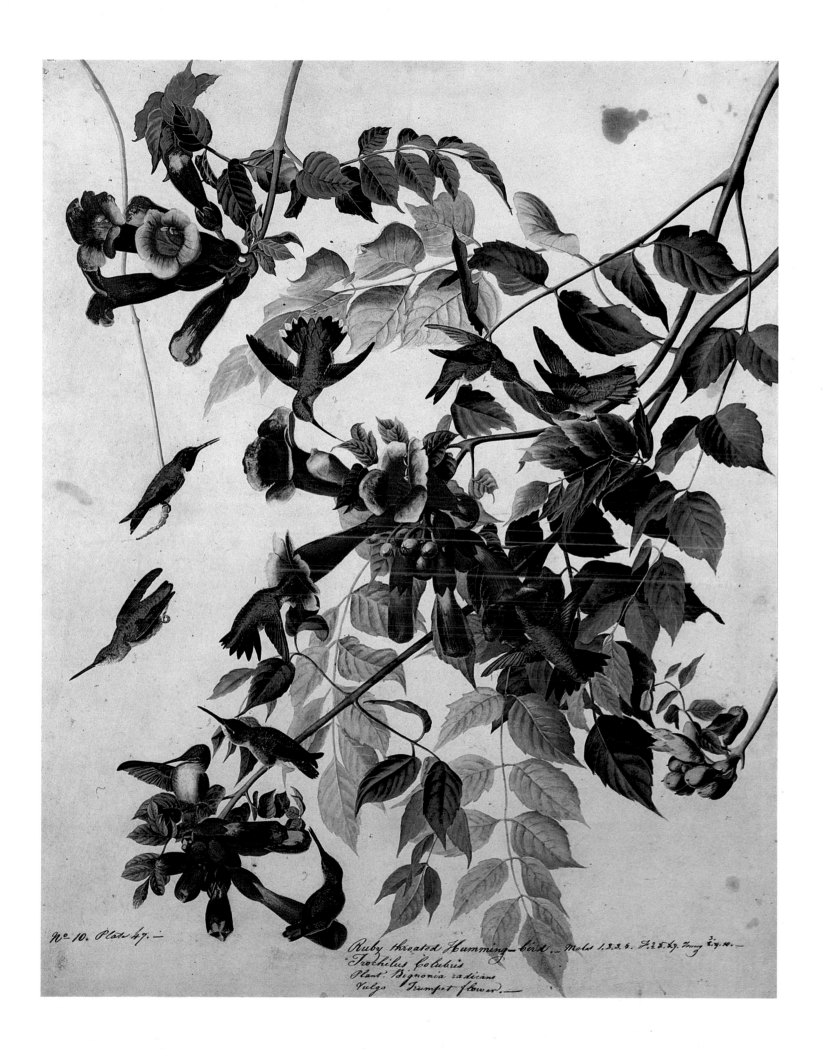

No. 10. Plate 47.—

Ruby throated Humming-bird.— Male 1.3.3.4. F.3.5.6.7. Young 2.4.4.—
Trochilus Colubris
Plant. Bignonia radicans
Vulgo Trumpet flower.—

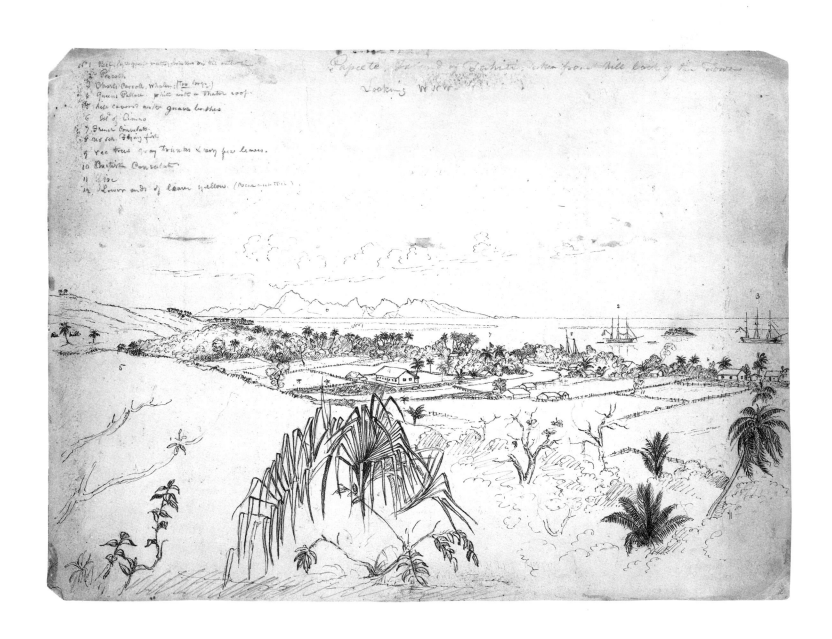

79. Titian Ramsay Peale. *Papeete, Island of Tahiti. Taken from Hill Back of the Town/Looking WNW*, 1839. Ink and pencil on paper, 10⅞ × 15 inches (27.6 × 38.1 cm). The American Museum of Natural History, New York.

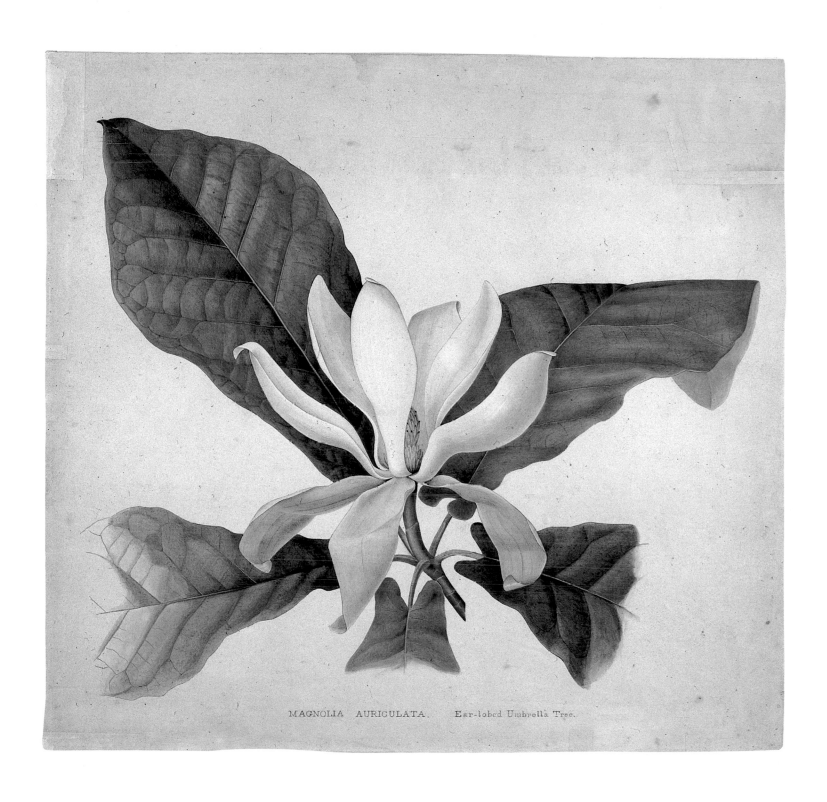

MAGNOLIA AURICULATA. Ear-lobed Umbrella Tree.

80. Isaac Sprague. *Magnolia auriculata, Ear-lobed Umbrella Tree,* 1849–52. Watercolor on paper, 13⅞ × 14⅞ inches (35.2 × 37.8 cm). Hunt Institute for Botanical Documentation, Carnegie-Mellon University, Pittsburgh.

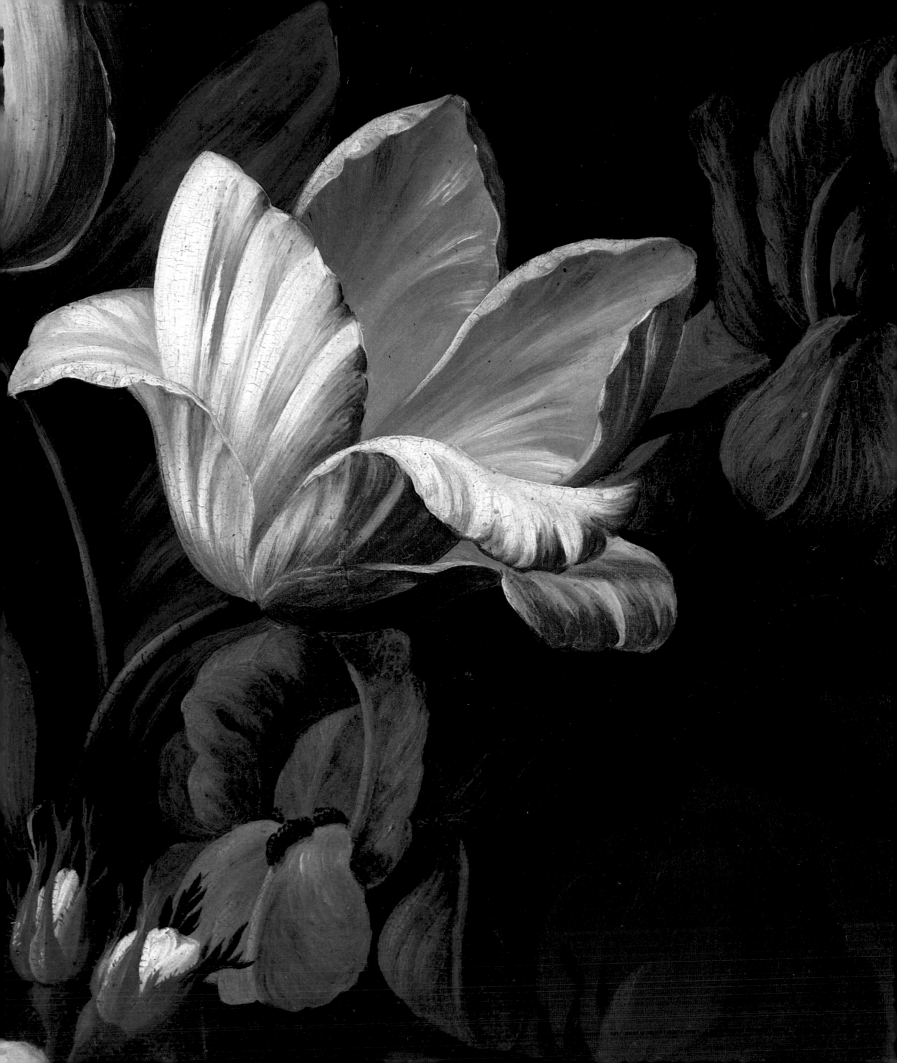

Floral Still Life

PAINTINGS OF FLOWERS in vases, either singly or in bouquet combinations, are generally called flower pieces and are grouped under the generic title of still life. A still-life painting, according to an accepted definition, "is a representation of objects which lack the ability to move (e.g., flower, shells, plate) and which are for artistic purposes grouped into a composition."[1] It was often the formal possibilities of these immobile objects that attracted artists to the genre. Almost every imaginable shape and color could be extracted from an eye-catching and mouth-watering assortment of live flowers, ripe fruits, and silver goblets.

Interest in still-life painting, a genre which historically occupied a position of minor status in America, developed during the nineteenth century primarily as a result of exposure to the European tradition. Although vases of flowers had served as accessories to portraits (particularly of female subjects) before that time, it was not until the mid-nineteenth century that American artists began to treat the floral world as an independent theme.

Since the roots of the still-life genre can be found in Northern Europe, it is not surprising that some of the most striking early flower pieces made in America came from the hand of a German immigrant. Severin Roesen produced a substantial body of work depicting flowers and fruits, either singly or together, and almost always gathered in interior settings. *Still Life: Flowers and Fruit* (Fig. 81) is one of his most elaborate and magnificent compositions. It presents an extraordinary panoply of fully blooming flowers assembled in a glass vase. To the right of the vase, a luscious display of fruits in a variety of colors and shapes competes with its floral counterpart for space on the marble ledge. With this painting, Roesen surely attempts to evoke wonder at the artistic potential of some of nature's common and exotic products. Although each item in the still life is described accurately, we have no doubt that Roesen followed the tradition of still-life painting and made his grouping for "artistic purposes." How else could fruits and flowers of different seasons appear on a single tabletop?

Roesen's work was not nearly so well known in his own day as the still-life

SEVERIN ROESEN, detail of *Still Life: Flowers and Fruit*, 1848 (see Fig. 82).

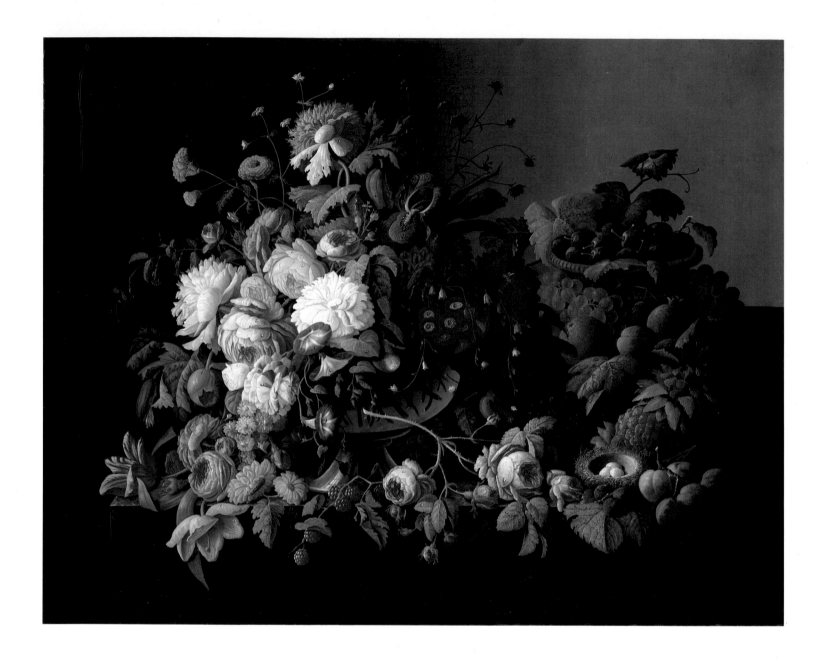

paintings of George Henry Hall. For an artist of this "minor" genre, Hall's work found a surprisingly brisk market. Critic Henry Tuckerman recorded with astonishment that "the large sum of twelve thousand dollars was obtained for seventy-five small but carefully elaborated fruit and flower-pieces."[2] Although "small but carefully elaborated" compositions are typical of Hall's work, *Still Life: Vase of Flowers and Watermelon* (Fig. 83) shows that the artist did, on occasion, attempt more complex arrangements. Both the setting and the subject of the painting reflect Hall's delight in the display of pattern and texture in paint. The elaborate wall covering and carved tabletop embrace a luxuriant combination of flowers and fruit. In the selection of specimens for his bouquet, Hall follows the Dutch taste in gathering the showiest of garden flowers: the rose, iris, daphne, tulip, and the exotic red glory-pea. The artist tempts us to run our finger through the pink, juicy syrup of the watermelon, which has spilled in glistening splendor onto the polished surface of the table.

While the formal challenge of the flower piece remains constant, the selection of specimens for the bouquet is more variable. The rose was the runaway favorite in nineteenth-century American painting and gardens. In Western art, it is the one flower that seems never to have lost its popularity. For the Renaissance painter the rose was the symbol of love, but by the late nineteenth century the charms of the flower were deemed more aesthetic than symbolic. George Cochran Lambdin, a cultivator as well as a painter of roses, felt that the flower had no match in its combination of "such beauty of form and color with such exquisite delicacy of texture and such delicious perfume."[3] All but the perfume is painted in Julian Alden Weir's *Flower Piece* (Fig. 85).

Peonies and chrysanthemums captured the imagination of many late nineteenth-century American flower painters. The appearance of these flowers in the work of such artists as Thomas Hovenden and William Merritt Chase (Figs. 86, 87) reflects the influence of Oriental art and horticultural fashion.[4] The chrysanthemum, widely cultivated in China, Japan, and Korea, was selected as one of the Four Noble Plants by the scholar-artists of the Ming Dynasty. This flower, along with the bamboo, plum blossom, and orchid, represented quintessential specimens of nature.[5] Chase's remarkable yellow bouquet was not purchased directly from the Japanese market depicted in Robert Blum's painting (Fig. 88), but the taste for the flower did come from that part of the world.

While the milkweed is a plant that seems to have elicited the interest of at least a few artists in every generation from John White to Ellsworth Kelly (Fig. 140), the fortunes of the calla lily were less constant. George Cochran Lambdin cultivated callas in pots and also liked to set off their elegant contours against a black background (Fig. 89); John Henry Hill scrutinized a single specimen *in situ* (Fig. 90). But it was not until two generations later that the flower was back in vogue. Among other twentieth-century artists, Marsden Hartley, Charles Demuth, and Georgia O'Keeffe painted the calla lily. O'Keeffe chose pink as the proper background color to set off its exotic quality (Fig. 137). Exactly what it was about the calla that appealed to O'Keeffe and her contemporaries, even critic Henry McBride could not precisely say, "other than the fact that it was considered vulgar a generation ago . . . but possibly that in itself is sufficient reason."[6]

Whatever flowers occupied the vase, the arrangement of them was treated with increasing naturalism as the nineteenth century drew to a close. This development was in part due to an increased interest in exploring flowers in natural light and even in combination with outdoor settings. John La Farge placed a bowl of cut flowers at a window to study the reflections of sunlight on their

81. SEVERIN ROESEN. *Still Life: Flowers and Fruit*, c. 1855. Oil on canvas, 40 × 50⅜ inches (101.6 × 128 cm). The Metropolitan Museum of Art, New York; Charles Allen Munn Bequest; Fosburgh Fund, Inc. Gift; Mr. and Mrs. J. William Middendorf II Gift; and Henry G. Keasbey Bequest.

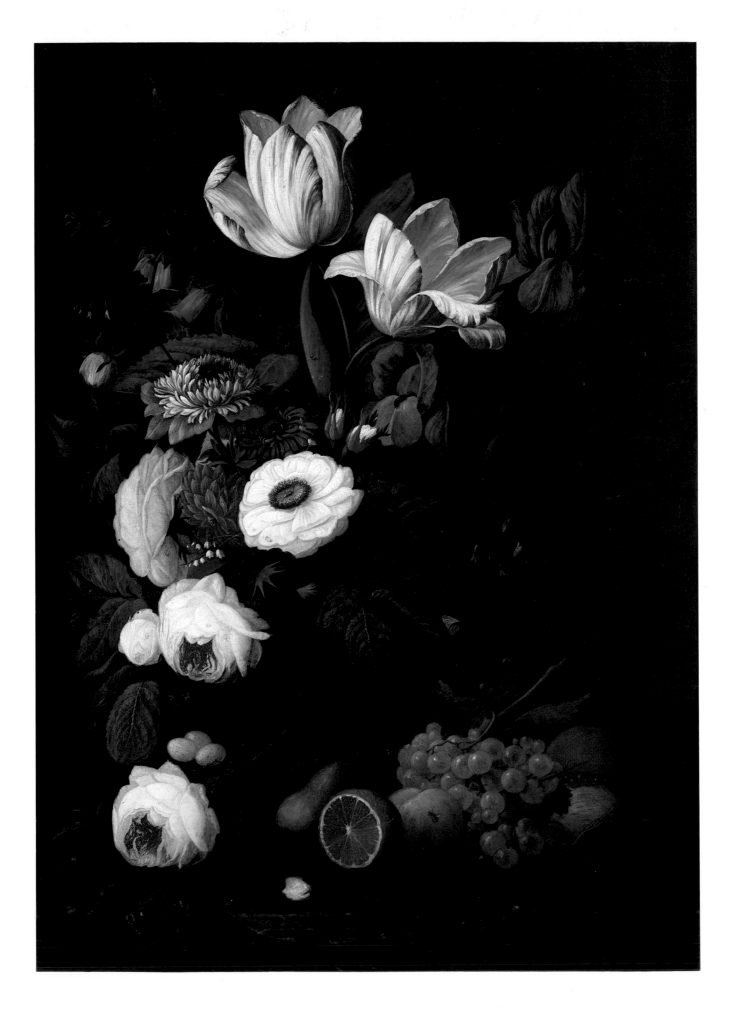

petals (Fig. 91). Ellen Robbins built her brilliantly colored flower piece on an outdoor ledge, set off by a landscape of trees in the background (Fig. 92).

The motif of the potted plant had been used as a decorative accessory in early nineteenth-century American art (Fig. 22), but it reemerged in connection with the developing naturalism of late nineteenth-century flower painting. It was the lively growth quality of the potted plant that interested William T. Richards, who produced many intricate studies of such plants. He often noted down on the drawings the name, color, and measurements of the various specimens. Such careful scrutiny of the plant world enabled him to endow the intricate contours of the ferns in *Conservatory* (Fig. 93) with the vigorous freshness of growing things.

Other artists, such as George Cochran Lambdin and John Henry Twachtman, chose the greenhouse environment for their images of potted flowers (Figs. 94, 95). Natural light penetrates the glass enclosures, drawing attention to the growth properties of these cultivated specimens and almost simulating an outdoor setting.

The distinction between flower piece and landscape vignette can become obscure, particularly in the work of artists inspired by the Ruskinian aesthetic. It would be difficult to say whether *Bird's Nest and Dogroses* (Fig. 33) by John William Hill, an American Pre-Raphaelite artist, should be categorized as a still life in a natural setting or as a landscape painting.[7] This close-up view of nature appears extremely naturalistic except that the wild roses have been cut and neatly arranged around the bird's nest. Hill's informal ordering of nature in this painting bears comparison with the Victorian cottage garden—a horticultural world far removed from the elaborate formal gardens of seventeenth-century Holland that filled the bouquets of the early floral still lifes.

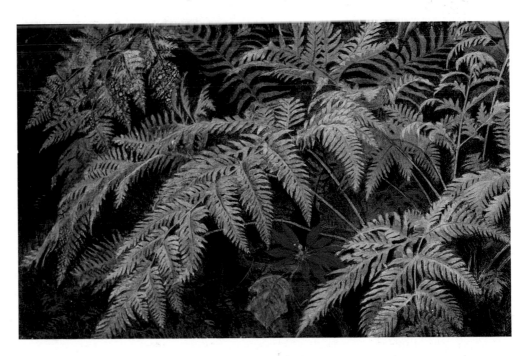

82. SEVERIN ROESEN. *Still Life: Flowers and Fruit,* 1848. Oil on canvas, 36 × 26 inches (91.4 × 66 cm). The Corcoran Gallery of Art, Washington, D.C., Museum Purchase through the gift of the Honorable Orme Wilson.

WILLIAM T. RICHARDS, detail of *Conservatory,* 1860 (see Fig. 93).

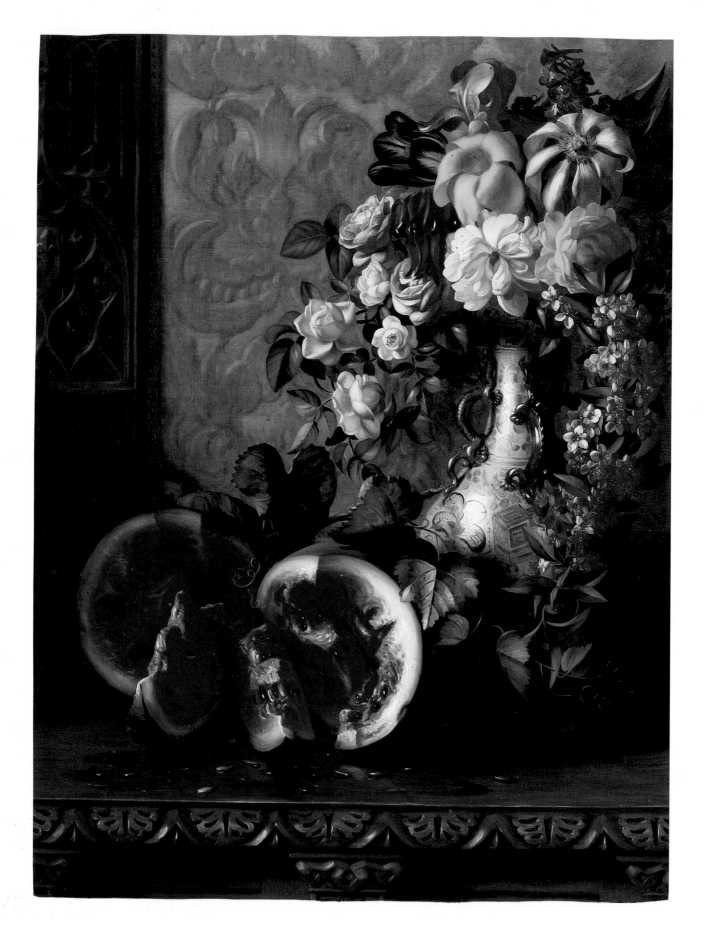

83. GEORGE HENRY HALL. *Still Life: Vase of Flowers and Watermelon*, 1865. Oil on canvas, 40⅝ × 30⅜ inches
(103.2 × 77.2 cm). Albrecht Art Museum, St. Joseph, Missouri; The Enid and Crosby Kemper Foundation Collection.

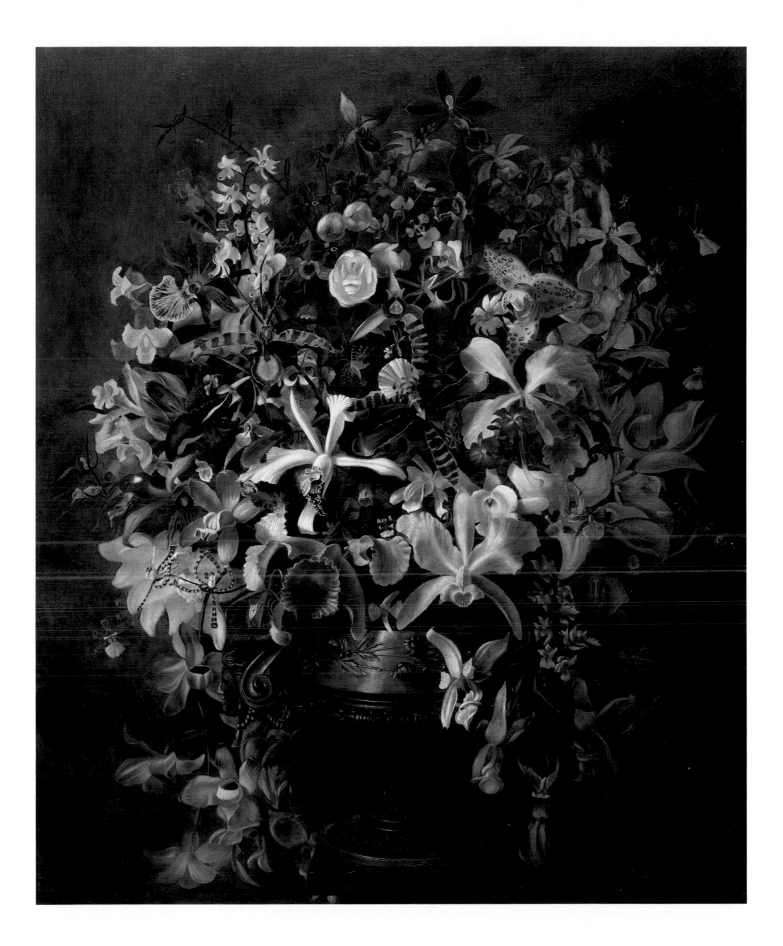

84. WILLIAM JACOB HAYS. *Bouquet of Orchids*, 1871. Oil on fabric, 36 × 30 inches (91:4 × 76.2 cm).
Collection of Mr. James M. and Dr. Edith Hays Walton-Myers.

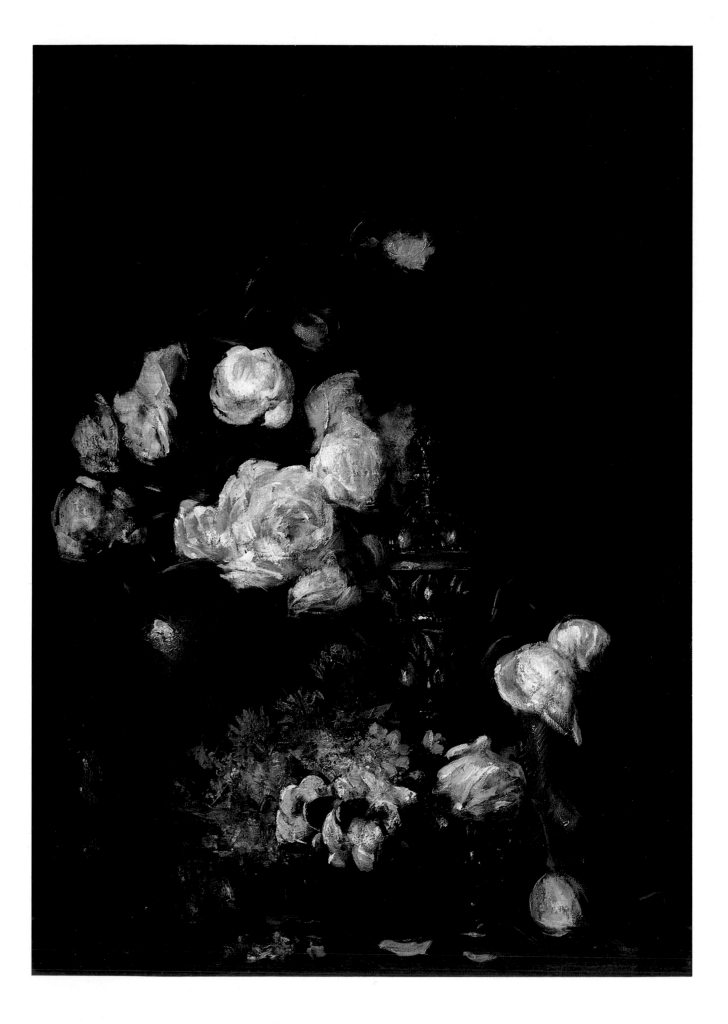

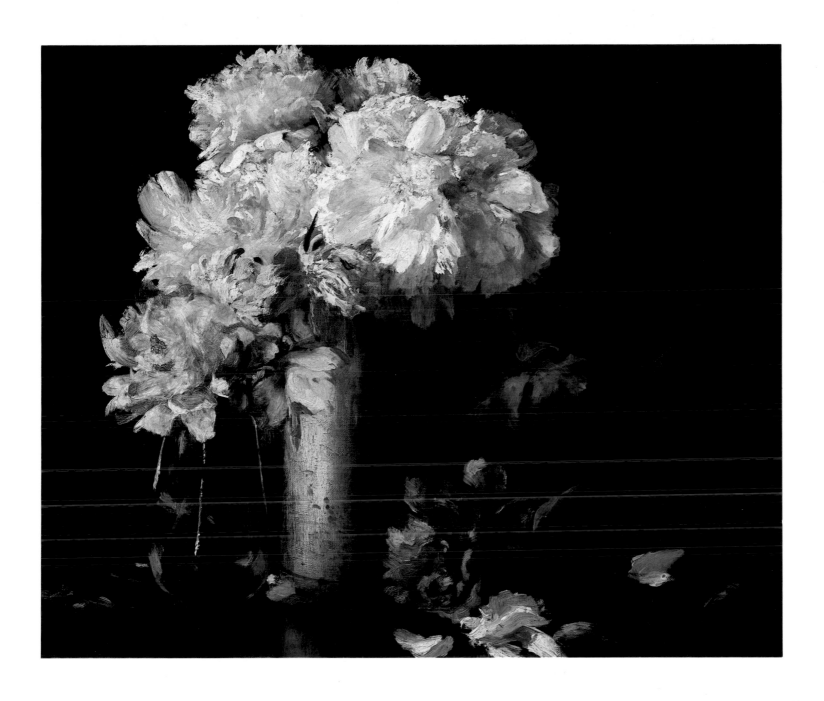

85. JULIAN ALDEN WEIR. *Flower Piece*, 1882. Oil on canvas, 29⅝ × 21½ inches
(75.2 × 54.6 cm). Portland Art Museum, Oregon.

86. THOMAS HOVENDEN. *Peonies*, 1886. Oil on canvas, 20 × 24 inches (50.8 × 61 cm).
Pennsylvania Academy of the Fine Arts, Philadelphia; Gift of Mrs. Edward H. Coates
in memory of Mr. Coates.

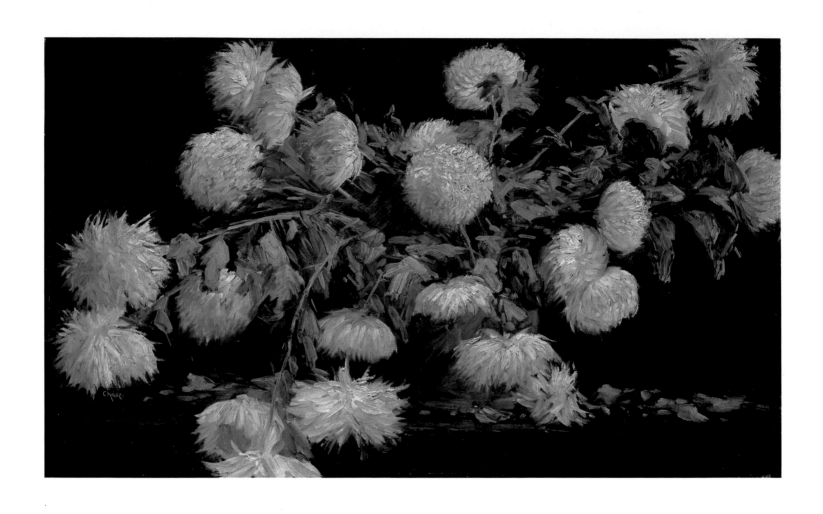

87. WILLIAM MERRITT CHASE. *Chrysanthemums*, c. 1878. Oil on canvas,
26⅞ × 44¾ inches (68.3 × 113.7 cm). National Gallery of Art, Washington, D.C.;
Gift of Chester Dale.

88. ROBERT F. BLUM. *The Flower Market*, c. 1891. Oil on canvas, 31⅝ × 25⅜ inches
(80.3 × 64.5 cm). Collection of James Maroney.

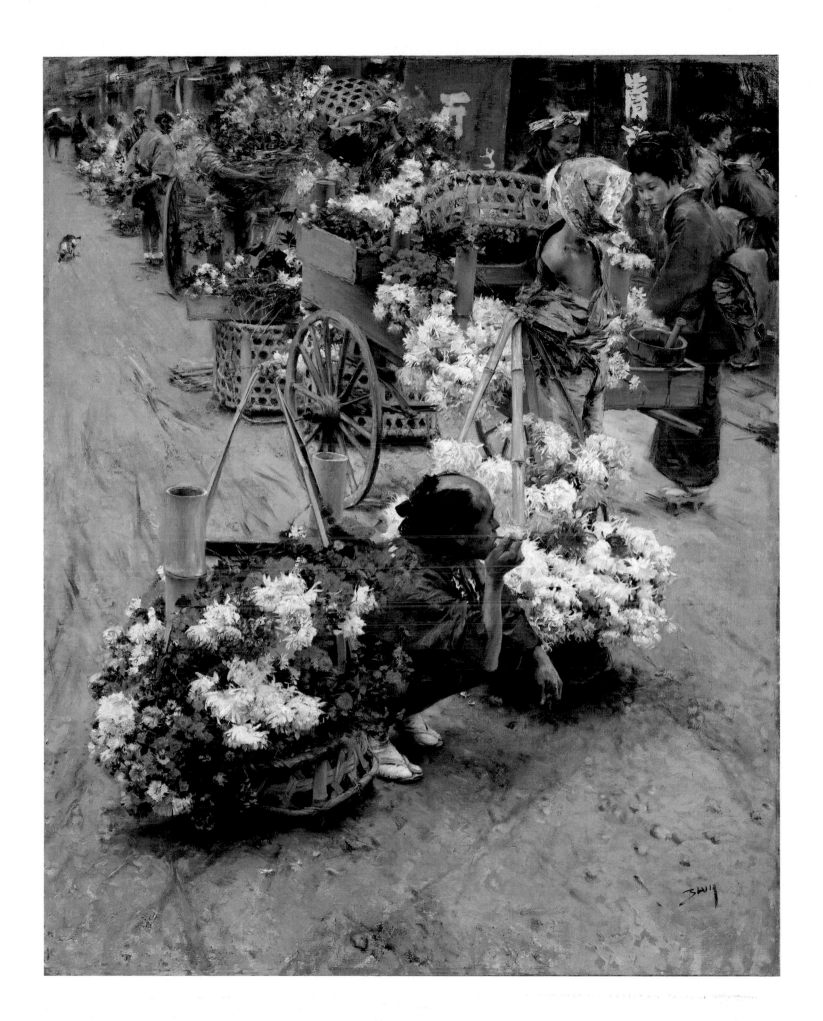

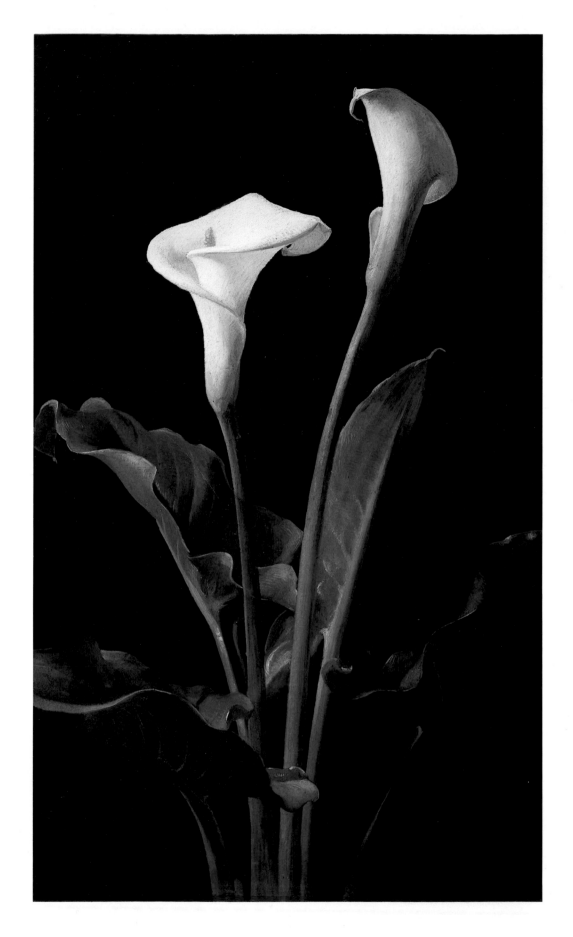

89. GEORGE COCHRAN LAMBDIN. *Calla Lilies*, 1874. Oil on panel,
20 × 11⅞ inches (50.8 × 30.2 cm). Berry-Hill Galleries, New York.

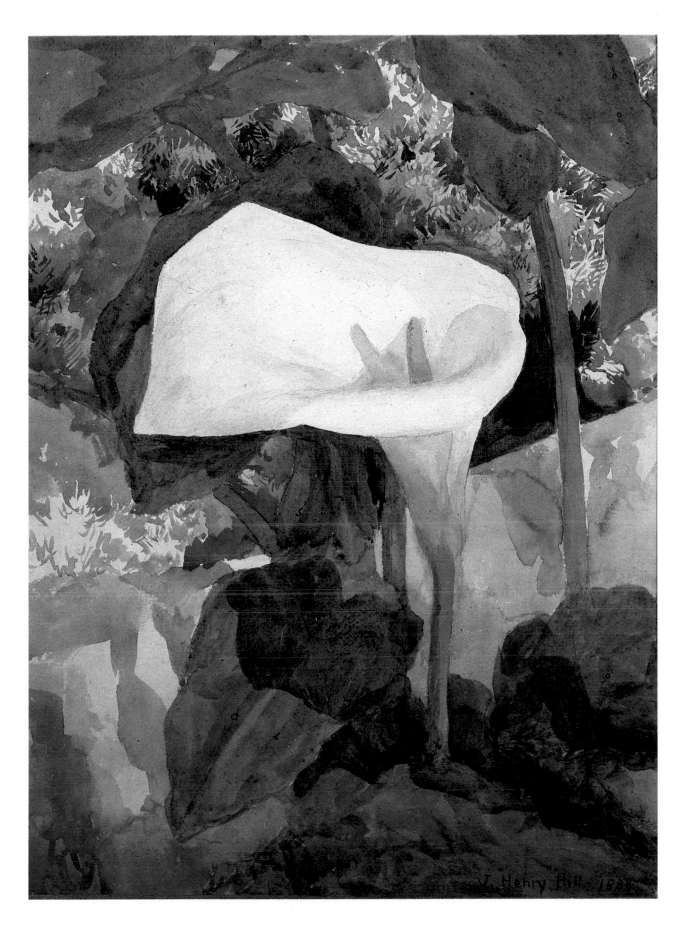

90. JOHN HENRY HILL. *Calla*, 1888. Watercolor on paper, 13 × 9 inches (33 × 22.9 cm).
Collection of Judith and Wilbur Ross.

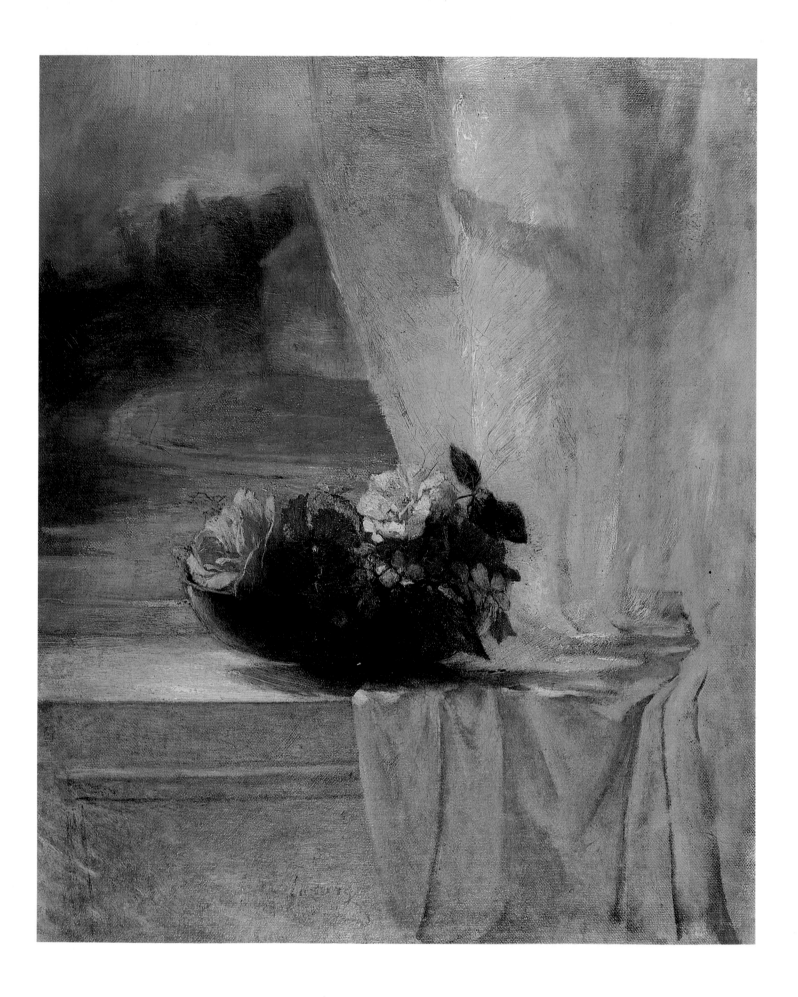

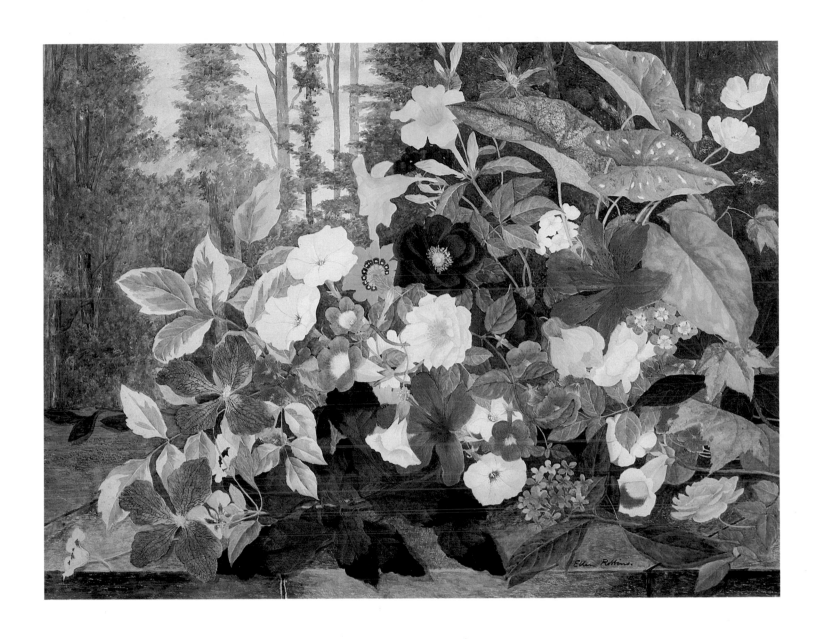

91. JOHN LA FARGE. *Flowers on a Window Ledge*, c. 1862. Oil on canvas, 24 × 20 inches
(61 × 50.8 cm). The Corcoran Gallery of Art, Washington, D.C.; Museum Purchase,
The Anna E. Clark Fund.

92. ELLEN ROBBINS. *Flowers in a Wood*, c. 1875. Watercolor on paper, 18½ × 28 inches
(47 × 71.1 cm). Collection of Mr. and Mrs. Arie L. Kopelman.

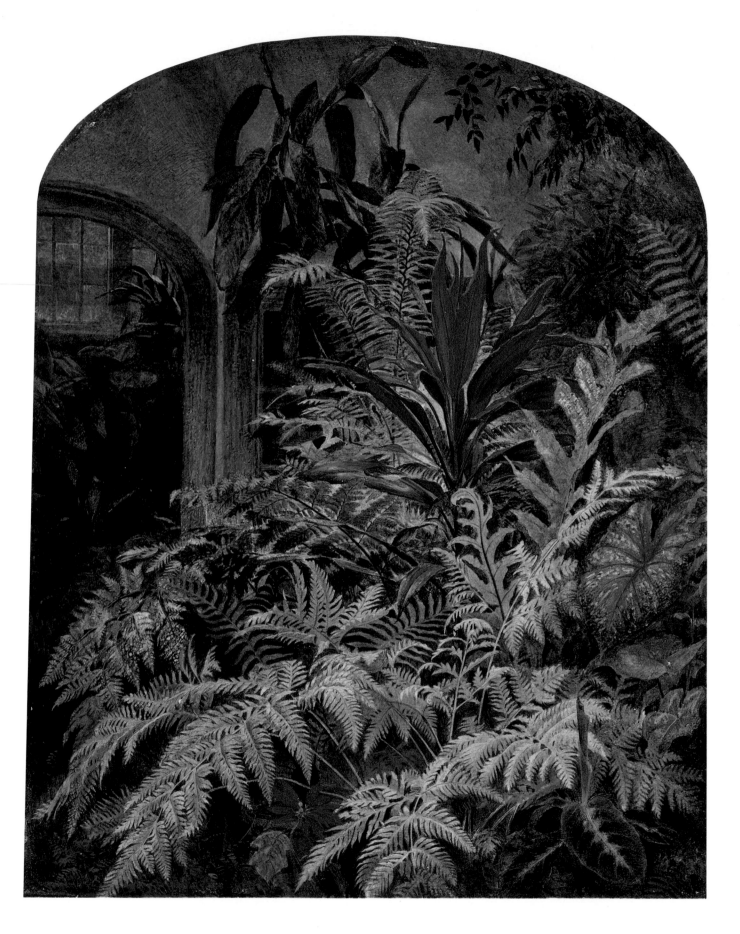

93. WILLIAM T. RICHARDS. *Conservatory*, 1860. Oil on wood,
10⅞ × 8⁹⁄₁₆ inches (27.6 × 21.7 cm). Private collection.

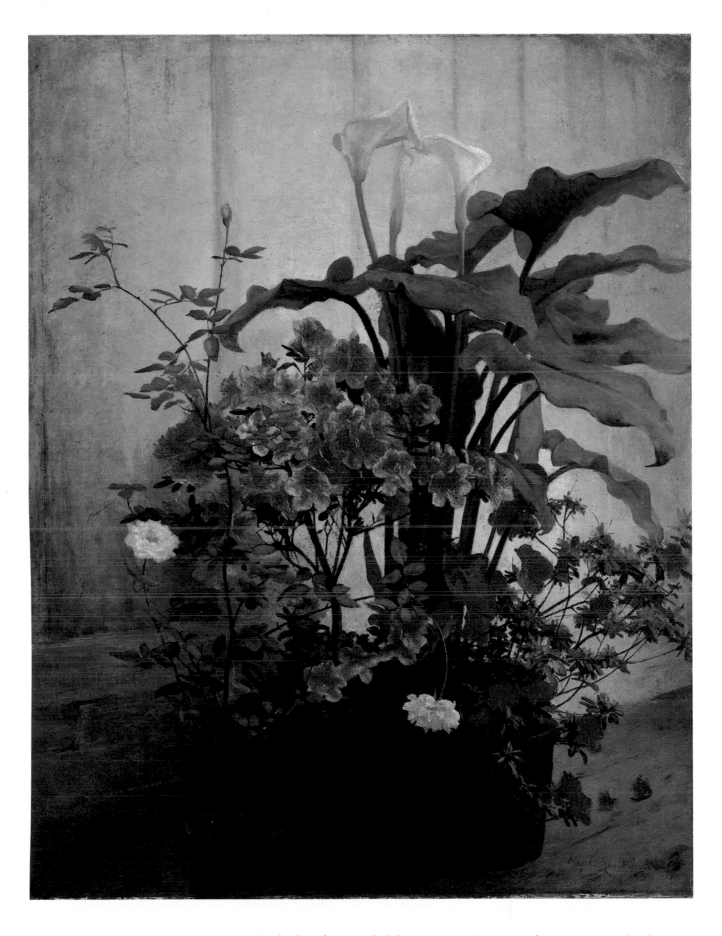

94. GEORGE COCHRAN LAMBDIN. *In the Greenhouse*, n.d. Oil on canvas, 31 3/16 × 40 inches (79.2 × 101.6 cm).
The Metropolitan Museum of Art, New York; Gift of Mrs. J. Augustus Barnard.

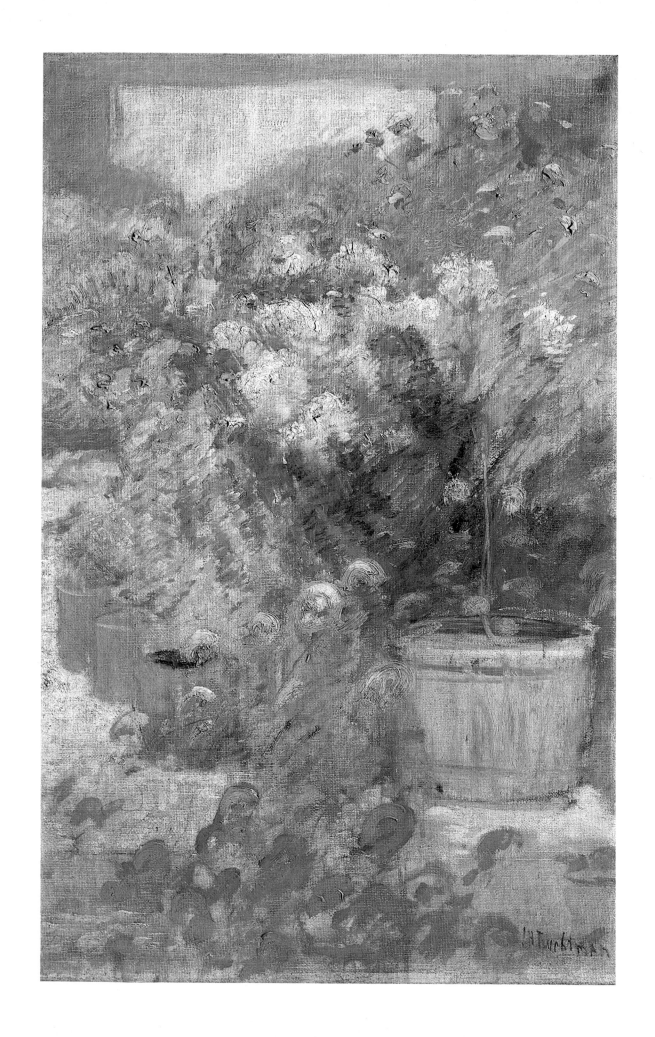

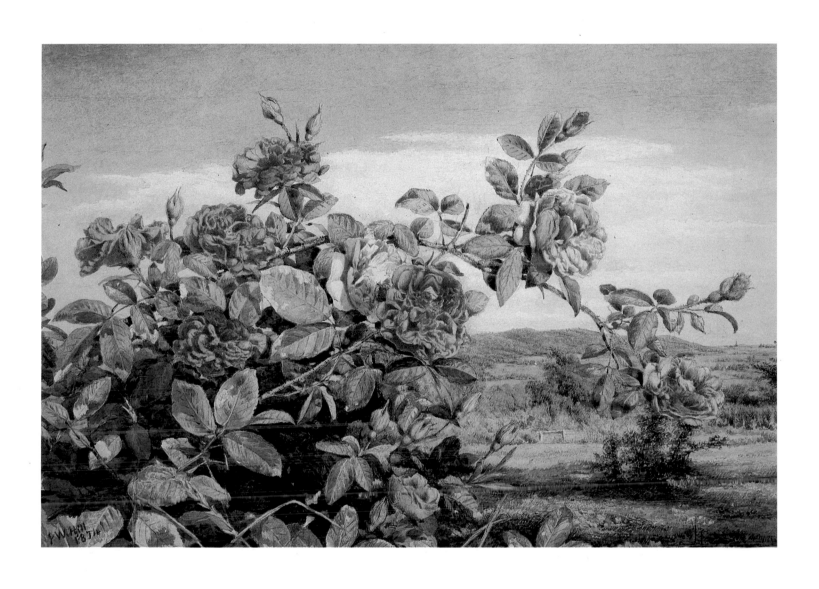

95. JOHN HENRY TWACHTMAN. *In the Greenhouse*, c. 1890–1902. Oil on canvas,
25 × 16 inches (63.5 × 40.6 cm). North Carolina Museum of Art, Raleigh.

96. JOHN WILLIAM HILL. *Tearoses in Landscape*, 1874. Watercolor on paper,
14 × 20 inches (35.6 × 50.8 cm). Collection of Stephen Rubin.

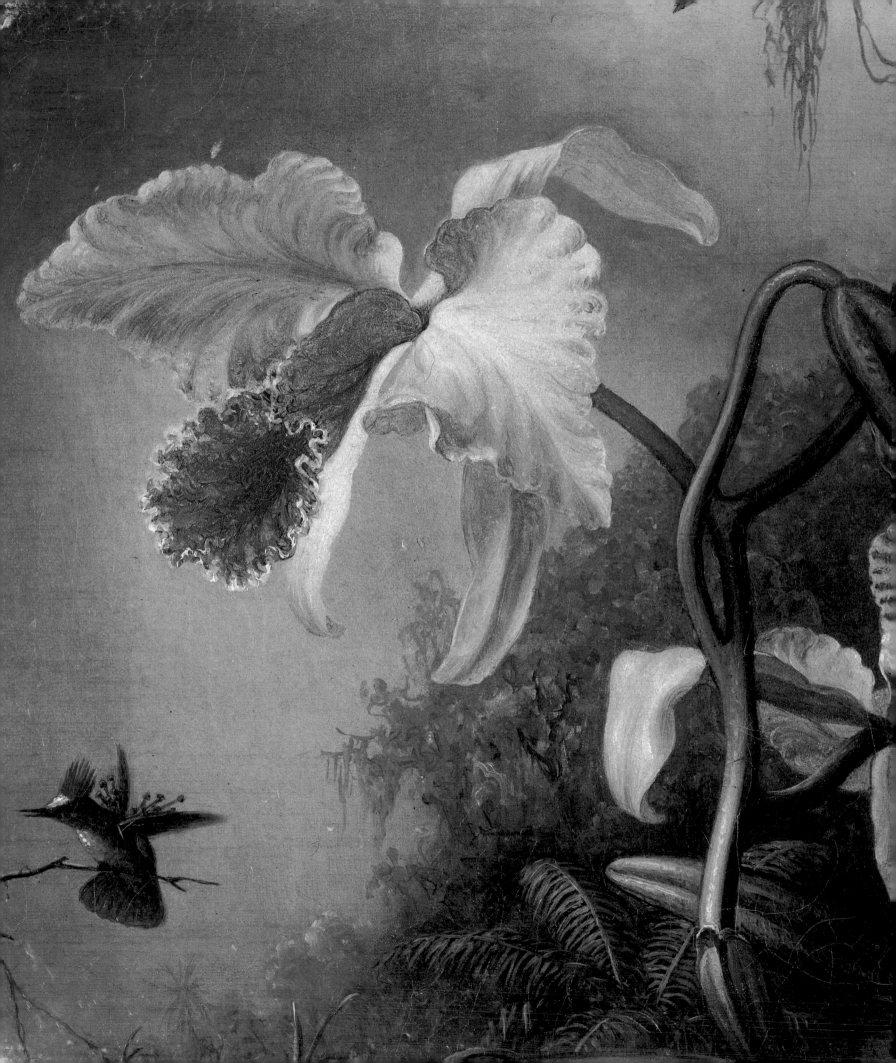

Flowers and Landscape

A VARIETY OF IMAGES of flowers in a natural environment emerged in nineteenth-century American painting, stimulated by magazine articles which advised artists to eschew the depiction of flowers in vases in favor of painting "a free, wild, vigorous plant as it grows."[1] Although in botanical drawings specimens could be surrounded with landscape details and some still-life arrangements found their way outdoors, it was in connection with landscape painting—the century's preeminent genre—that the representation of flowers *in situ* developed fully.

Hudson River School artists planted the foregrounds of their landscape compositions with meticulously described plants and flowers. The authenticity of these organic details depended upon sketches of live specimens produced on the spot: the site might be a botanical garden or a secluded place in the Catskills. Thomas Cole and other first-generation landscape artists characteristically used pencil for their plant drawings.[2] Jasper F. Cropsey, whose library was filled with popular botany books, produced exquisite studies of single plant specimens, such as the skunk cabbage (Figs. 97, 98), and some oil sketches of floral clusters (Fig. 99). Cropsey seems to have followed the advice of his fellow landscape painter Asher B. Durand in the selection of common local flowers for his artistic scrutiny: "Go not abroad then in search of material for the exercise of your pencil," wrote Durand, in his influential essay "Letters on Landscape Painting." "Many are the flowers in our untrodden wilds that have blushed too long unseen, and their original freshness will reward your research with a higher and purer satisfaction, than appertains to the display of the most brilliant exotic."[3]

Some artists, nevertheless, could not resist the artistic allure of the "most brilliant exotic." The saturated colors and eloquent shapes of tropical specimens figure prominently in oil sketches of flowers by Frederic E. Church and Martin Johnson Heade. Church clusters his *Jamaican Flowers* (Fig. 100) as if he had happened upon this felicitously colored grouping growing at the side of a path, while Heade usually clips the specimens for his flower drawings to create more

MARTIN JOHNSON HEADE, detail of *Two Fighting Hummingbirds and Two Orchids*, 1875 (see Fig. 41).

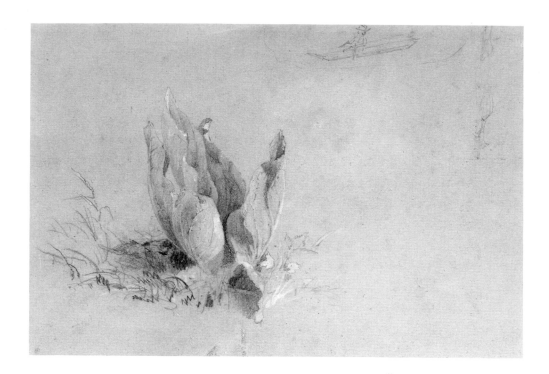

finished replicas for subsequent use in his floral landscapes and still lifes (Figs. 102–105).

Landscape paintings that featured flowers as the central motif rather than as foreground detail became the dominant type in late nineteenth-century American flower painting. Heade gave grandiose prominence to the spectacle of exotic orchids and passionflowers set in tropical environments, while Fidelia Bridges captured the delicate contours of ordinary field flowers such as *Queen Anne's Lace* (Fig. 109).

Bridges worked directly from nature in preparing studies for her finished images of flowers in landscape. Like John William Hill (Fig. 96), she was inspired by Ruskin's dictum about the proper way for an artist to perceive the floral world: "A flower is to be watched as it grows, in its association with the earth, the air, and the dew," Ruskin had declared. "Its leaves are to be seen as they expand in sunshine; its colours, as they embroider the field, or illumine the forest."[4] The process of working *within* nature was slow and painstaking because, as Bridges remarked, "it always takes some time to get fairly at work out of doors."[5] The joyful component of Bridges' close scrutiny of nature, which she also acknowledged in her writing, finds visual expression in two exquisite *Studies for a Picture of Field Flowers Against an Evening Sky* (Fig. 110).

Close-up renderings of field flowers on larger canvases appealed to artists of an Impressionist persuasion. This type of flower offered a kind of outdoor laboratory for the study of the interaction of light and color. John Henry Twachtman captured the blending of pastel tints under the hot glare of sunlight in *Meadow Flowers* (Fig. 115). The identity of individual specimens is further dissolved by

97. JASPER F. CROPSEY. *Leaf Study*, n.d. Gouache and pencil on paper, 6⅞ × 9⅞ inches (17.5 × 25.1 cm). Newington-Cropsey Foundation, Hastings-on-Hudson, New York.

98. JASPER F. CROPSEY. *Skunk Cabbage*, 1851..Oil on canvas, 8¹⁄₁₆ × 11½ inches (20.5 × 29.2 cm). Newington-Cropsey Foundation, Hastings-on-Hudson, New York.

the artist's feathery brushwork. Joseph Raphael, a San Francisco artist, used a more emphatic stroke to represent a profusion of luxuriant rhododendron blossoms, which seem to crowd the field with the fragrance of paint (Fig. 116).

Maria Oakey Dewing, George Cochran Lambdin, and John Henry Twachtman were all ardent gardeners, so it is not surprising that their cultivated creations entered their art (Figs. 45, 94, 95). The garden was a favorite subject of the Impressionists. Childe Hassam, like Ernest Lawson (Fig. 117), developed an interest in the subject on trips to France, but Hassam found an equal inspiration on this side of the Atlantic in the garden of his friend Celia Thaxter. Planted with "the old-fashioned flowers our grandmothers loved," Thaxter's array of poppies in almost endless variety, of hollyhocks, larkspurs, and many other species embellish some of Hassam's freshest watercolor images (Fig. 48).[6] It was the brilliant colors and unusual shapes of tropical flora that lured Winslow Homer on a rare excursion into the flower genre. In 1899 he recorded a brilliant bed of red and yellow cannas in a garden right outside the door of a bungalow he rented in Bermuda (Fig. 118).

Whether artists traveled far to find exotic flowers for their art or merely looked to their own backyard gardens, they considered it important to surround their subjects with a natural outdoor setting. While a number of reasons for this development can be suggested, perhaps the simplest was put forward by a New England conservationist and amateur flower painter. "Nature is a better suggestor as to backgrounds than our own unassisted ideas," asserted Mabel Loomis Todd. "Her flowers always seem to be in just the one place and position which above all others is most appropriate."[7]

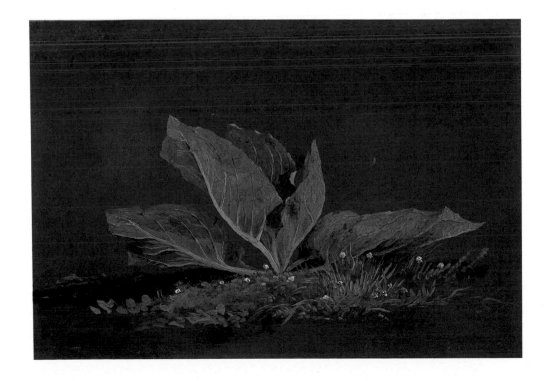

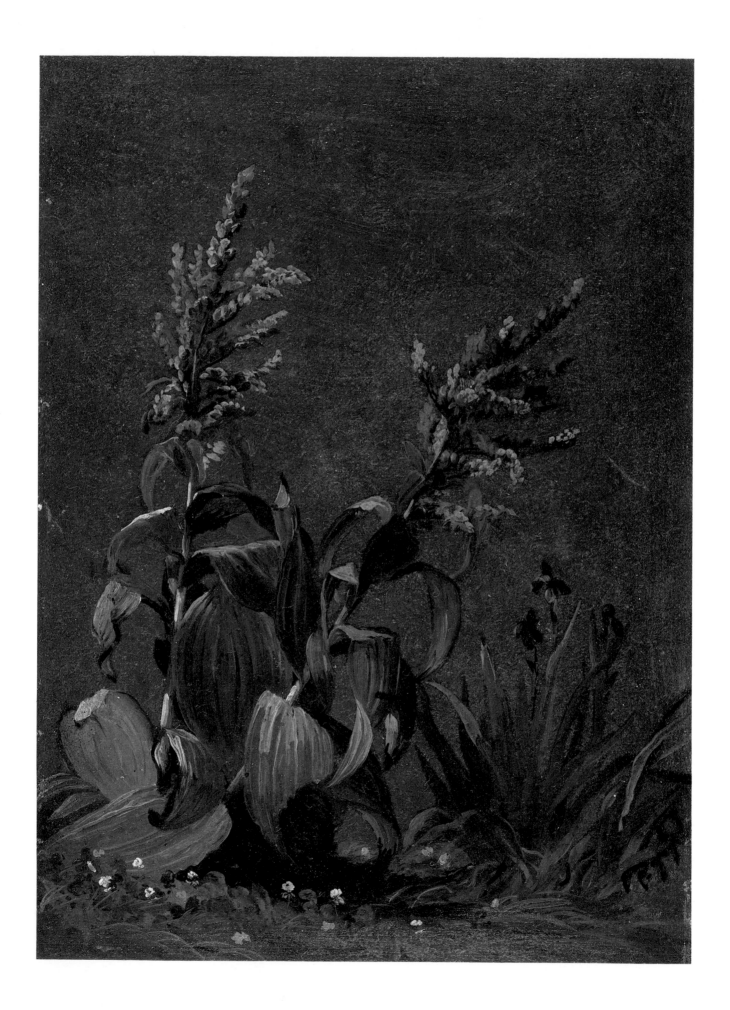

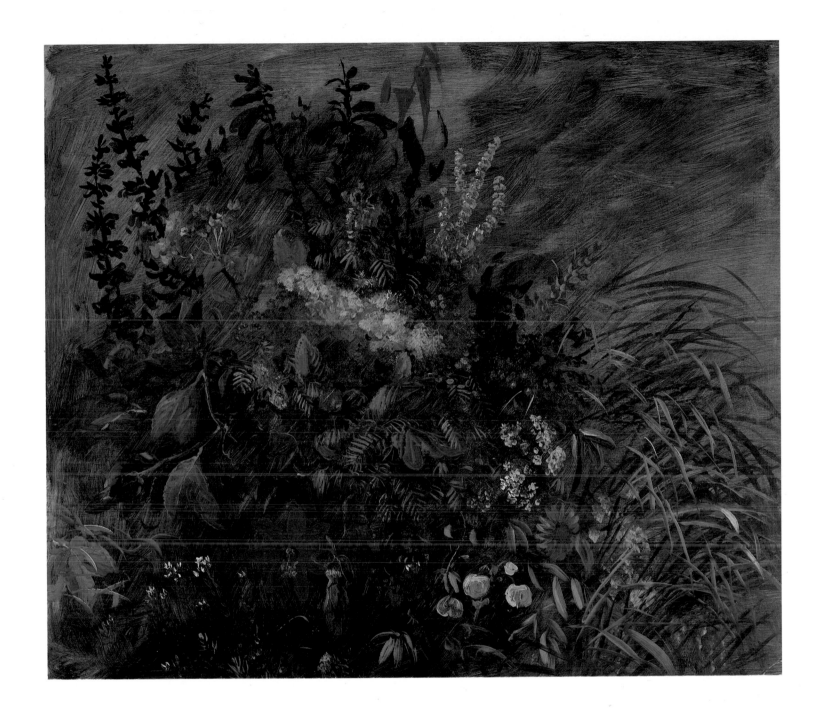

99. Jasper F. Cropsey. *Hellebore, Iris and Violets*, 1851. Oil on academy board mounted on canvas, 10⅝ × 7 inches (27 × 17.8 cm). Munson-Williams-Proctor Institute, Utica, New York; Gift of Mr. and Mrs. Ferdinand H. Davis.

100. Frederic E. Church. *Jamaican Flowers*, 1865. Oil on paperboard, 13⅝ × 15⅝ inches (34.6 × 39.7 cm). Cooper-Hewitt Museum, The Smithsonian Institution's National Museum of Design, New York.

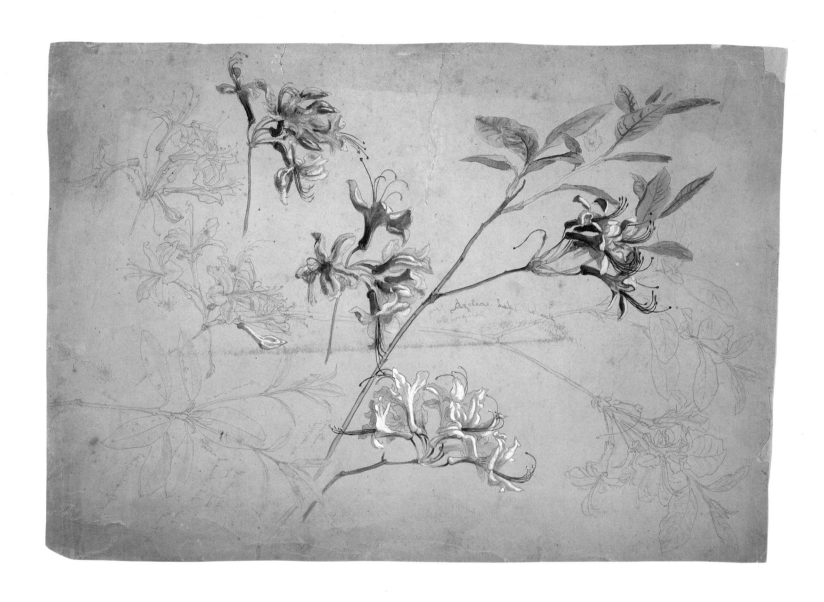

101. SAMUEL COLMAN. *Azaleas,* 1876. Watercolor and pencil on light brown paper, 14¼ × 22¼ inches (36.2 × 56.5 cm). Cooper-Hewitt Museum, The Smithsonian Institution's National Museum of Design, New York.

102. MARTIN JOHNSON HEADE. *Study of Varied Flowers with a Hummingbird,* 1870s. Oil on canvas, 14¾ × 19½ inches (37.5 × 49.5 cm). St. Augustine Historical Society, Florida.

103. MARTIN JOHNSON HEADE. *Branches of Cherokee Roses,* c. 1880. Oil on canvas, 10 × 17 inches (25.4 × 43.2 cm). St. Augustine Historical Society, Florida.

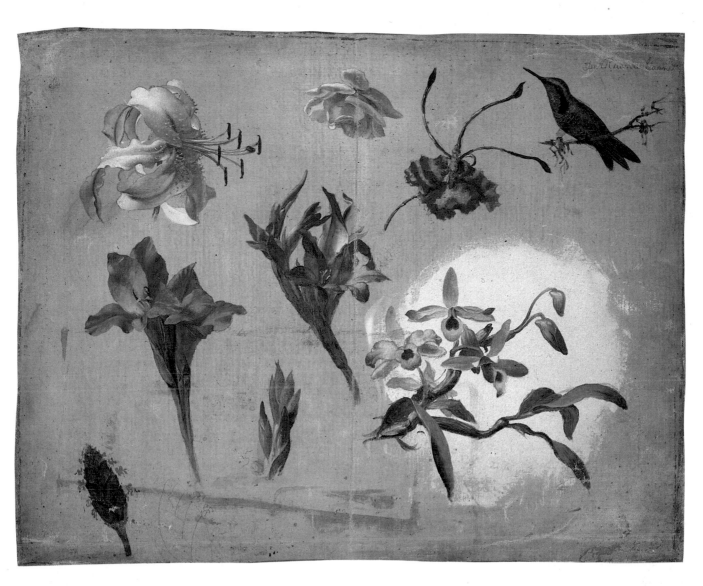

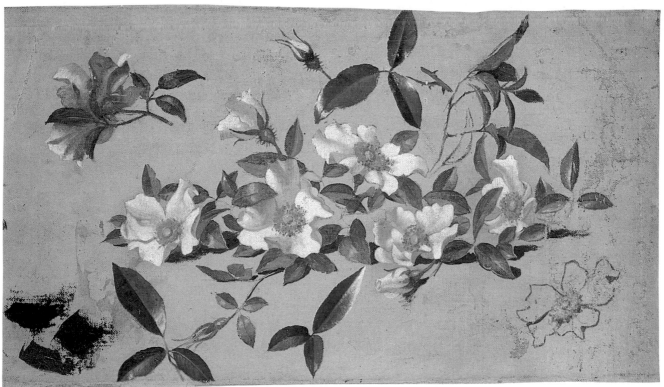

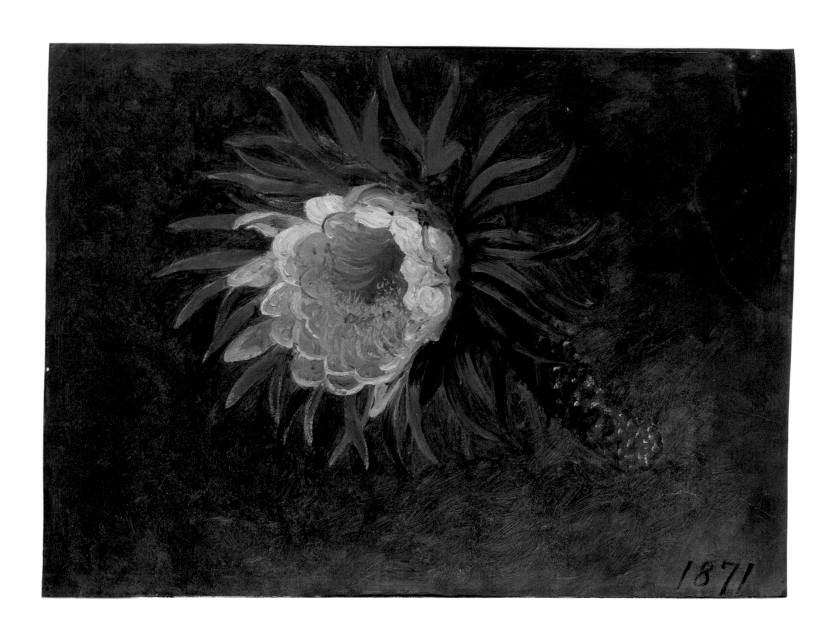

104. MARTIN JOHNSON HEADE. *Study of a Yellow Flower*, 1871. Oil on canvas, 11¼ × 14¼ inches (28.6 × 36.2 cm). St. Augustine Historical Society, Florida.

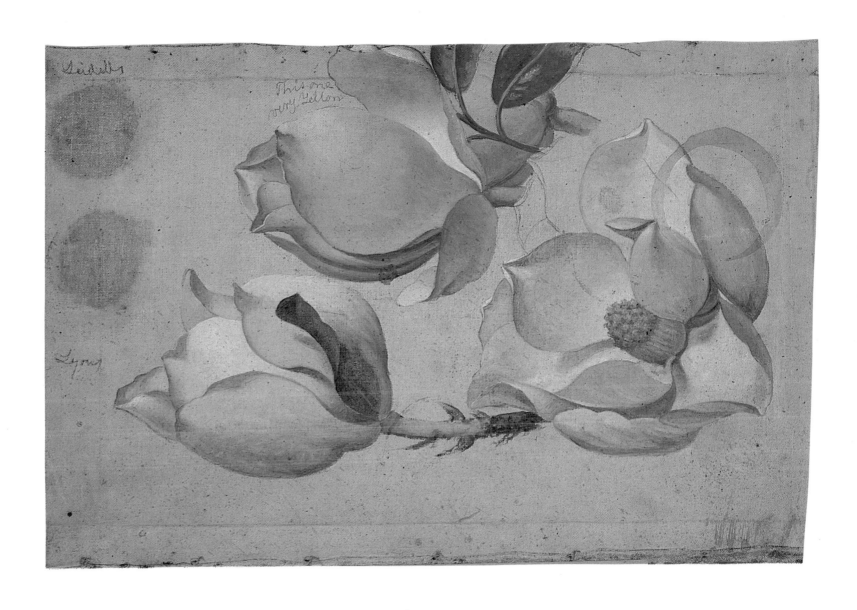

105. MARTIN JOHNSON HEADE. *Study of Three Blossoms of Magnolia,* c. 1880. Oil on canvas,
10¼ × 14½ inches (26 × 36.8 cm). St. Augustine Historical Society, Florida.

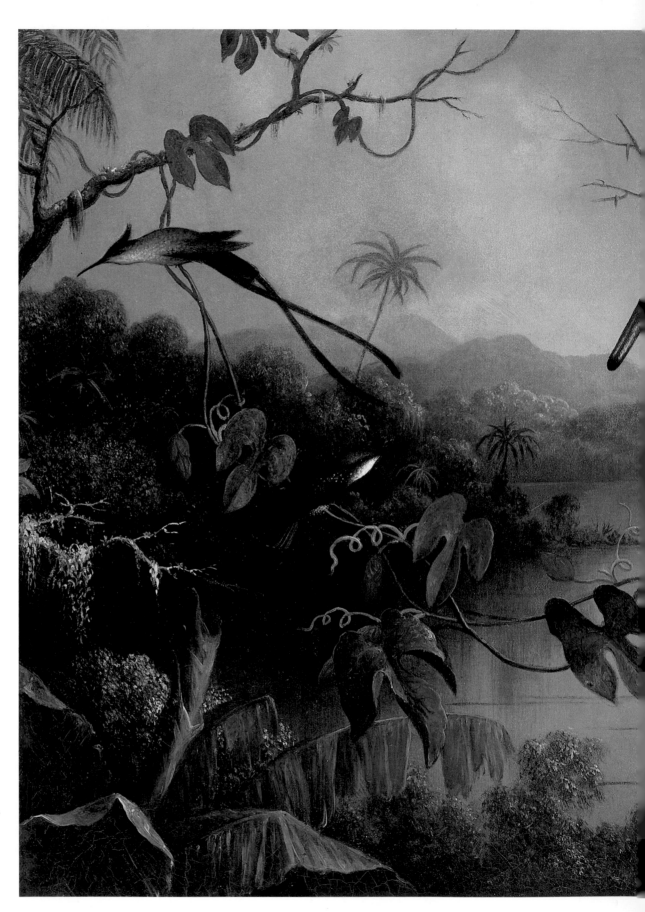

106. MARTIN JOHNSON HEADE.
Tropical Landscape with Ten
Hummingbirds, 1870. Oil on
canvas, 18 × 30 inches
(45.7 × 76.2 cm).
Private collection.

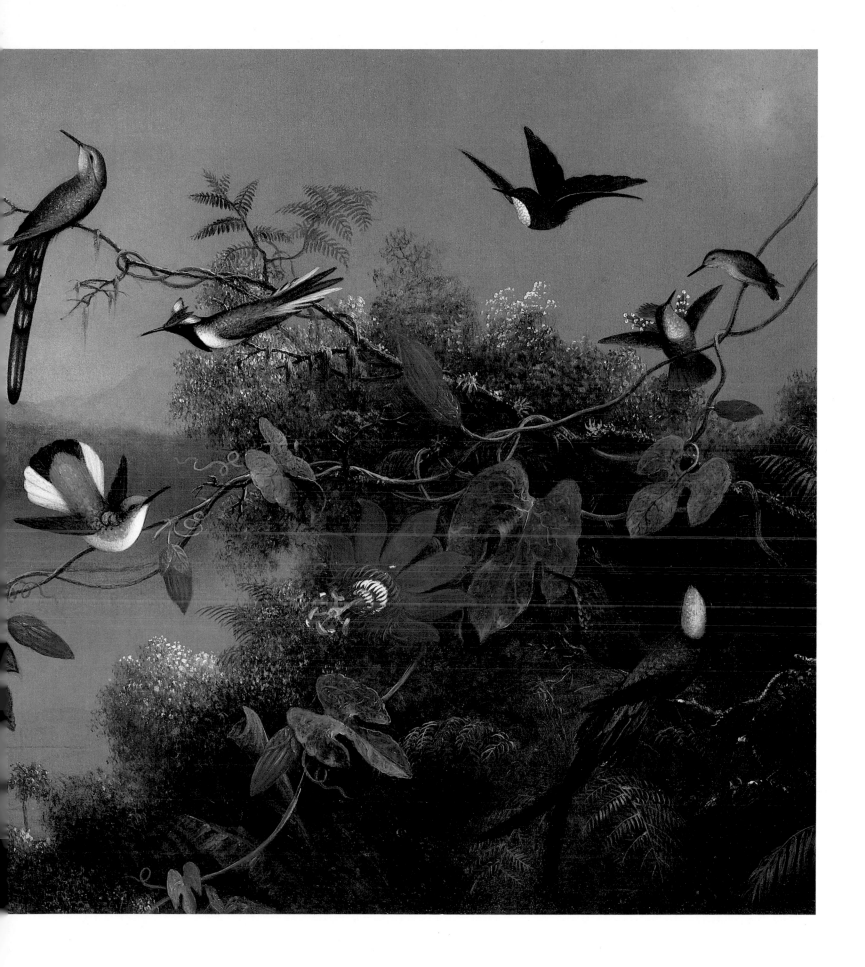

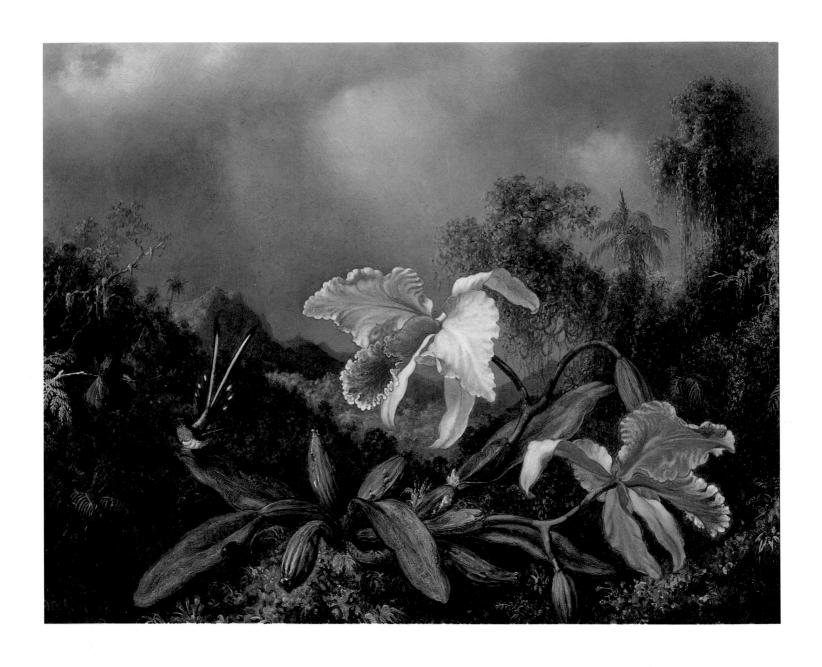

107. MARTIN JOHNSON HEADE. *Jungle Orchids and Hummingbirds,* 1872. Oil on canvas, 18 × 23 inches (45.7 × 58.4 cm).
Yale University Art Gallery, New Haven, Connecticut; Christian A. Zabriskie and Francis P. Garvan Funds.

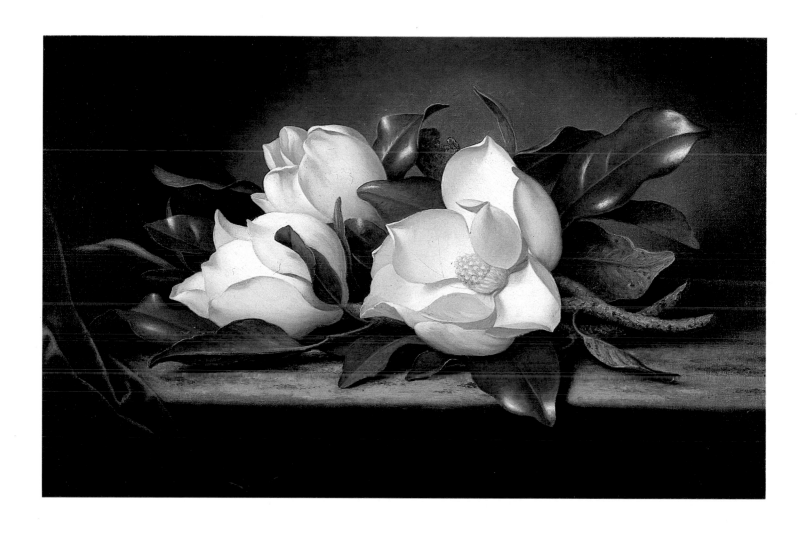

108. MARTIN JOHNSON HEADE. *Giant Magnolias*, c. 1885–95. Oil on canvas, 15¼ × 24 inches (38.7 × 61 cm).
The R. W. Norton Art Gallery, Shreveport, Louisiana.

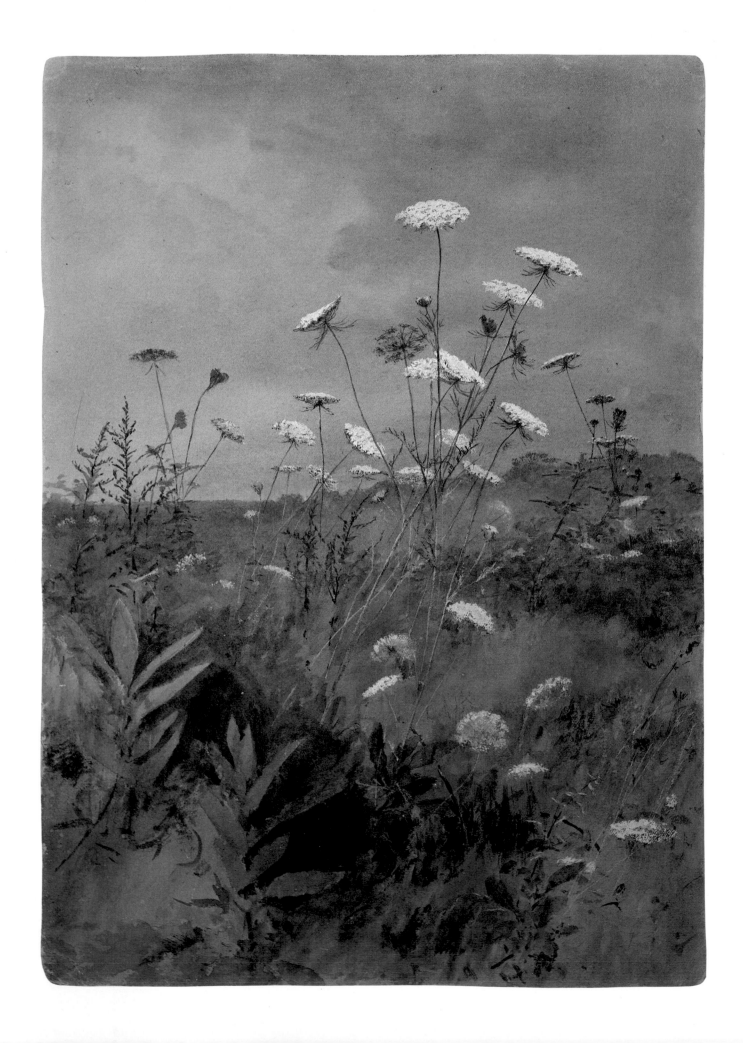

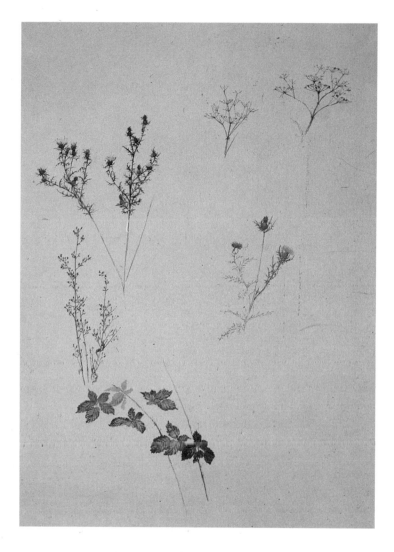

109. FIDELIA BRIDGES. *Queen Anne's Lace in a Landscape*, c. 1870. Watercolor on paper, 14 × 10 inches (35.6 × 25.4 cm). Private collection.

110. FIDELIA BRIDGES. *Studies for a Picture of Field Flowers Against an Evening Sky*, c. 1865. Watercolor and pencil on paper, two sheets: left, 12½ × 8½ inches (31.8 × 21.6 cm); right, 12 × 8½ inches (30.5 × 21.6 cm). Collection of Mr. and Mrs. Wilbur Ross.

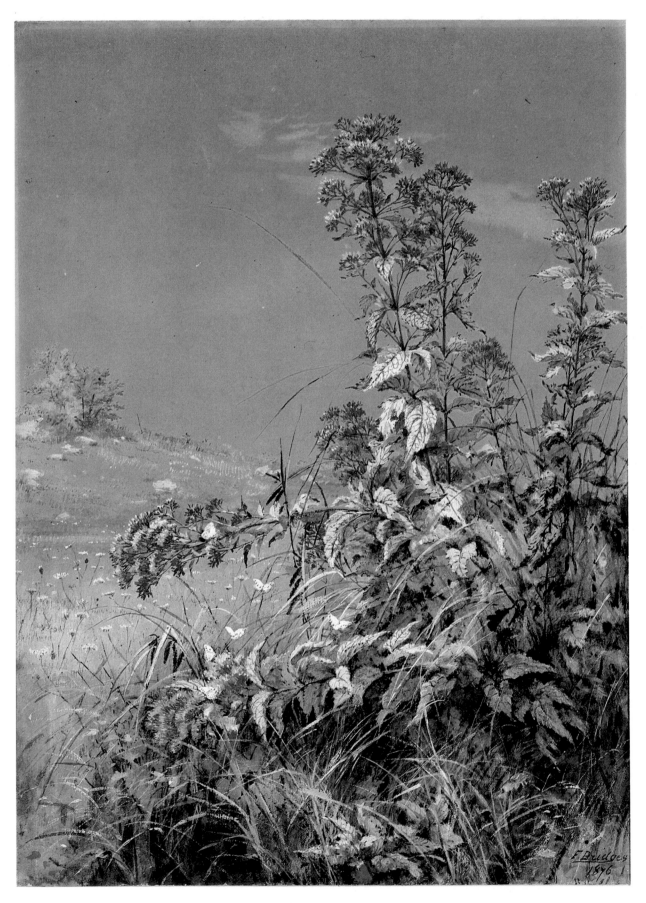

III. FIDELIA BRIDGES. *Untitled* (Joe-pye weed), 1876. Watercolor on paper, 13⅞ × 9⁵⁄₁₆ inches (35.2 × 23.7 cm). National Museum of American Art, Smithsonian Institution, Washington, D.C.; Gift in memory of Charles Downing Lay and Laura Gill Lay by their children.

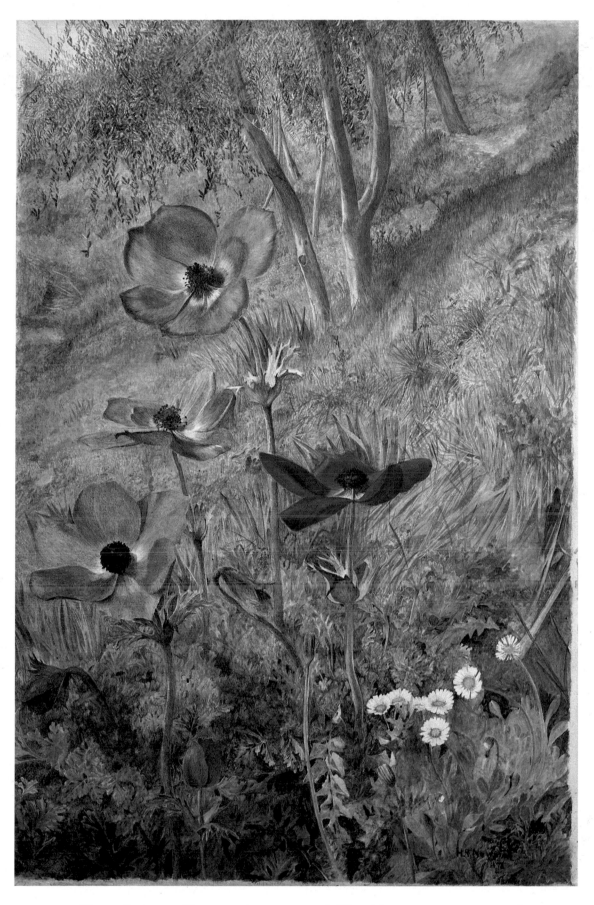

112. HENRY RODERICK NEWMAN. *Anemones,* 1876. Watercolor on paper, 18 × 11¾ inches (45.7 × 29.8 cm). Private collection.

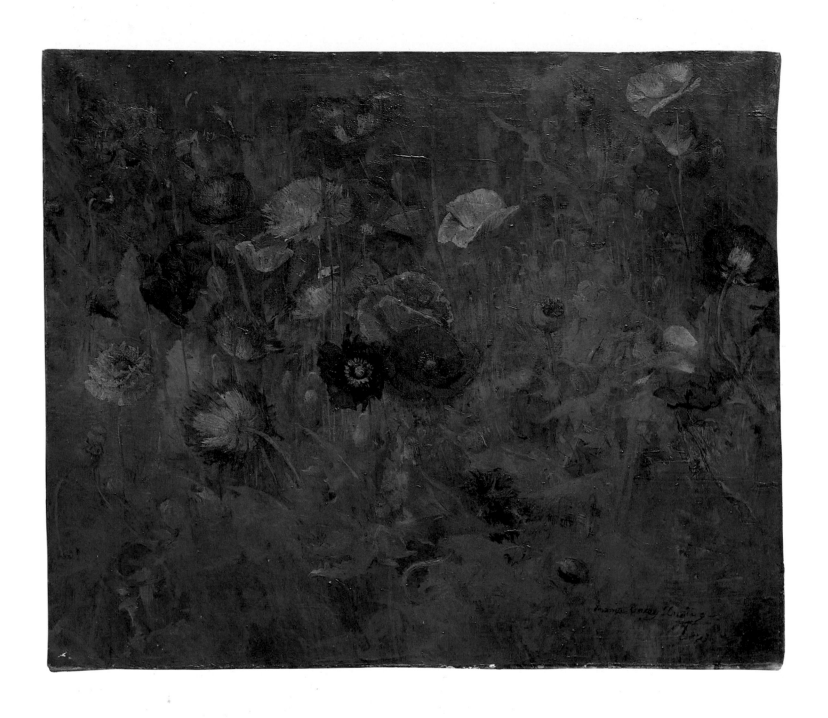

113. MARIA OAKEY DEWING. *Bed of Poppies*, 1909. Oil on canvas, 25 × 30 inches (63.5 × 76.2 cm). Addison Gallery of American Art, Phillips Academy, Andover, Massachusetts.

114. JOHN LA FARGE. *Irises and Wild Roses*, 1887. Watercolor on paper, 12⅝ × 10⅛ inches (32.1 × 25.7 cm). The Metropolitan Museum of Art, New York; Gift of Priscilla A. B. Henderson in memory of her grandfather, Russell St. Sturgis, a founder of the Metropolitan Museum.

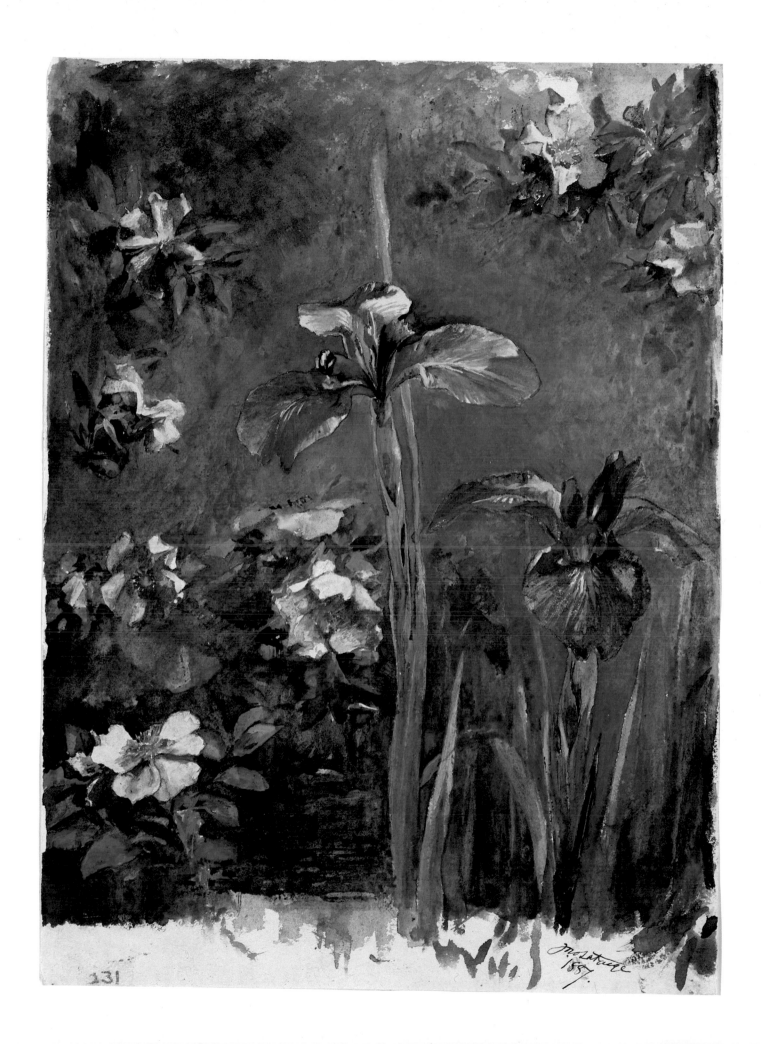

231

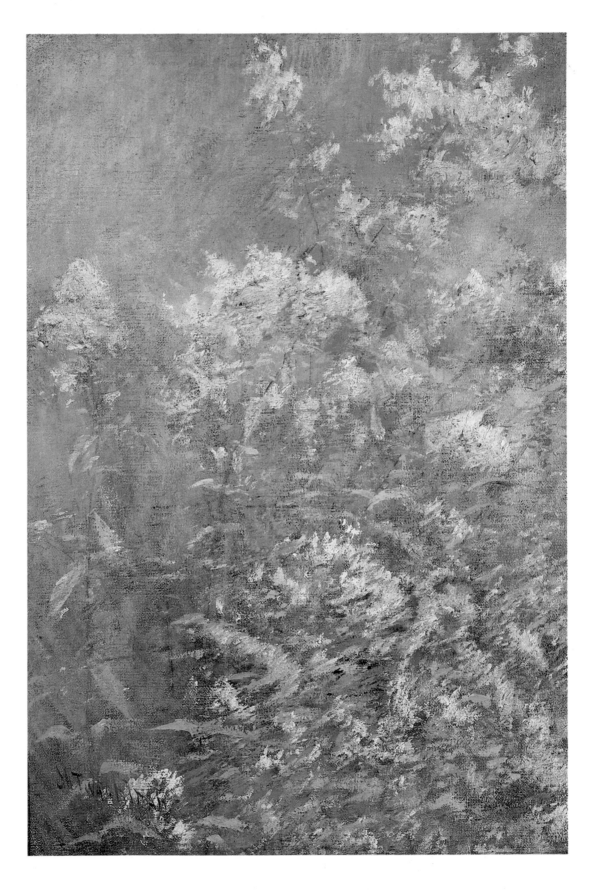

115. JOHN HENRY TWACHTMAN. *Meadow Flowers*, c. 1890–1900. Oil on canvas,
33⅟₁₆ × 22⅟₁₆ inches (84 × 56 cm). The Brooklyn Museum; Caroline H. Polhemus Fund.

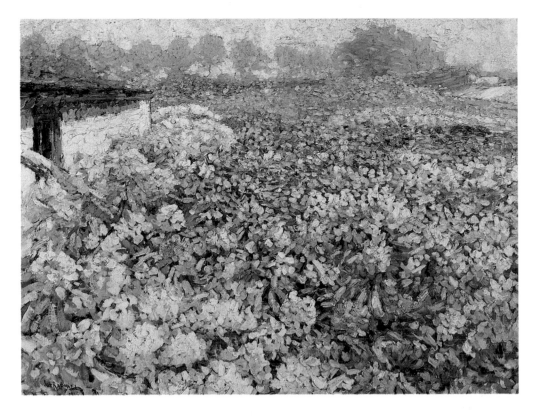

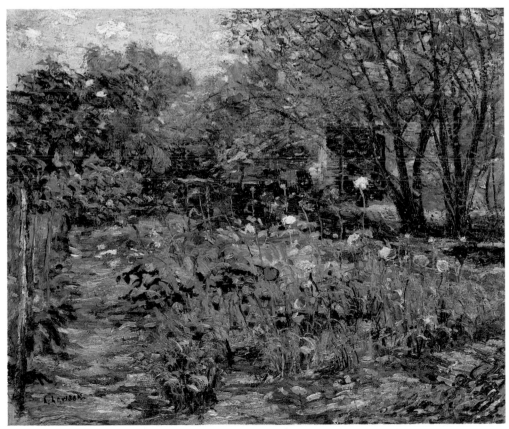

116. JOSEPH RAPHAEL. *Rhododendron Field*, 1915. Oil on canvas, 30 × 40 inches (76.2 × 101.6 cm). The Oakland Museum; Gift of William S. Porter.

117. ERNEST LAWSON. *Garden Landscape*, n.d. Oil on canvas, 20 × 24 inches (50.8 × 61 cm). The Brooklyn Museum; Bequest of Laura L. Barnes.

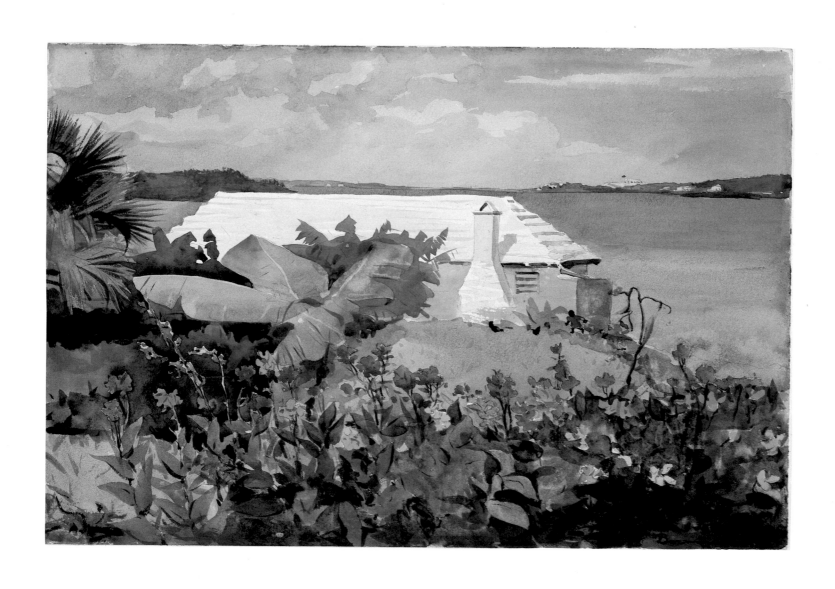

118. WINSLOW HOMER. *Flower Garden and Bungalow, Bermuda,* 1899. Watercolor on paper, 14 × 21 inches (35.6 × 53.3 cm). The Metropolitan Museum of Art, New York; Amelia B. Lazarus Fund.

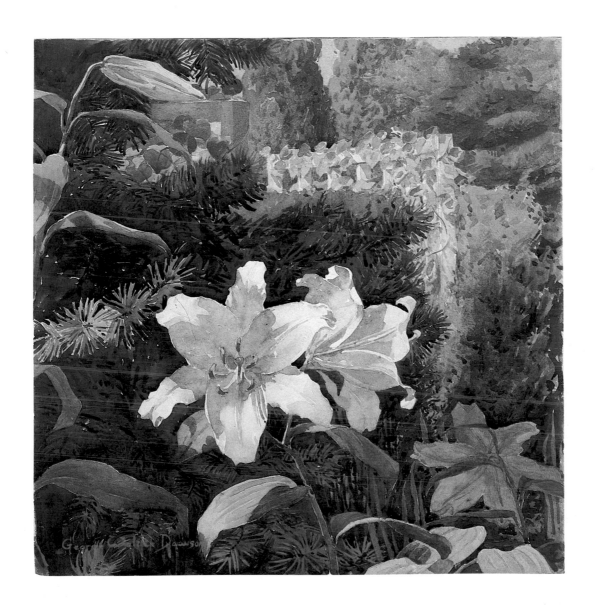

119. GEORGE WALTER DAWSON. *Auratum Lilies,* 1935. Watercolor on paper, 16 × 16 inches (40.6 × 40.6 cm).
Pennsylvania Academy of the Fine Arts, Philadelphia; Presented by friends of the artist.

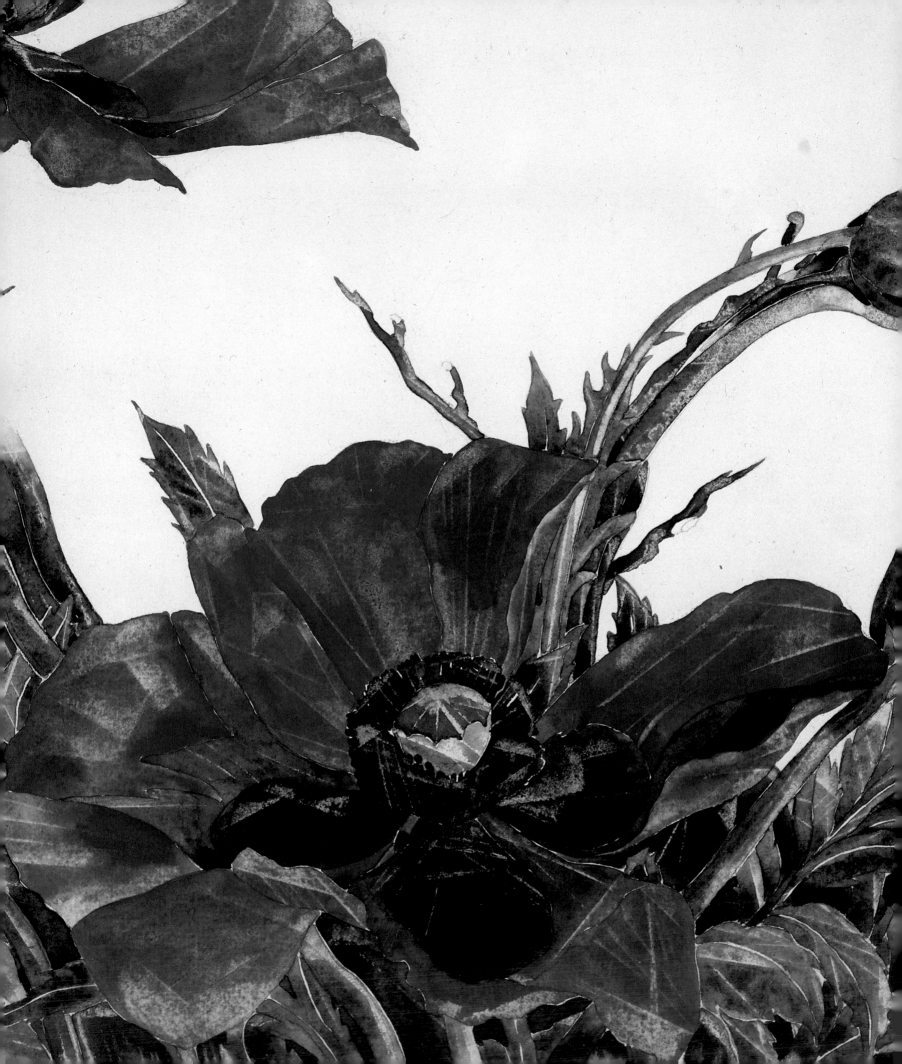

Twentieth-Century Flower Art

Twentieth-century artists often produce images of flowers which appear very different from those of earlier American artists. Because it is sometimes difficult even to identify the flower represented, we might imagine that nature is no longer an important inspiration.[1] However, many abstract and representational artists feel themselves to be part of a tradition of American nature painting. Ellsworth Kelly, for example, was impressed by the formal qualities of John James Audubon's work. Kelly particularly admired the naturalist's use of collage to arrange landscape details, such as plant specimens, on his watercolor drawings. Audubon had used paste-ups for a practical purpose: to create a finished design for his engraver (a practice that Catesby had employed a century earlier). It was not the pragmatism of Audubon's approach, but its formal implication— an attention to shape and design—which corresponded to Kelly's own aesthetic focus. Again, it was Audubon's work which convinced Marsden Hartley that "a painting of life in the natural world may also be a work of art, and lose none of its scientific veracity."[2] Theodoros Stamos found inspiration in the intimate feeling for nature expressed in the landscape art of the Hudson River School. According to Stamos, "the inheritance of America's great nature painting" served as a fundamental component of his aesthetic.[3] The ties to nature appear so strong in the work of Morris Graves, the painter of *Iceland Poppies—A Triumph of Hybridization* (Fig. 120), that one critic wryly suggested the artist might be "the child of a lady ornithologist by a geologist father."[4]

Floral and plant themes occupy the artistic vocabulary of many early American modernist painters of Hartley's generation. In their experimentation with abstract modes of representation, the organic world provided a paradisiacal array of design possibilities along with a comforting tie to reality. Hartley's own *Flower Abstraction* (Fig. 121) represents one of the earliest and most radically abstracted floral images produced by an American artist. Combining a Synthetic Cubist vocabulary with the flat color and emblematic design of military pageantry, the work submits its flower subject to stringent formal reduction. Fellow

CHARLES DEMUTH, detail of *Red Poppies*, 1929 (see Fig. 51).

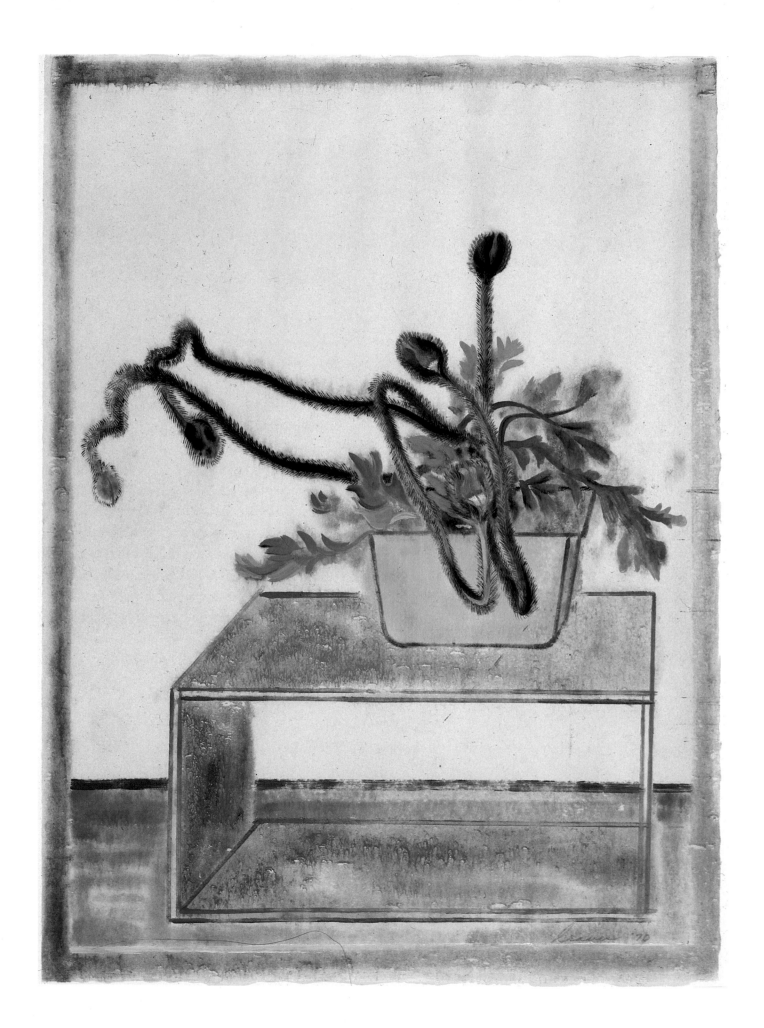

modernist Arthur G. Dove exhibits a similar interest in the geometrical structuring of the organic world in *Plant Forms* (Fig. 122), but the artist retains the local color of vegetation and earth and indications of the natural world's three-dimensional structure.

Preoccupation with the formal potential of flower subjects did not necessarily result in abstract renderings. We can clearly recognize the zinnia in Charles Sheeler's *Flower in a Bowl* (Fig. 126), but his concern with the placement of the specimen and the highlighting of its silhouette against an unmodulated blue ground is equally striking. An earlier photograph of the same subject (Fig. 127) shows a more rigorous ordering of organic specimens for design purposes: the unnaturally erect zinnia is shown in combination with the leaves of another flower (nasturtium), whose dark waxy surface and rounded contours complement the frontal blossom. A similarly stringent subordination of natural forms to an abstract framework of flattened design is evident in Sheeler's later oil paintings of *Geranium* and *Cactus* (Figs. 128, 129). In the latter work, the artist contrasts the subtle curves and pliable texture of the succulent plant with the streamlined edges and metallic surfaces of photographic equipment. Under the glare of the hooded lights, the cactus appears as an object of interrogation. Like many of his contemporaries, Sheeler was attracted to the divergent formal possibilities of organic and man-made industrial objects. "I would arrive at the picture," wrote Sheeler, ". . . through a conception of form architectural in its structure, whether flowers or buildings are the theme, set forth with the utmost clarity by means of craftsmanship so adequate as to be unobtrusive."[5]

A more subjective approach to the floral world emerges in the work of Joseph Stella, Charles Burchfield, and Georgia O'Keeffe, artists who shared with Sheeler a dual interest in the forms of nature and urban culture. In *Tree of My Life* (Fig. 131), Joseph Stella unleashes a display of personal fantasy in the deluge of plant life which, despite its whimsical appearance, is based upon accurate flower studies.[6] His swarming array of organic specimens, distorted in scale and shape for expressive purposes, is barely contained within the symmetrical and stylized ordering of his composition. A more tranquil conjunction of abstract design with the sensuous expressive power of the plant world can be found in Stella's *Song of Barbados* (Fig. 132), one of the artist's many excursions into tropical imagery.

In Charles Burchfield's *Rogues' Gallery* (Fig. 134), a line of sunflowers, exhibiting the curling contours of advanced stages of bloom, wind in contrapuntal contrast to the erect geometry of the architectural forms behind them. Burchfield loved both the shape and the expressive power of the sunflower, particularly when it is past its prime: ". . . the sunflower . . . seems more alive, at least artistically," according to Burchfield, "when quite dead."[7] Perhaps most poignantly, Burchfield elicits the pain of the life process from the stalk of a single *Dead Sunflower* (Fig. 135). By contrast, he suggests the effervescence of life's

120. MORRIS GRAVES. *Iceland Poppies—A Triumph of Hybridization*, 1970. Tempera on paper, 22½ × 16½ inches (57.2 × 41.9 cm). Collection of Herschel and Caryl Roman.

pleasures in the cottony texture and party-favor design of dandelion clocks in *Dandelion Seed Heads and the Moon* (Fig. 136).

For Georgia O'Keeffe, it was the *Black Iris* (Fig. 138) which contained the mystery and the architecture that are shared by art and life. The extraordinary quality of the flower led her in a persistent search for specimens in the New York flower market. During the short season of its availability (only about two weeks in the spring), O'Keeffe worked intensively with the iris, painting it "many times—year after year."[8] In her artistic conception of the flower, she captures its monumental, if imperfect, symmetry of structure, and the allusive and evocative coloring of the soft-textured petals. O'Keeffe manages to draw both the formal power and the expressive organicism of nature from the blossom of a single iris.

More recent images of flowers continue to project a distillation of the form or the experience of flora. Ellsworth Kelly and Lee Krasner represent opposite approaches to the plant world: Kelly emphasizes an objective, formalist approach, whereas Krasner draws subjective experience from nature. The milkweed plant serves both artists as an inspirational model (Figs. 139, 140). With these two images we can understand the incredible range of aesthetic results that the flower subject continues to elicit from artists of our century.

In his milkweed drawing, Ellsworth Kelly uses a pen to excerpt in outline the shape of the plant viewed from above. This perspective appealed to the artist because of its formal possibilities. Looking down on the milkweed, said Kelly, allowed him to extract the "expanding shape relationships" of the various plant parts.[9] From the panoply of visual information available to him in this direct transcription of a live specimen, Kelly sought the essence of the flower through a condensed view of its shape. In his approach, Kelly no doubt unwittingly followed the guidelines of the eleventh-century Chinese artist Kuo Hsi. According to this revered painter, whose sayings inspired generations of artists: "He who learns to paint flowers takes a stalk of the flower, places it in a deep hole in the ground and examines it from above; in this way the flower may be completely grasped."[10]

Lee Krasner, in her aesthetic response to the plant world, eschews direct experience. It is clear that her collage painting of *Milkweed* does not record the specific shapes of the plant from any point of view. She relies upon a subjective and unconscious amalgamation of memory, experience, and art to construct an aesthetic translation of nature on canvas. The milkweed occupied the fields near her childhood home; she came to know the plant even better as an enthusiastic gardener later in life. As an artist, however, she was vigorously opposed to the idea of "representing flowers." In her view, realistic reproduction limits the role of the unconscious.[11] Collage is the perfect medium for a flower artist who combines her response to nature with her conception of the artistic process. "I cannot conceive of anything outside of nature,"[12] said Krasner. Ellsworth Kelly, although his images of plant life are very different, I think would agree with her.

121. MARSDEN HARTLEY. *Flower Abstraction*, 1914. Oil on canvas, 49⅜ × 42½ inches (125.4 × 108 cm). Collection of Mr. and Mrs. Meyer P. Potamkin.

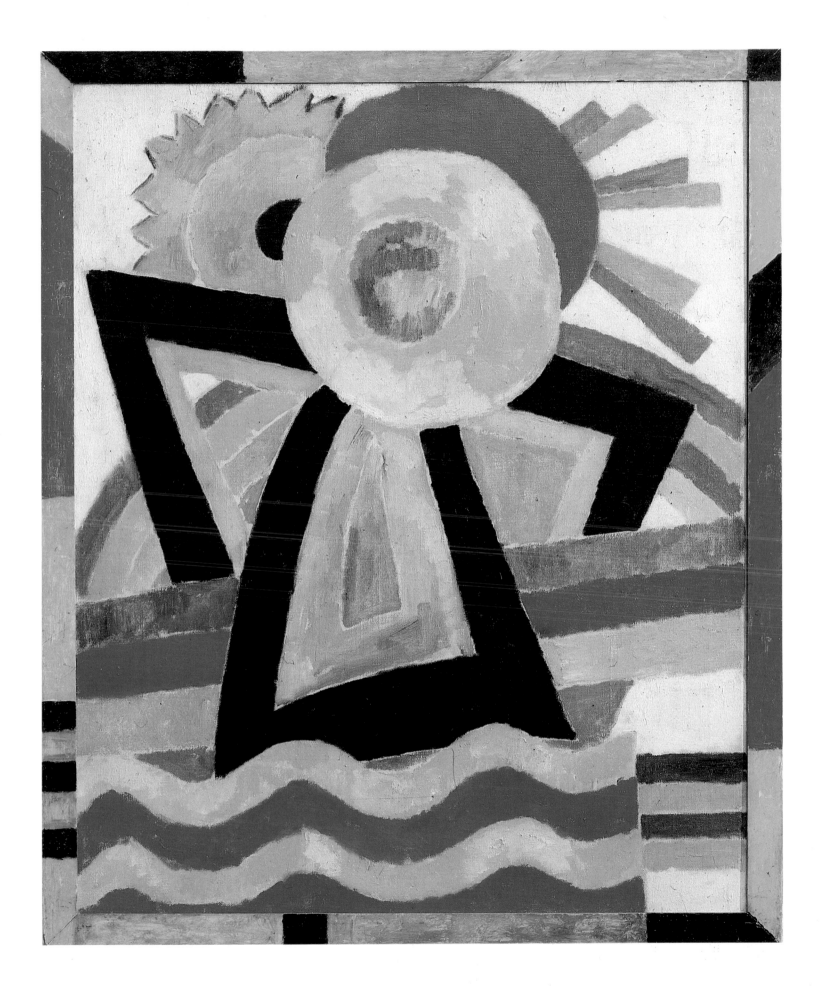

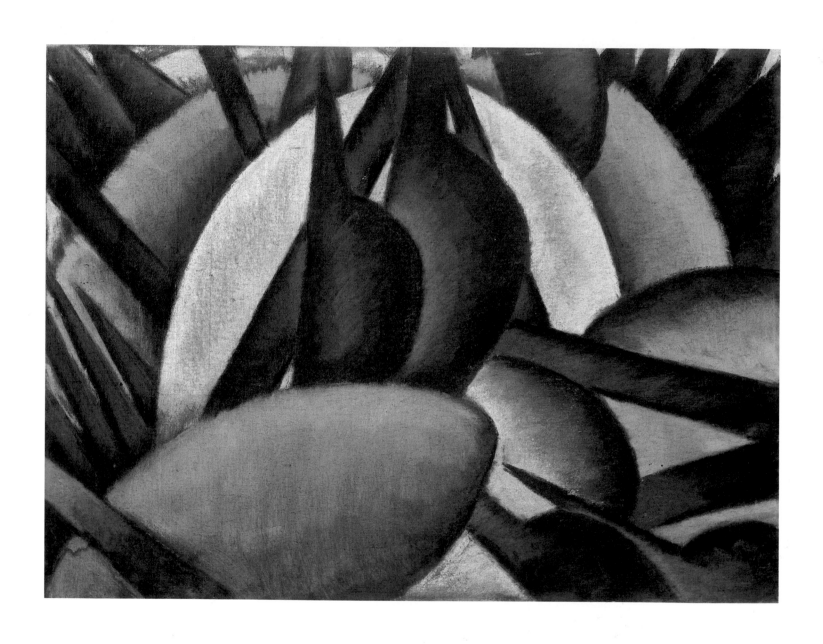

122. ARTHUR G. DOVE. *Plant Forms*, 1915. Pastel on canvas, 17¼ × 23⅞ inches (43.8 × 60.6 cm). Whitney Museum of American Art, New York; Gift of Mr. and Mrs. Roy R. Neuberger 51.20.

123. CHARLES DEMUTH. *Yellow and Blue*, 1915. Watercolor on paper, 14 × 10 inches (35.6 × 25.4 cm). The Metropolitan Museum of Art, New York; The Alfred Stieglitz Collection.

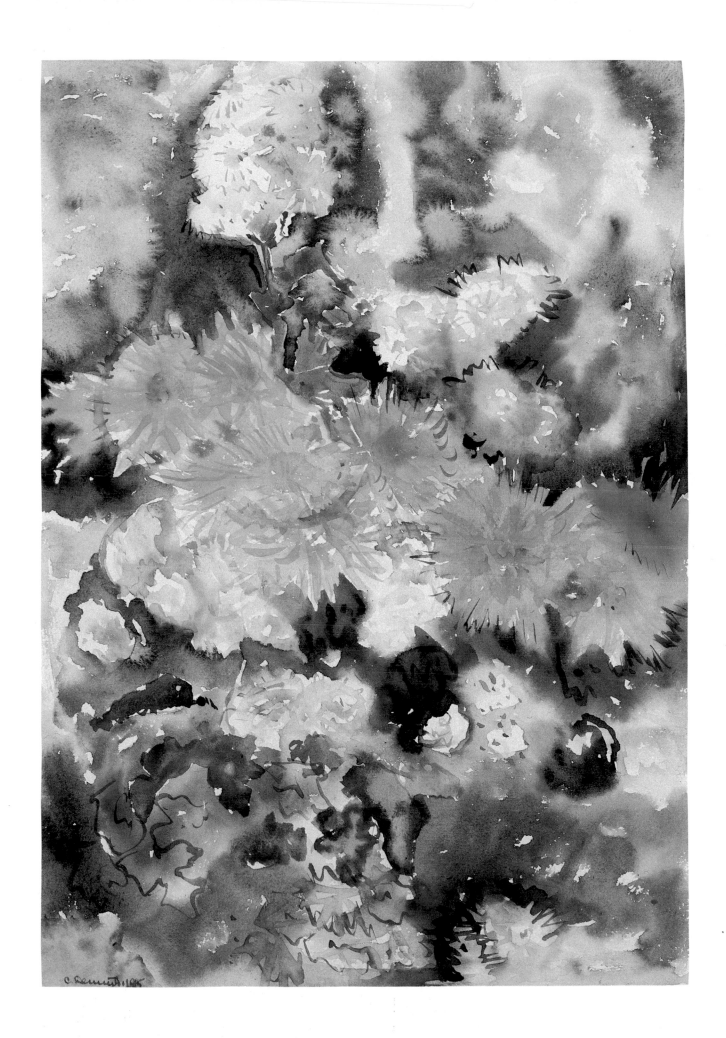

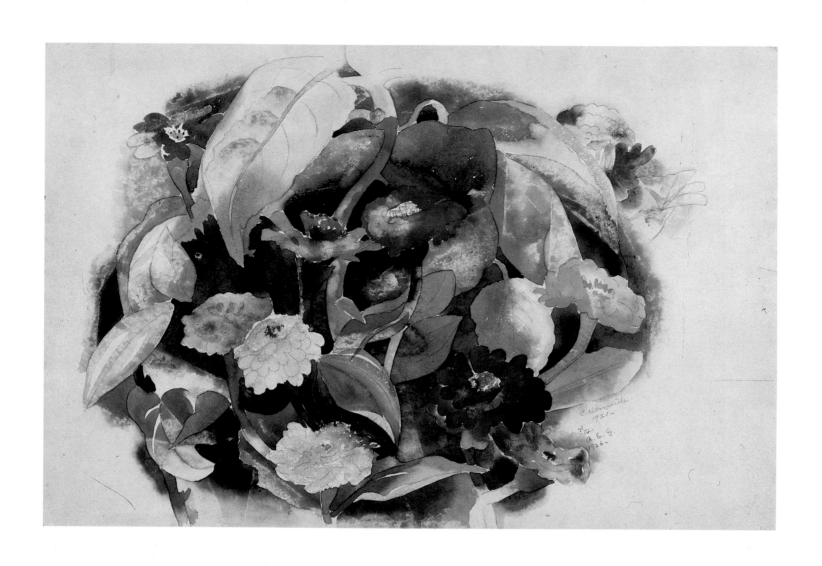

124. CHARLES DEMUTH. *Zinnias,* 1921. Watercolor on paper, 11⅞ × 18 inches (30.2 × 45.7 cm). Philadelphia Museum of Art; A. E. Gallatin Collection.

125. CHARLES SHEELER. *Chrysanthemums,* 1912. Oil on canvas, 24 × 20 inches (61 × 50.8 cm). Whitney Museum of American Art, New York; Gift of the artist 55.24.

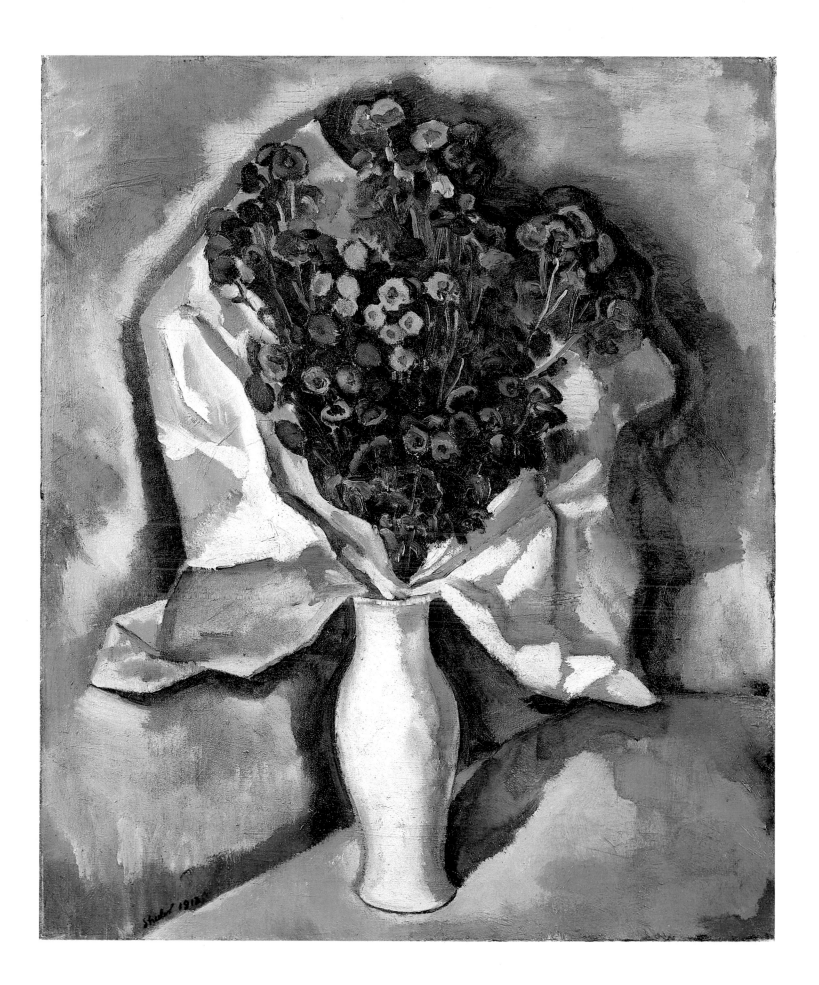

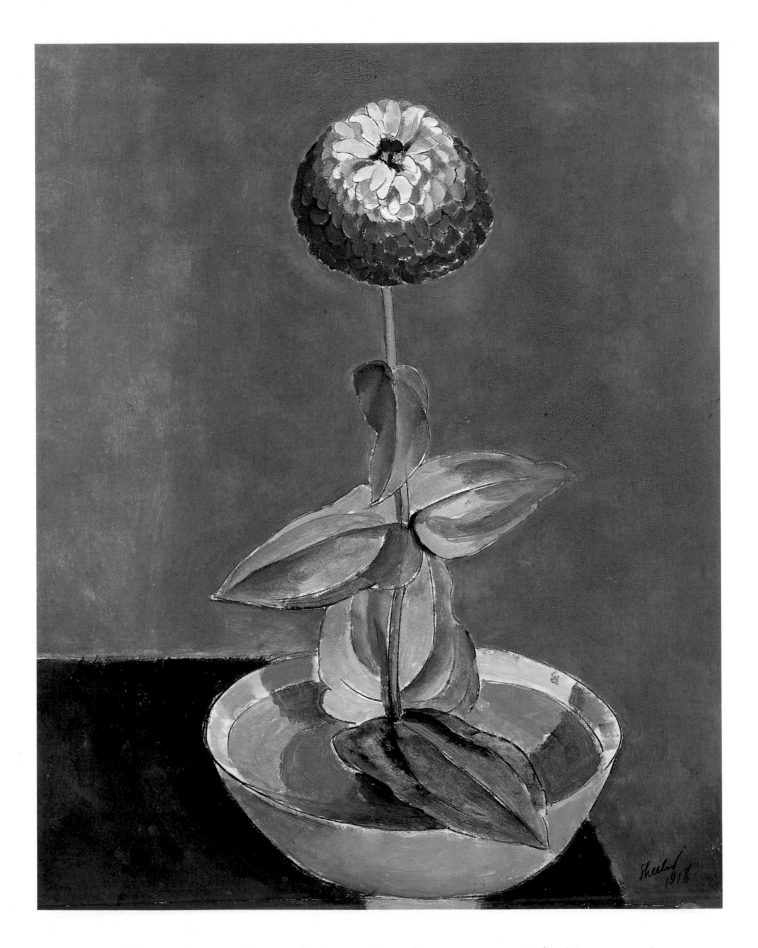

126. CHARLES SHEELER. *Flower in a Bowl,* 1918. Watercolor on paper, 15 × 12 inches (38.1 × 30.5 cm). Collection of Warren Adelson.

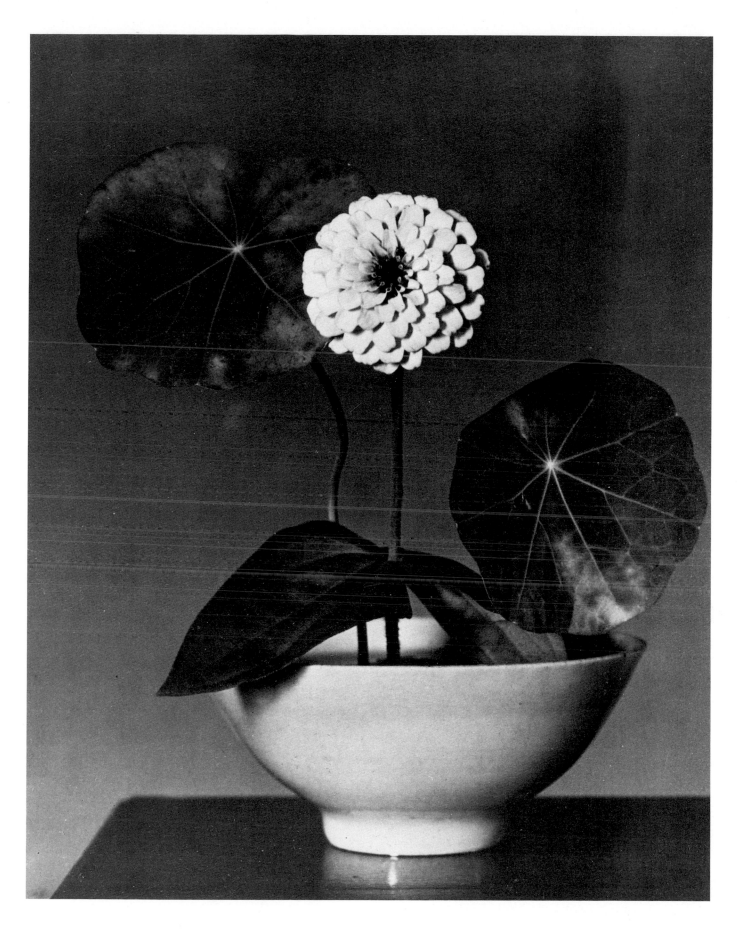

127. CHARLES SHEELER. *Zinnia and Nasturtium Leaves*, 1915. Silver-print photograph, 9⅝ × 7¹¹⁄₁₆ inches
(24.4 × 19.5 cm). Worcester Art Museum, Massachusetts; Anonymous gift.

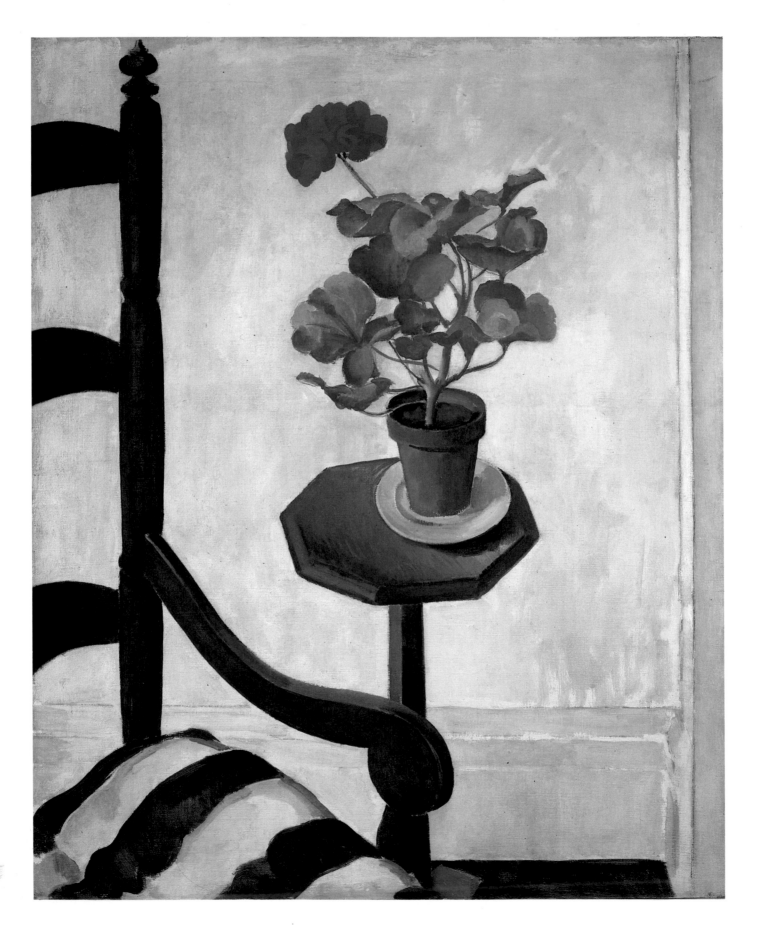

128. CHARLES SHEELER. *Geranium*, c. 1926. Oil on canvas, 32 × 26 inches (81.3 × 66 cm). Whitney Museum of American Art, New York; Gift of Gertrude Vanderbilt Whitney   31.343.

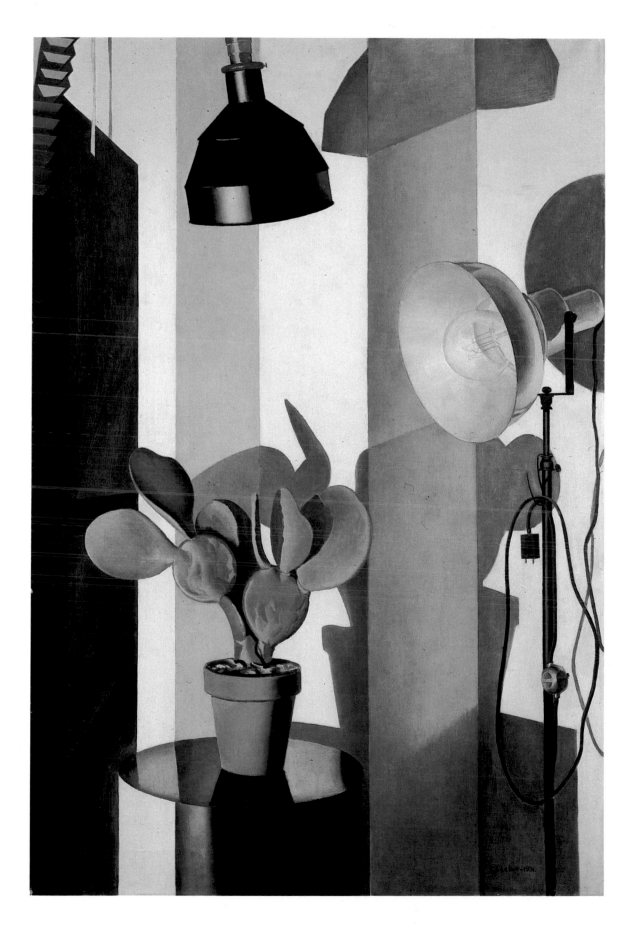

129. CHARLES SHEELER. *Cactus,* 1931. Oil on canvas, 45⅛ × 30 inches (114.6 × 76.2 cm).
Philadelphia Museum of Art; The Louise and Walter Arensberg Collection.

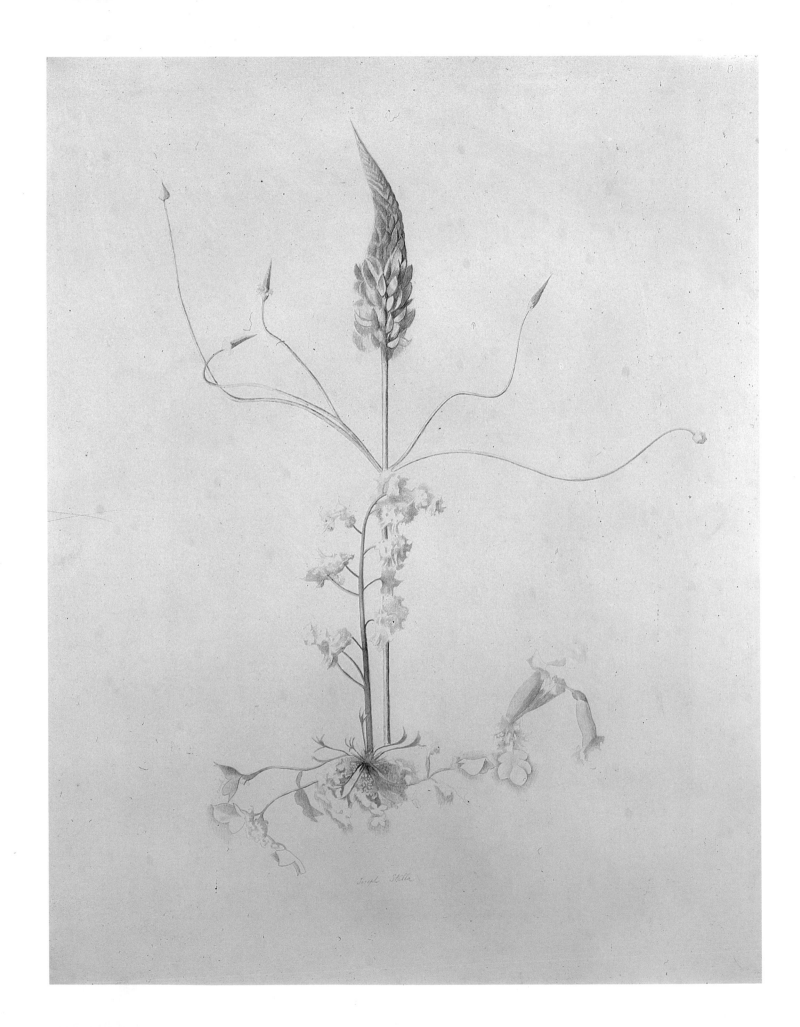

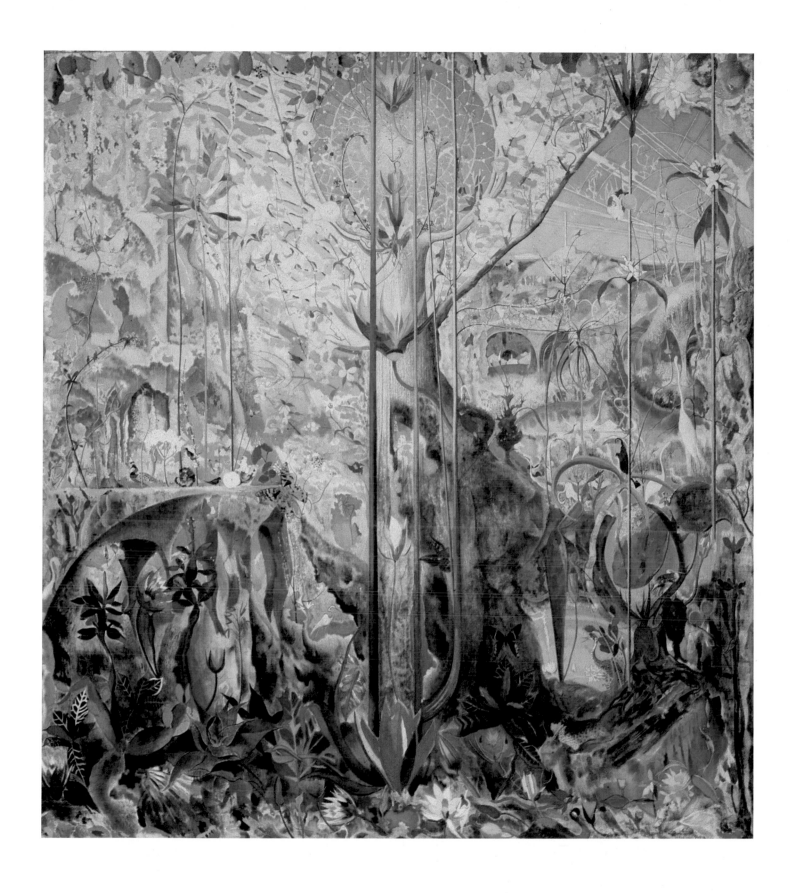

130. JOSEPH STELLA. *Lupine*, c. 1919. Pastel on paper, 27½ × 21½ inches (69.9 × 54.6 cm).
Collection of Robert Tobin.

131. JOSEPH STELLA. *Tree of My Life*, 1919. Oil on canvas, 83½ × 75½ inches
(212.1 × 191.8 cm). Iowa State Education Association, Des Moines.

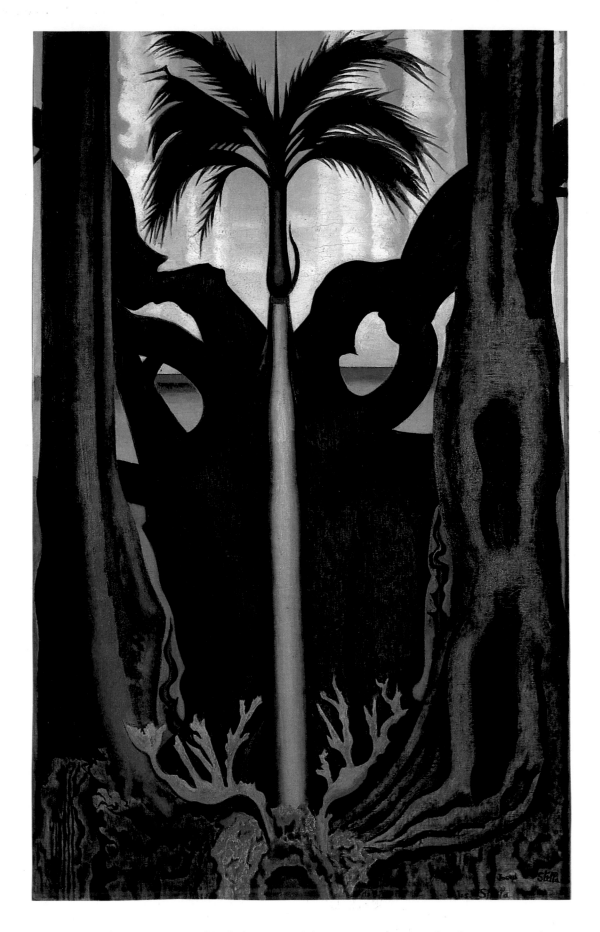

132. JOSEPH STELLA. *Song of Barbados*, 1938. Oil on canvas, 58 × 37 inches (147.3 × 94 cm).
Collection of Mr. and Mrs. James A. Fisher.

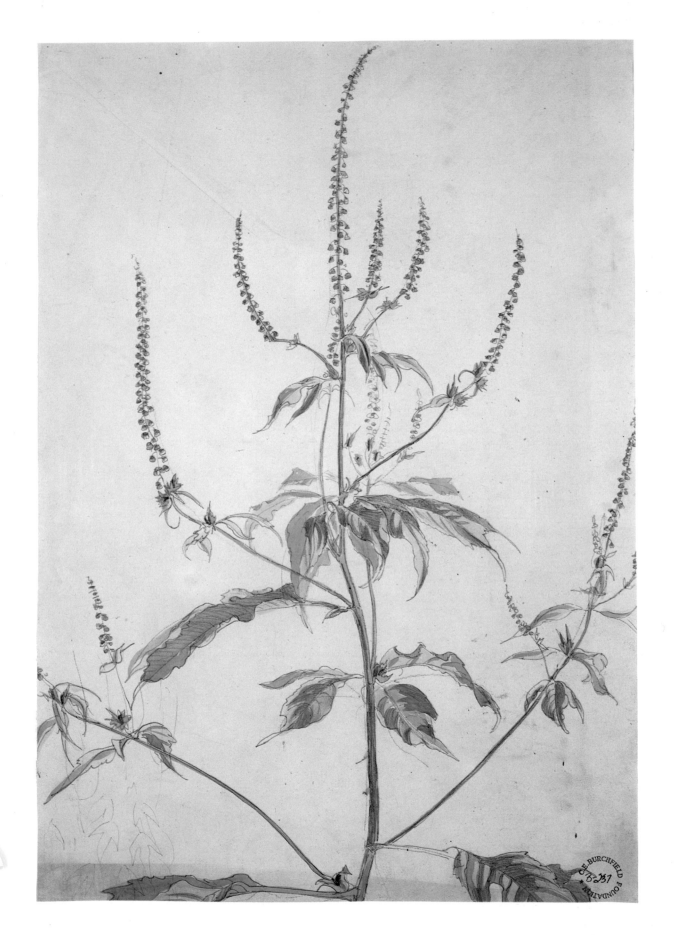

133. CHARLES BURCHFIELD. *Wild Flower Study*, 1911–12. Watercolor on paper, 20 × 14 inches
(50.8 × 35.6 cm). Kennedy Galleries, New York.

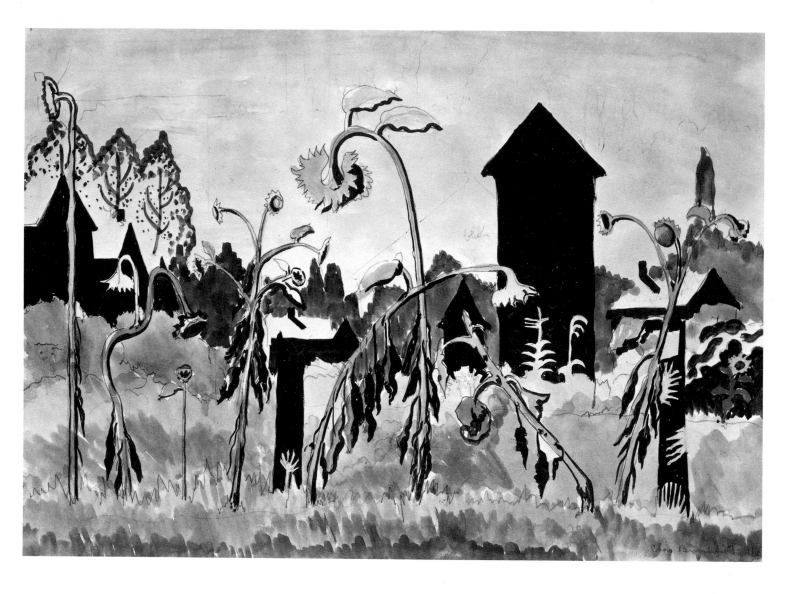

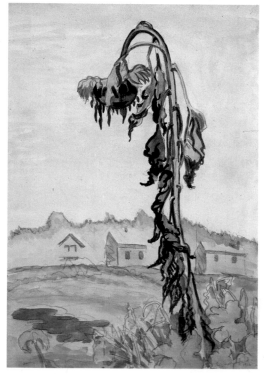

134. CHARLES BURCHFIELD. *Rogues' Gallery*, 1916. Watercolor on paper,
13½ × 19⅝ inches (34.3 × 49.8 cm). The Museum of Modern Art, New York;
Gift of Abby Aldrich Rockefeller.

135. CHARLES BURCHFIELD. *Dead Sunflower*, 1917. Watercolor on paper,
19⅞ × 13⅞ inches (50.5 × 35.2 cm). Munson-Williams-Proctor Institute, Utica,
New York; Edward W. Root Bequest.

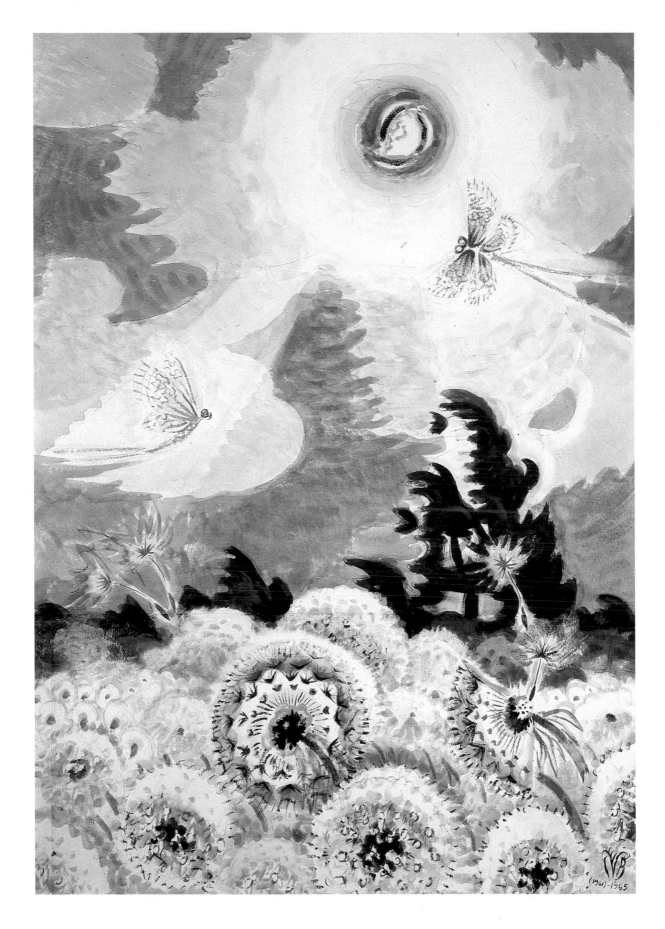

136. CHARLES BURCHFIELD. *Dandelion Seed Heads and the Moon*, 1961–65. Watercolor on paper,
54¼ × 38½ inches (137.8 × 97.8 cm). Collection of Dr. Irwin Goldstein.

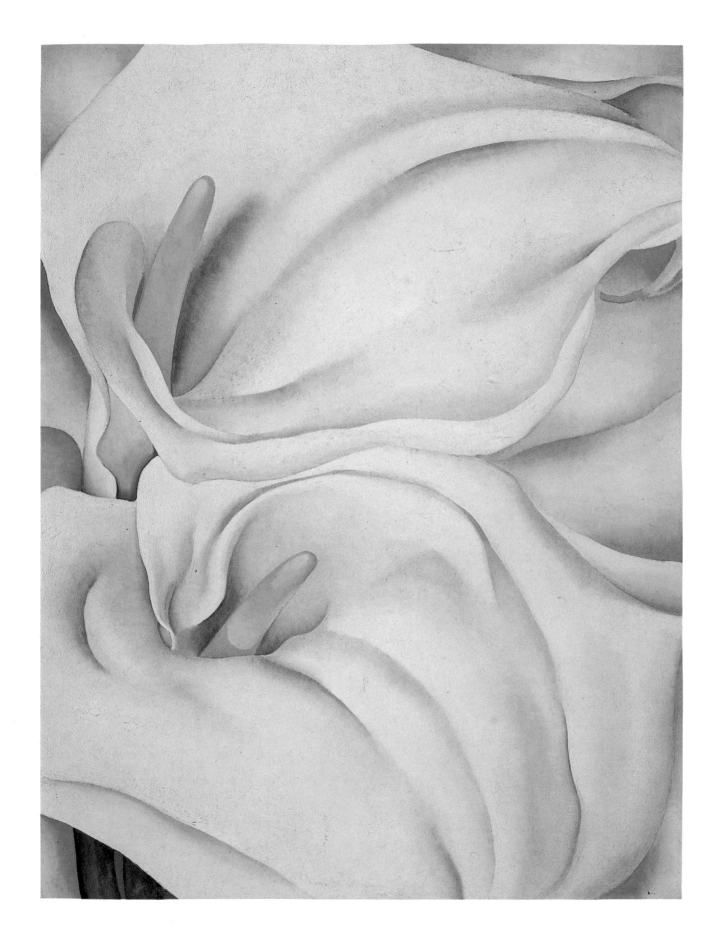

137. GEORGIA O'KEEFFE. *Two Calla Lilies on Pink,* 1928. Oil on canvas, 40 × 30 inches (101.6 × 76.2 cm). Collection of the artist.

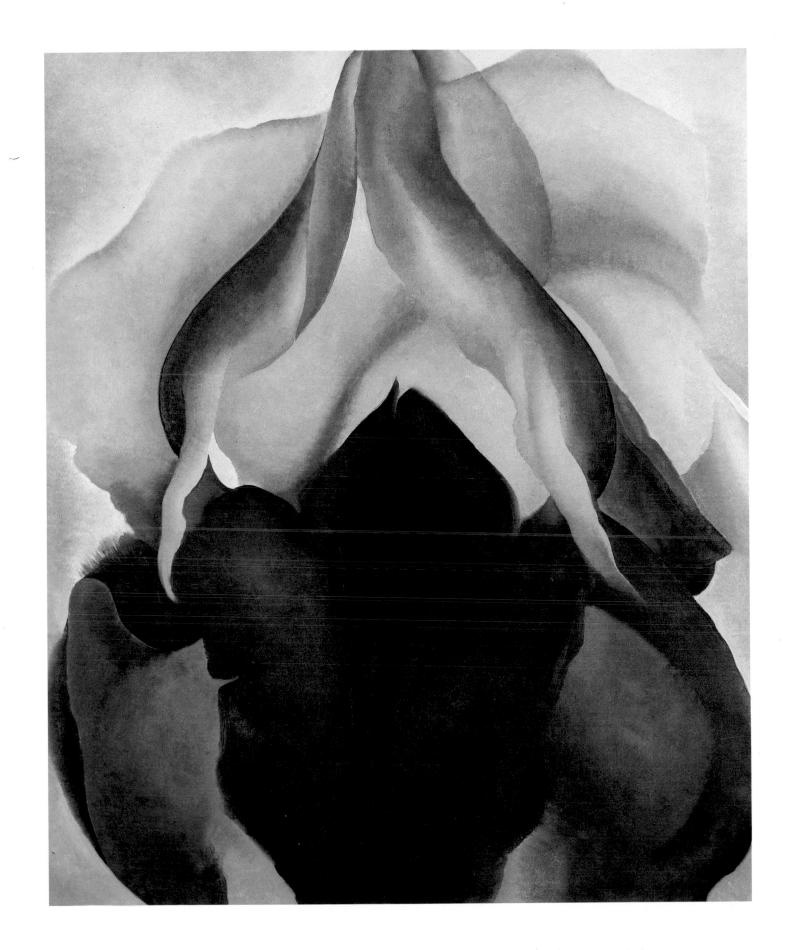

138. GEORGIA O'KEEFFE. *Black Iris,* 1926. Oil on canvas, 36 × 29⅞ inches (91.4 × 75.9 cm).
The Metropolitan Museum of Art, New York; The Alfred Stieglitz Collection.

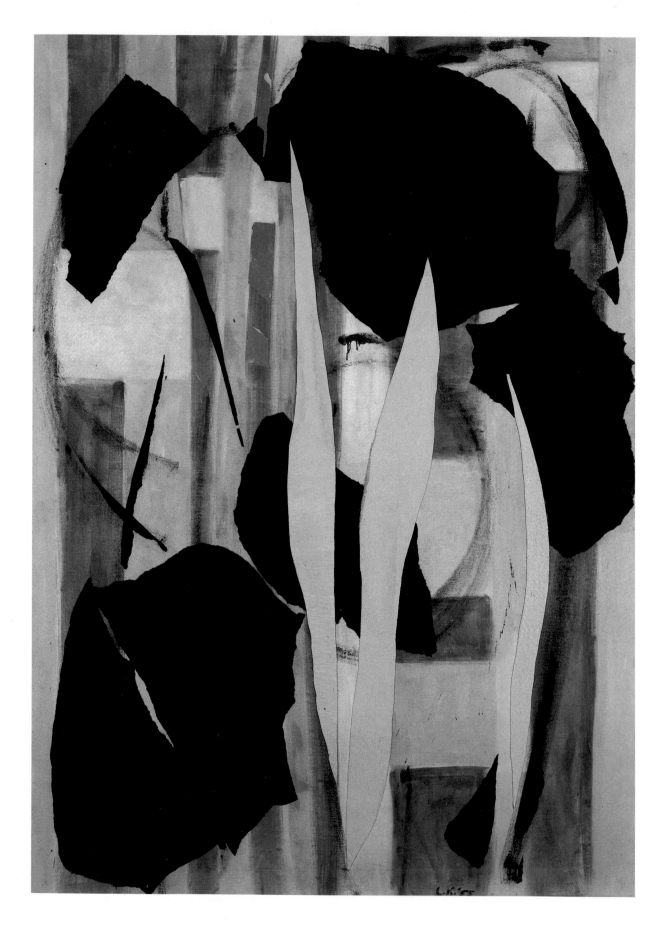

139. Lee Krasner. *Milkweed*, 1955. Oil, paper, and canvas collage on canvas, 82⅜ × 57¾ inches
(209.2 × 146.7 cm). Albright-Knox Art Gallery, Buffalo; Gift of Seymour H. Knox.

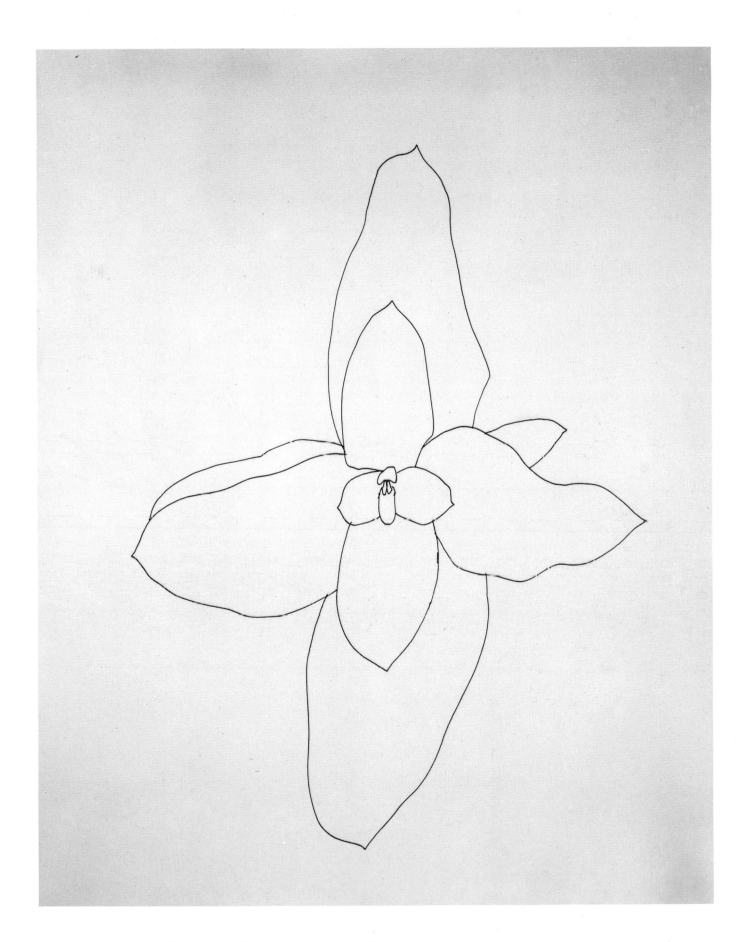

140. ELLSWORTH KELLY. *Milkweed*, 1969. Ink on paper, 29 × 23 inches (73.7 × 58.4 cm).
Private collection.

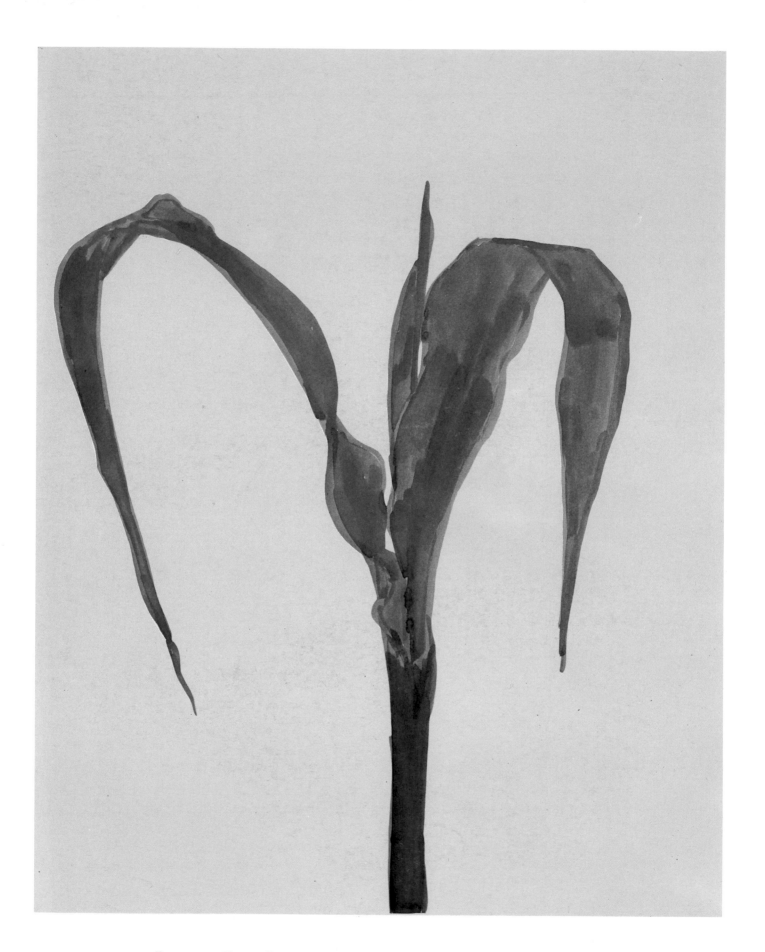

141. ELLSWORTH KELLY. *Corn*, 1959. Watercolor on paper, 18½ × 22½ inches (47 × 57.2 cm). Private collection.

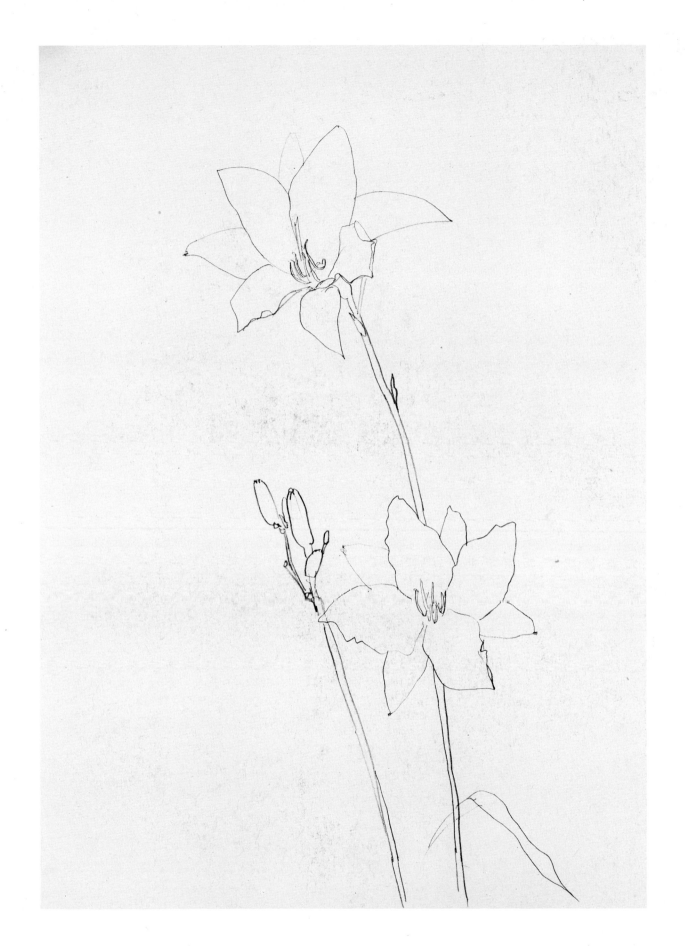

142. ELLSWORTH KELLY. *Lilies,* 1980. Pencil on paper, 30 × 20 inches (76.2 × 50.8 cm).
Private collection.

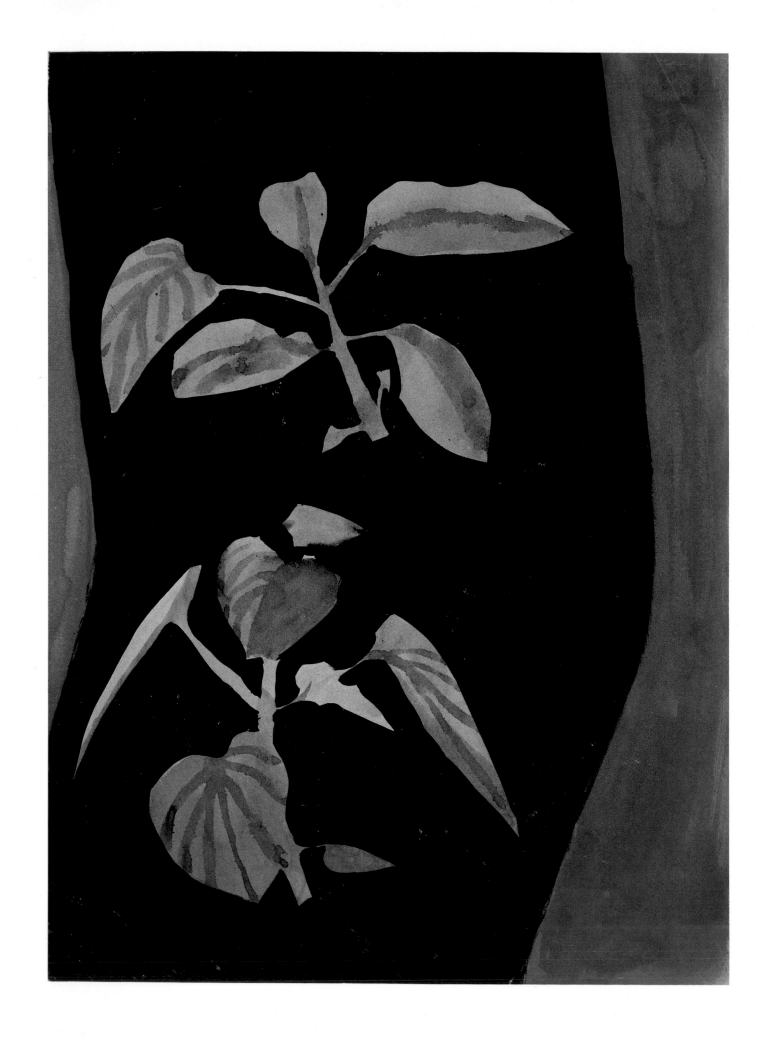

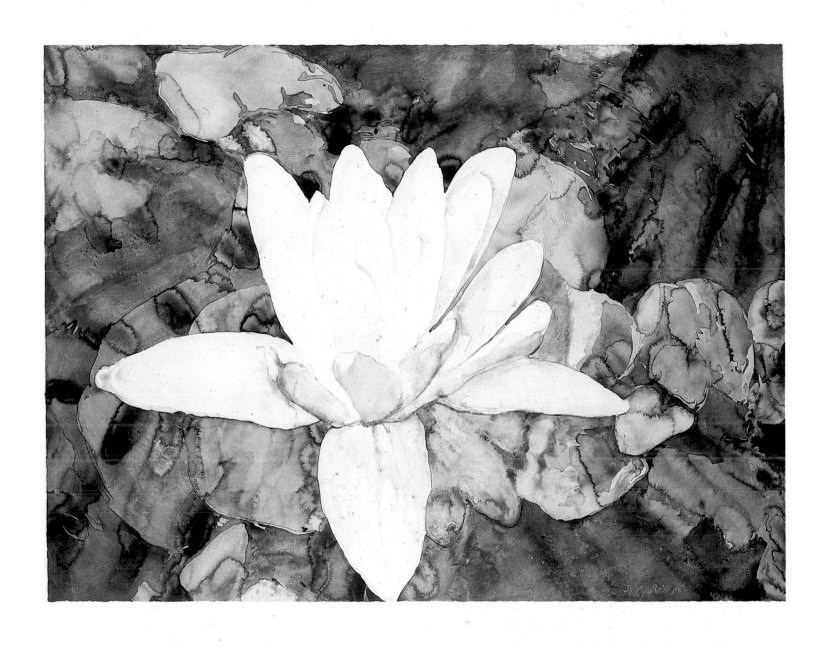

143. ELLSWORTH KELLY. *Trunk with Leaves,* 1949. Ink on paper, 10½ × 8⅛ inches (26.7 × 20.6 cm). Private collection.

144. JOSEPH RAFFAEL. *Large Mystic Lily,* 1976. Watercolor on paper, 28½ × 38 inches (72.4 × 96.5 cm). Collection of Frank and Betsy Goodyear.

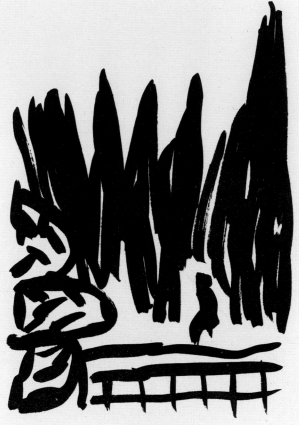

145. JENNIFER BARTLETT. *In the Garden #10*, 1980. Ink on paper, 19½ × 26 inches (49.5 × 66 cm). Collection of Rose and Morton Landowne.

146. JENNIFER BARTLETT. *In the Garden #65*, 1980. Pencil on paper, 26 × 19½ inches (66 × 49.5 cm). Collection of Mr. and Mrs. Mason Adams.

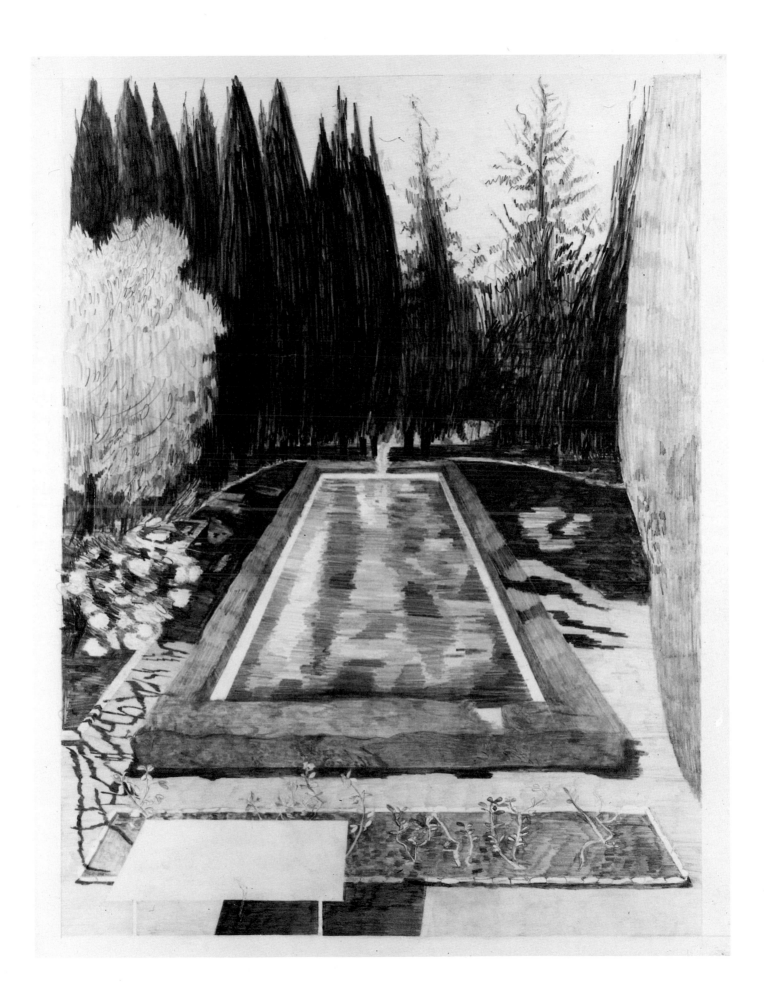

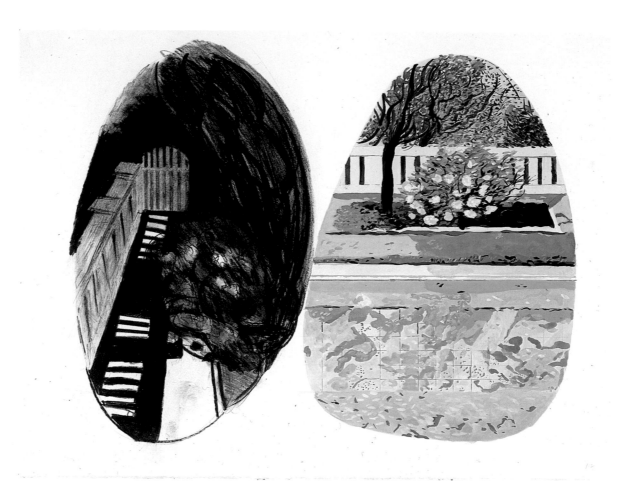

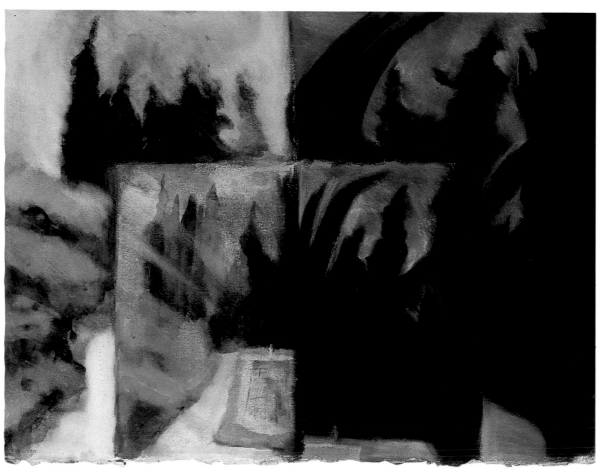

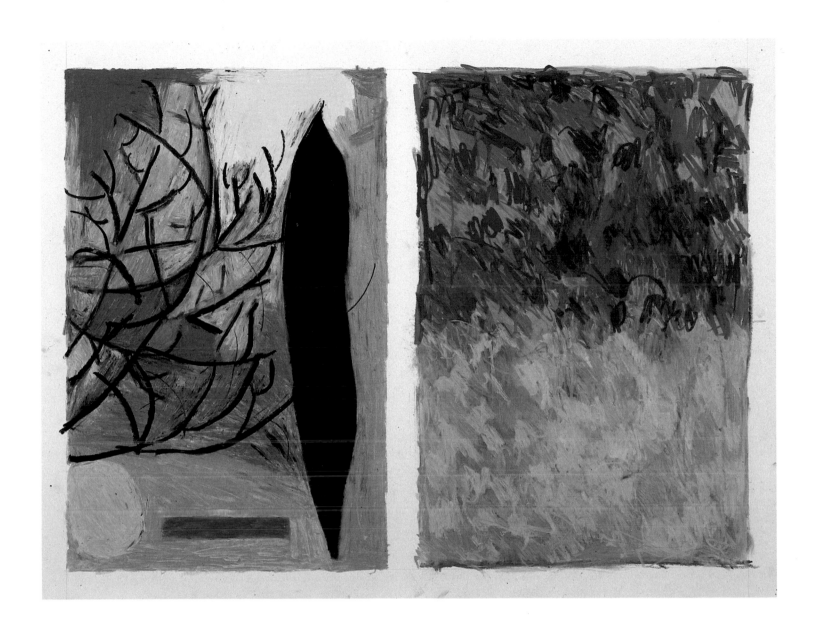

147. JENNIFER BARTLETT. *In the Garden #112*, 1980. Charcoal and gouache on paper,
19¾ × 26 inches (50.2 × 66 cm). Collection of Wendy and Richard Hokin.

148. JENNIFER BARTLETT. *In the Garden #118*, 1980. Watercolor and pastel on paper,
19¾ × 26 inches (50.2 × 66 cm). Private collection.

149. JENNIFER BARTLETT. *In the Garden #174*, 1980. Oil pastel on paper, 19¾ × 26 inches
(50.2 × 66 cm). Collection of Steven and Sue Antebi.

Notes

Reflections of Nature: Flowers in American Art

1. Sir Joshua Reynolds, *Discourses on Art* (London, 1797; rpt., ed. Robert Wark, San Marino, Calif.: Huntington Library Publications, 1959), pp. 70–71. For Reynolds, flower painting could offer the young artist a confined format for studying "the art of colouring, and the skilful management of light and shadow."

2. John Ruskin, *Modern Painters*, 5 vols., 5th ed. (London, 1851–60), vol. 5, p. 95.

3. Pliny the Elder, *Natural History*, XXV, 4; trans. and ed. W. H. S. Jones (Cambridge, Mass.: Harvard University Press, 1956), pp. 140–41.

4. The post-classical centuries of plant illustration have been described as "a history of degradation rather than of progress"; see Agnes Arber, *Herbals, Their Origin and Evolution: A Chapter in the History of Botany, 1470–1670* (London: Cambridge University Press, 1938), p. 186.

5. John Ruskin was so impressed by the naturalism and aesthetic quality of the drawings in Rinio's herbal that he copied one of them for his students. He encouraged them to study the Venetian manuscript because, as he told them, it "contains the earliest botanical drawings I know, of approximate accuracy"; *The Complete Works of John Ruskin*, ed. E. T. Cook and Alexander Wedderburn, 39 vols. (London: George Allen; New York: Longmans, Green & Co., 1906), vol. 21, pp. 142–43.

6. Paul Hulton and Lawrence Smith, *Flowers in Art from East and West* (London: British Museum Publications, 1979), p. 16. According to the authors, this definition appeared in the earliest English printed book on plants, published in 1525.

7. The flowers are identified in Millard Meiss, *French Painting in the Time of Jean de Berry: The Limbourgs and Their Contemporaries*, 2 vols. (New York: George Braziller and the Pierpont Morgan Library, 1974), vol. 1, p. 193.

8. For the relationship between fifteenth-century French and Italian artists in the development of a realistic projection of nature in landscape art, see Otto Pächt, "Early Italian Nature Studies and the Early Calendar Landscape," *Journal of the Warburg and Courtauld Institutes*, 13 (January–June 1950), pp. 13–47.

9. Ibid., p. 17, n. 2. Pächt makes the distinction between nature studies which have the character of "stilled life" and those which approach the reproduction of "life." In Pächt's opinion, most of Dürer's work retains this *nature morte* quality despite the artist's lifelong "struggle for the mastery of organic movement." Leonardo, on the other hand, "seems to have been able to combine the faculty of presenting a 'still' with an imagination producing convincing images of intense movement."

10. Kenneth Clark, Introduction to Carlo Pedretti, *Leonardo da Vinci Nature Studies from the Royal Library at Windsor Castle*, exhibition catalogue (London: Johnson Reprint Corporation for the J. Paul Getty Museum and the Metropolitan Museum of Art, 1980), p. 9. The record of these flower studies, which have not survived, appears in the *Codex Atlanticus*.

11. In her edition of *The Notebooks of Leonardo da Vinci* (New York, London, and Scarborough, Ontario: Plume Books, 1960), p. 12, Pamela Taylor describes these botanical phenomena. Leonardo devoted the sixth book of his *Treatise on Painting* to a study of "Botany for Painters and Elements of Landscape Painting."

12. Leonardo da Vinci, *Treatise on Painting [Codex Urbinas Latinus 1270]*, trans. A. Philip McMahon, 2 vols. (Princeton, N.J.: Princeton University Press, 1956), vol. 1, p. 293.

13. Henry David Thoreau, "Natural History of Massachusetts," *The Dial*, 3 (July 1842), p. 22.

14. The circumstances for the making of Dürer's drawing are described in Sebastian Killerman, *A. Dürers Pflanzen- und Tierzeichnungen und Ihre Bedeutung für die Naturgeschichte* (Strassburg: J. H. E. Heitz [Heitz & Mündel], 1910), p. 32.

15. Leonardo, *Treatise on Painting*, p. 41.

16. The flowers are identified in L. J. Bol, *The Bosschaert Dynasty* (Leigh-on-Sea, England: F. Lewis, 1960), p. 20. I am grateful to the New York Botanical Garden Library for the confirmation of this information.

17. Crispin van de Passe the Younger provided the engraved

illustrations to accompany the botanical texts written by Dodanaeas and Clusius for the *Hortus floridus* (Utrecht, 1614; Arnheim, 1616).

18. Friedrich Schlie, "Sieben Briefe und eine Quittung von Jan van Huysum," *Oud-Holland*, 18 (1900), pp. 137–38. The translation of these letters was kindly provided by Ottho Heldring. In another letter, van Huysum explained that he would have to wait until the following summer to obtain a specimen of a yellow rose for the completion of a painting. The popularity of this artist in mid-nineteenth-century America is demonstrated in the article "John van Huysum," *The Illustrated Magazine of Art*, 3 (February 1854), pp. 129–42.

19. I am grateful to Professor Susan Donahue Kuretsky, Vassar College, for her expert guidance through the complexities of Dutch still-life painting.

20. Ingvar Bergström, *Dutch Still-Life Painting in the Seventeenth Century*, trans. Christina Hedström and Gerald Taylor (New York: Thomas Yoseloff, 1956), p. 48.

21. The concept of "disguised symbolism" in Netherlandish painting was first and most eloquently explored by Erwin Panofsky, *Early Netherlandish Painting: Its Origins and Character*, 2 vols. (Cambridge, Mass.: Harvard University Press, 1955).

22. Gerhard Langemeyer and Hans-Albert Peters, *Stilleben in Europa*, exhibition catalogue (Münster: Landschaftsverband Westfalen-Lippe, 1979), p. 308.

23. It is important to note that while many of the natural and artificial curiosities pictured in van Kessel's *America* are native to the continent, several are not. The sixteen landscape panels surrounding the central image, for instance, include a number of Old World beasts such as elephants, giraffes, and zebra; see Hugh Honour, *The European Vision of America*, exhibition catalogue (Cleveland: The Cleveland Museum of Art, 1975), pp. 136–37.

24. Giovanni da Verrazzano, letter to King Francis I of France, July 8, 1524, trans. Susan Tarrow, in Lawrence C. Wroth, *The Voyages of Giovanni da Verrazzano, 1524–1528* (New Haven, Conn., and London: Yale University Press for the Pierpont Morgan Library, 1970), pp. 136–37.

25. Hulton and Smith, *Flowers in Art*, p. 29.

26. Paul Hulton, *The Work of Jacques Le Moyne de Morgues: A Huguenot Artist in France, Florida and England*, 2 vols. (London: The Trustees of the British Museum, British Museum Publications, 1977), vol. 1, p. 57.

27. Autograph title of manuscript volume containing the John White drawings; British Museum, London. Neither of John White's dates in this title can be taken as accurate, according to Paul Hulton and David Beers Quinn, *The American Drawings of John White, 1577–1590: With Drawings of European and Oriental Subjects* (London: The Trustees of the British Museum; Chapel Hill, N.C.: University of North Carolina Press, 1964), p. 65.

28. It is this empirical approach to nature that allows the schol-

ars of John White to say that "he has some substantial claim to be the first to make a North American contribution to the great achievement of the Renaissance in exploring, identifying and recording the flora and fauna of the planet, an achievement which was a major element in the establishment of the scientific outlook and the making of modern man"; Hulton and Quinn, *The American Drawings of John White*, p. 47.

29. Mark Catesby copied seven of White's drawings when he was compiling his *Natural History*, but he makes an acknowledgment of only one of them, and that is to Raleigh; see Hulton and Quinn, *The American Drawings of John White*, p. 7.

30. Mark Catesby, *The Natural History of Carolina, Florida and the Bahama Islands*, 2 vols. (London, 1731–43), vol. 1, p. vi.

31. Ibid., pl. 27.

32. Quoted in William M. Smallwood and Mabel S. C. Smallwood, *Natural History and the American Mind* (New York: Columbia University Press, 1941), p. 26.

33. Catesby noted, in connection with his drawing of the *Magnolia flore albo*, that "Mr. Bartram of Pennsylvania has discovered many of them in that province, from the seeds of which I am in hopes of raising some"; Catesby, *The Natural History of Carolina*, vol. 2, appendix p. 15.

34. Kalm recorded a very favorable impression of the American naturalist as a man of remarkable learning. "He has acquired a great knowledge of natural philosophy and history," Kalm wrote of John Bartram, "and seems to be born with a peculiar genius for these sciences"; Peter Kalm, *Travels into North America; Containing Its Natural History and a Circumstantial Account of Its Plantations and Agriculture in General*, trans. John Reinhold Forster, 3 vols. (Warrington, England, 1770), vol. 1, p. 83.

35. Peter Collinson, letter to John Bartram, London, February 25, 1741, in *Memorials of John Bartram and Humphrey Marshall with Notices of Their Botanical Contemporaries*, ed. William Darlington (Philadelphia, 1849), p. 141.

36. The exact identification of the flower in Bartram's lapel continues to be a subject of debate, as does its specific association with the botanist; see William Howard Adams, ed., *The Eye of Jefferson*, exhibition catalogue (Washington, D.C.: National Gallery of Art, 1976), p. 345, fig. 599.

37. Peter Collinson, letter to William Bartram, July 28, 1767, in *Memorials of John Bartram*, p. 290.

38. Carl Linnaeus, *Systema naturae* (Leiden, 1735); trans. M. S. J. Engel-Lederboer and H. Engel (Amsterdam: Nieuwkoop B. de Graff, 1964), p. 22.

39. Charles F. Jenkins, "The Historical Background of Franklin's Tree," *The Pennsylvania Magazine of History and Biography*, 57, no. 3 (1933), pp. 196, 202.

40. Numerous references to William Bartram's thorough knowledge of the Linnaean system can be found in the definitive study by Joseph Ewan, *William Bartram: Botanical and Zoological Drawings*,

1756–1788 (Philadelphia: The American Philosophical Society, 1968), and in William Bartram, *Travels Through North and South Carolina, Georgia, East and West Florida* (Philadelphia, 1791).

41. I am deeply grateful to Dr. Rupert Barneby, Mrs. Lothian Lynas, and Thomas Everett of the New York Botanical Garden for their botanical judgments, which are reflected throughout this work.

42. The discussion of this drawing first appeared in Ella M. Foshay, "Charles Darwin and the Development of American Flower Imagery," *Winterthur Portfolio: A Journal of American Material Culture*, 15 (Winter 1980), pp. 300–1.

43. Quoted in George Brown Goode, "The Beginnings of Natural History in America," *Proceedings of the Biological Society of Washington*, 3 (July 1, 1884–February 6, 1886), p. 89.

44. Charles Coleman Sellers, *Charles Willson Peale*, 2 vols. (Philadelphia: The American Philosophical Society, 1947), vol. 2, p. 270. The engraved ticket, which bears this inscription on a festoon suspended between two trees, is crowned with an opened Book of Nature encircled by rays of light. Various animals and birds inhabit the trees and landscape. In an advertisement for Peale's Museum that appeared in Poulson's *American Daily Advertiser*, November 3, 1821, the inscription on the open book reads "Nature and Art."

45. Adams, *The Eye of Jefferson*, p. 346, fig. 600.

46. Barbara Novak has explored the relationships of art, science, and religion in the American view of nature in a number of scholarly publications. Most recently, in *Nature and Culture: American Landscape and Painting, 1825–1875* (New York: Oxford University Press, 1980), p. 47, she wrote that if "the Trinity of God, Man, and Nature was central to the nineteenth-century universe," then "Nature itself was illuminated by another Trinity: art, science and religion." Noting that an undiluted scientific approach to the natural world was resisted—it threatened faith in the creation of the universe by God—she recalled Thoreau's warning (p. 114): "The mystery of the life of plants is kindred with that of our own lives, and the physiologist must not presume to explain their growth according to mechanical laws, or as he might explain some machinery of his own making"; Henry David Thoreau, *The Journal of Henry D. Thoreau*, ed. Bradford Torrey and Francis H. Allen (Boston, 1906; rpt., 2 vols., New York: Dover Publications, 1962), rpt. vol. 2, p. 1439.

47. James Jackson Jarves, *The Art-Idea* (New York, 1864; rpt., ed. Benjamin Rowland, Jr., Cambridge, Mass.: Harvard University Press, Belknap Press, 1960), p. 40.

48. Ibid., p. 42.

49. Ralph Waldo Emerson, *The Complete Works of Ralph Waldo Emerson*, vol. 10: *Lectures and Biographical Sketches* (Boston and New York: Houghton Mifflin Co., 1904), p. 132.

50. Ralph Waldo Emerson, *The Complete Works of Ralph Waldo Emerson*, vol. 1: *Nature: Addresses and Lectures* (Boston and New York: Houghton Mifflin Co., 1903), pp. 25–35.

51. *Godey's Lady's Book* and other popular journals of the period were filled with illustrations of flowers, including stylish bouquets (Fig. 24), symbolic renderings, decorative designs for ladies' handiwork, and botanical drawings. In 1857, the *Cosmopolitan Art Journal*, 1 (June 1857), p. 111, lamented that "the illustration mania is upon our people." In the gift books, the nineteenth century's version of emblem books, illustrations of flowers illuminated a complex system of symbolic associations. Often serving as accompaniments to sentimental love poetry, the significance of individual flowers could vary according to placement: "the marigold, for example: placed upon the head, it signifies 'distress of mind'; upon the heart 'the pains of love'; upon the breast 'ennui'"; see Frances S. Osgood, ed., *The Poetry of Flowers and Flowers of Poetry: To Which Are Added, a Simple Treatise on Botany, with Familiar Examples, and a Copious Floral Dictionary* (New York, 1841), p. 25. The influence of popular floral symbolism in contemporary professional flower painting is difficult to document because of the variability of the symbolic inference attached to each flower.

52. Henry T. Tuckerman, "Flowers," *Godey's Lady's Book*, 40 (January 1850), p. 13.

53. The moral and spiritual benefit of nature study was clearly expressed in an article promoting the introduction of the study of natural history as a required component of the school curriculum. "It cannot be doubted that the proper study of nature begets devout affections," the anonymous author wrote, "and this truth has given rise to the common maxim, that 'a true naturalist cannot be a bad man'"; "The Study of Natural History," *The Knickerbocker*, 15 (April 1845), p. 292.

54. Jim White at the Hunt Botanical Institute has kindly provided botanical identifications for the flowers in Hollen's bouquet: *Centaurea s.p.* (cornflower), *Dianthus s.p.* (pink), and *Trifolium pratense L.* (red clover).

55. Probably trained as a porcelain and enamel painter in Cologne, Severin Roesen immigrated to America in 1848. Publications by William Gerdts, Maurice Mook, and Lois Goldreich Marcus on Severin Roesen have enlarged our knowledge of that artist's life and work (see Bibliography). See also the pioneering study by Richard B. Stone, "Not Quite Forgotten: A Study of the Williamsport Painter, S. Roesen," *Lycoming Historical Society: Proceedings and Papers*, 9 (November 1951), pp. 2–40.

56. Since the seventeenth century, German still-life painting had been strongly influenced by the Netherlandish school; see Bergström, *Dutch Still-Life Painting*, p. 293. Exhibition records show that Roesen was but one of a growing number of artists producing flower pieces in the Dutch tradition in mid-nineteenth-century America.

57. Information supplied by the plant information service at the Brooklyn Botanic Garden.

58. Emma C. Embury, *American Wild Flowers in Their Native Haunts* (New York, 1845), p. 10.

59. Edwin Whitefield's diary entry for April 1842 shows that

he moved to Hudson, New York, from Albany in 1842 for the purpose of making "a complete collection of American wild flowers"; Edwin Whitefield Manuscripts, Print Room, Boston Public Library. We also learn from Whitefield's papers that he was involved with flowers in other ways, both practical and artistic. His accounts for May 3, 1840, show that he spent money on plants for his garden: scarlet runners, China asters, parsley, sweet Williams. Whitefield also taught art. The prospectus for his lessons listed several techniques in which the student could choose instruction: perspective, sketching from nature, watercolors, flower colors, and oil painting.

60. This comparison of the Edwin Whitefield drawings first appeared in Foshay, "Charles Darwin," pp. 303–4.

61. Much of what is known about the life of Otto Marseus van Schriek was documented in Arnold Houbraken, *De Groote Schouburgh der Nederlandsche Konstschilders en Schilderessen*, 3 vols. (Amsterdam, 1718–21); rpt., 2 vols. (Maasricht: Leiter-Nypels, n.v., 1943–44), vol. 1, pp. 282, 345. There it is suggested that the artist kept a kind of open-air terrarium in which he preserved his live zoological and botanical specimens for study. One interpretation of van Schriek's animal and plant paintings suggests that personal fantasy played a significant role in these seemingly documentary works; see V. Curt Habicht, "Ein vergessener Phantast der holländischen Malerei," *Oud-Holland*, 41 (1923–24), pp. 31–37.

62. Eugène Delacroix, letter to Constant Dutilleux, February 6, 1849, in *Correspondence générale de Eugène Delacroix, 1804–1837*, 5 vols. (Paris: Librairie Plon, 1936), vol. 2, p. 373.

63. Thoreau, "Natural History of Massachusetts," p. 22. The impact of Ruskin is discussed in William Gerdts' "The Influence of Ruskin and Pre-Raphaelitism on American Still-Life Painting," *The American Art Journal*, 1 (Fall 1969), pp. 80–97; and Roger B. Stein, *John Ruskin and Aesthetic Thought in America, 1840–1900* (Cambridge, Mass.: Harvard University Press, 1967).

64. Ruskin, *Complete Works*, vol. 3, p. 624. Allen Staley suggests that a distinguishing feature of Ruskin's aesthetic view of nature was his preference for particular truths over general truths. To master the particulars, it was necessary to gain control of the fine details of nature and to reproduce them with care and finish; see Staley's *The Pre-Raphaelite Landscape* (Oxford: Clarendon Press, 1973), p. 9.

65. There are numerous references in Ruskin's writings to the innately superior beauty of wild flowers. Many appear in a chapter of *Proserpina* called "Of Wildness in Flowers": "To this class of true wild flowers," wrote Ruskin, "belong the most beautiful plants in the world"; Ruskin, *Complete Works*, vol. 25, p. 535.

66. John Ruskin, "The British Villa," in *Complete Works*, vol. 1, p. 156. The particular species of cultivated flowers which inspired Ruskin's most vehement disapprobation were those that most frequently appear in Dutch still-life painting. For example, such flowers as "dahlias, tulips and ranunculi," he cautioned, "should be avoided like garlic" (p. 157).

67. John Ruskin, *Praeterita*, 3 vols. (London, 1899), vol. 2, p. 300. Ruskin's remark appears in chapter 10, "Crossmount," and is dated 1846–47.

68. An exhibition organized by Theodore Stebbins displayed an illuminating sampling of the oil sketches of Frederic Church and several other American artists such as Thomas Cole, William Sidney Mount, and William Whittredge. See Theodore E. Stebbins, Jr., *Close Observation: Selected Oil Sketches by Frederic E. Church*, exhibition catalogue (Washington, D.C.: Smithsonian Institution Press for the Cooper-Hewitt Museum, 1978).

69. Henry T. Tuckerman, *Book of the Artists: American Artist Life, Comprising Biographical and Critical Sketches of American Artists, Preceded by an Historical Account of the Rise and Progress of Art in America* (New York, 1867), p. 386.

70. Ibid. Tuckerman could have been describing a Church landscape of 1866, *Rainy Season in the Tropics*, another painting in which the artist made use of his Jamaican sketches.

71. "Domestic Art Gossip," *The Crayon*, 6 (September 1860), p. 264.

72. The growing seasons and preferred climates of the corn lily (*Clintonia*) and the heliotrope (*Valeriana officinalis*) are documented in Harold Ricket, *Wild Flowers of the United States*, 6 vols. (New York: The New York Botanical Garden and McGraw-Hill Book Co., 1964–73), vol. 1, pp. 34, 338.

73. Heade was probably first drawn to the subject of orchids for his art through his interest in hummingbirds, which had fascinated him since his childhood. In 1863, he went to Brazil to do a book on the hummingbirds of that country, to be called "The Gems of Brazil," which was to have identified and illustrated the major species. In one of his articles, Heade declared that "from early boyhood I have been almost a monomaniac on hummingbirds"; see Heade's "Taming Hummingbirds," *Forest and Stream*, 38 (April 14, 1892), p. 348; also quoted in Theodore E. Stebbins, Jr., *The Life and Works of Martin Johnson Heade* (New Haven, Conn.: Yale University Press, 1975), p. 120.

74. Stebbins, *The Life and Works of Martin Johnson Heade*, pp. 146–47.

75. Ibid., pp. 145–46. Stebbins noted the correspondence of these works.

76. Stebbins described the originality of Heade's orchid and hummingbird pictures: "The combination of these birds with flowers and landscape was new to the American public, and the first person to adapt it to painting was Heade." And further on he added, "There are quite simply no other paintings like these known in America or elsewhere"; *The Life and Works of Martin Johnson Heade*, pp. 130, 148.

77. Heade's exposure to the work of Charles Darwin is discussed in Foshay, "Charles Darwin," where many of these ideas about the connection between science and late nineteenth-century American painting first appeared.

78. Charles Darwin, *The Various Contrivances by Which British and Foreign Orchids Are Fertilised by Insects and on the Good Effects of Intercrossing*, 2nd ed. (London, 1877), p. 284.

79. Darwin was acquainted with the population theory of Robert Malthus, whose views were published in *An Essay on the Principle of Population as It Affects the Future Improvement of Society* (1798). The Malthusian thesis that population tends to increase proportionally faster than the supply of food influenced Darwin's theory of natural selection.

80. Clearly stated summaries of Darwin's theory of evolution, from which this general explanation is drawn, can be found in Paul F. Boller, *American Thought in Transition: The Impact of Evolutionary Naturalism, 1865–1900*, The Rand McNally Series on the History of American Thought and Culture, ed. David D. Van Tassel (Chicago: Rand McNally & Co., 1969), pp. 1–2; and Ernst Mayr, "Evolution," *Scientific American*, 239 (September 1978), pp. 47–55. I am also very much indebted to Professor Loren Graham for his exposition of Darwinian thought in his lectures (and private discussions) at Columbia University.

81. The study of the *Passifloraceae* family of plants appears in Charles Darwin, "The Movements and Habits of Climbing Plants," *Journal of the Linnean Society*, 9 (1865); rev. ed. published as *The Movements and Habits of Climbing Plants* (London, 1876), pp. 153–58.

82. Charles Darwin, *The Effects of Cross and Self Fertilisation in the Vegetable Kingdom* (London, 1876), pp. 370–71.

83. Charles Darwin, *On the Origin of Species by Means of Natural Selection; or, The Preservation of Favoured Races in the Struggle for Life*, rev. ed. (New York, 1860), pp. 423–24.

84. An important recent study of the character and development of the flower painting in John La Farge's oeuvre is Kathleen A. Foster's "The Still-Life Painting of John La Farge," *The American Art Journal*, 11 (July 1979), pp. 4–37.

85. *Catalogue of Mr. John La Farge's Library, Valuable Illustrated and Art Works, and General Literature*, auction catalogue (New York: Geo. A. Leavitt & Co., 1881).

86. *Catalogue of a Portion of the Library of John La Farge*, auction catalogue (New York: Anderson Auction Co., 1909); microfilm copy, Archives Division, Sterling Memorial Library, Yale University, New Haven, Connecticut.

87. "Introduction," *Bulletin of the Torrey Botanical Club*, 1 (January 1870), p. 1.

88. Quoted in Royal Cortissoz, *John La Farge: A Memoir and a Study* (Boston and New York: Houghton Mifflin Co., 1911), p. 136.

89. Quoted in Novak, *Nature and Culture*, p. 112.

90. John La Farge, paraphrased in *A John La Farge Reader*, ed. Thurston N. Davis and Joseph Small (New York: The America Press, 1956), p. 16.

91. Maria Oakey Dewing, "Flower Painters and What the Flower Offers to Art," *American Magazine of Art: Art and Progress*, 6 (June 1915), pp. 255–62. In this illuminating essay, Dewing set down what she considered to be the essential qualities of good flower art; she then judged the work of a selection of artists according to those criteria.

92. There is good evidence to show that popular and critical taste found much to admire in Dutch flower painting. For Henry Tuckerman, any work of art "to be at all valuable or significant, must be true," and he found the "literal truth" of Dutch art a viable mode of achieving status; Tuckerman, *Book of the Artists*, vol. 1, p. 24. The flower paintings of Jan van Huysum were particularly admired for "certain little details which would enable the botanist to recognize and name the myosotis, the fuchsia, and the blue campanula." His floral images showed that he "placed nature in the first rank," because they demonstrated "what art, what care is necessary for setting these pretty models, so that, whether seen in full or in profile, whether bending forwards or backwards, they may preserve the character and the form which we know to be peculiar to them"; see "John van Huysum," pp. 130–33.

93. Dewing, "Flower Painters," p. 262.

94. Dewing recognized John La Farge's profound debt to Japanese art, but she saw his use of an integrated background in flower painting as an essential departure from his much-admired model; see "Flower Painters," p. 258.

95. Ibid., p. 262.

96. Quoted in Kermit S. Champa, *Studies in Early Impressionism* (New Haven, Conn.: Yale University Press, 1973), p. 41.

97. Hassam's *Celia Thaxter in Her Garden* served as the frontispiece to her book *An Island Garden* (Boston and New York, 1894). Hassam was one of a number of artists and writers who made frequent summer visits to Thaxter's home on the island of Appledore in the Isles of Shoals. Miss Thaxter's garden, renowned for its beauty, became the subject of a number of works by Hassam, some of which served as illustrations to *An Island Garden*. A catalogue raisonné of Hassam's work, now in preparation by Stuart P. Feld and Kathleen M. Burnside, will be an invaluable reference. I thank the authors for sharing their research with me.

98. Quoted in Thaxter, *An Island Garden*, pp. 81–82.

99. Celia Thaxter, letter to Annie Fields, in *Letters of Celia Thaxter*, ed. A. F. and R. L. (Boston, 1895), pp. 129–30.

100. Stuart Davis, "The Cube Root," *Art News*, 41 (February 1, 1943), p. 33.

101. Clement Greenberg, "Modernist Painting," in Gregory Battcock, ed., *The New Art: A Critical Anthology* (New York: E. P. Dutton & Co., 1966), p. 193.

102. John Graham, *John Graham's System and Dialectics of Art*, ed. Marcia Epstein Allentuck (Baltimore: The Johns Hopkins Press, 1971), p. 117.

103. Quoted in Barbara Haskell, *Arthur Dove*, exhibition catalogue (San Francisco: San Francisco Museum of Art, 1974), p. 136.

104. Quoted in Francis V. O'Connor, *Jackson Pollock*, exhibition catalogue (New York: The Museum of Modern Art, 1967), p. 26. When queried about the possible relationship of his art to nature, Clyfford Still, another Abstract Expressionist artist, replied, "I paint only myself, not nature"; quoted in J. Benjamin Townsend, "An Interview with Clyfford Still," *Gallery Notes* (Albright-Knox Art Gallery, The Buffalo Fine Arts Academy), 24 (Summer 1961), p. 11.

105. Frank Stella and Donald Judd, "After Abstract Expressionism," in Barbara Rose, ed., *Readings in American Art Since 1900: A Documentary Survey* (New York and Washington, D.C.: Frederick A. Praeger, 1968), p. 179.

106. Whether or not it is possible to posit a valid relationship between the treatment of forms in art and the dominant attitude of science toward nature in the modern era is a matter of debate. The painter and designer Gyorgy Kepes, a professor of visual design at the Massachusetts Institute of Technology, asserts that such connections can and should be explored; see his *The New Landscape in Art and Science* (Chicago: Paul Theobold & Co., 1956) and *Structure in Art and Science* (New York: George Braziller, 1965). The art historian John I. H. Baur takes a more circumspect point of view about the validity of parallels between modern art and science. He asserts that the complexity of contemporary scientific concepts has removed them from the conscious experience of the contemporary artist; see his *Nature in Abstraction: The Relation of Abstract Painting and Sculpture to Nature in Twentieth-Century American Art*, exhibition catalogue (New York: The Macmillan Co. for the Whitney Museum of American Art, 1958), p. 7.

107. Lancelot L. Whyte, "Atomism, Structure and Form: A Report on the Natural Philosophy of Form," in Kepes, ed., *Structure in Art and Science*, p. 26.

108. Charles Sheeler, paper read at a symposium on photography, The Museum of Modern Art, New York, October 20, 1950, published as part of his "The Black Book," in *Charles Sheeler*, exhibition catalogue (Washington, D.C.: Smithsonian Institution Press for the National Collection of Fine Arts, 1968), p. 96.

109. Ibid., p. 97.

110. Certain fundamental achievements, such as artificial parthenogenesis, by the scientist Jacques Loeb and other "mechanists" at the beginning of the twentieth century helped lay the foundation for nascent fields of biochemistry and molecular biology; see Garland E. Allen, *Life Science in the Twentieth Century* (New York and London: John Wiley & Sons, 1975), pp. 147–48.

111. See J. Reynolds Green, *A History of Botany, 1860–1900* (New York: Russell & Russell, 1909; rpt., 1967), p. 505.

112. Quoted in Thomas E. Norton, ed., *Homage to Charles Demuth: Still Life Painter of Lancaster* (Ephrata, Pa.: Science Press, 1978), p. 108.

113. Henry McBride, "Charles Demuth, Artist," *Magazine of Art*, 31 (January 1938), p. 21.

114. The complementary imagery in the work of these men is not coincidental, as Williams and Demuth were close friends and aesthetic allies. The poem "Daisy" drew direct inspiration from Demuth's images of that flower. This relationship is explored in an unpublished thesis by Maryann Bruno, "The Influence of Painting on the Poetry of William Carlos Williams" (Vassar College, 1982), p. 14. The two men shared a personal identification with the floral world, which Williams once described: "I always had a feeling of identity with nature, but not assertive! I have always believed in keeping myself out of the picture. When I spoke of flowers, I was a flower, with all the prerogatives of flowers, especially the right to come alive in the Spring."

115. Emerson, *Nature: Addresses and Lectures*, p. 10.

116. Henry McBride, "Demuth," in *The Flow of Art: Essays and Criticisms of Henry McBride*, ed. Daniel Catton Rich (New York: Atheneum Publishers, 1975), p. 218.

117. Georgia O'Keeffe, *Georgia O'Keeffe* (New York: The Viking Press, A Studio Book, 1976), text facing pl. 100.

118. Ibid., text facing pl. 23.

119. Ibid., introductory essay, unpaginated.

120. Ibid.

121. O'Keeffe describes this progression: "The year I painted them I had gone to the lake early in March. Remembering the art lessons of my high school days, I looked at the Jacks with great interest. I did a set of six paintings of them. The first painting was very realistic. The last one had only the Jack from the flower"; ibid., text facing pl. 41.

122. See John I. H. Baur, *The Inlander: Life and Work of Charles Burchfield, 1893–1967* (Newark, Del.: University of Delaware Press; New York and London: Cornwall Books, 1982), chapter 14.

123. Of the year 1918, when he painted *White Violets and Coal Mine*, Burchfield wrote: "I knew my time for induction into the army was approaching. I tried to ignore it, but could not and I became melancholy about it. . . . My subjects changed but not my manner. I sought to superimpose my melancholy on scenes and objects—make a tree or woods look sad or even insane"; Charles Burchfield, "On the Middle Border," *Creative Art*, 3 (September 1928), p. xxix.

124. Charles Burchfield, journal entry for April 20, 1946, quoted in Baur, *The Inlander*, p. 203.

125. Charles Burchfield was an admirer of John James Audubon, both as an artist and as a writer. He expressed special fondness for Audubon's reactions to nature as expressed in the naturalist's journals; see John I. H. Baur, *Charles Burchfield* (New York: The Macmillan Co. for the Whitney Museum of American Art, 1956), p. 65.

126. Charles Burchfield, Foreword to *Charles Burchfield* (New York: American Artists Group, 1945), unpaginated.

127. Among a number of nineteenth-century volumes on natural history in Stamos' library were: *The Power of Movement in Plants*, by Darwin; *Gray's Botanical Textbook: Organography on the Basis of Morphology*; *Geology and Mineralogy, Considered with Ref-*

erence to *Natural Theology*, by William Buckland; *The Structural Development of Mosses and Ferns*, by Douglas Campbell; and *Seaside Studies in Natural History*, by Elizabeth and Alexander Agassiz; see Barbara Cavaliere, "Theodore Stamos in Perspective," *Arts Magazine*, 52 (December 1977), p. 106.

128. Two kinds of angular plant movements are diageotropism, which is gravity-related, and diaheliotropism, which is light-related; see Lester F. Ward, "Darwin as a Botanist," *Proceedings of the Biological Society of Washington*, 1 (November 29, 1880–May 26, 1882), p. 83.

129. Theodoros Stamos, handwritten statement, undated, Artists' Files, Whitney Museum of American Art, New York.

130. Margaret Stones, a leading botanical artist who is best known for her *Drawings of British Plants* (1948) and *The Endemic Flora of Tasmania* (1967–78), has observed numerous dissected plant parts in the late works of Arshile Gorky. Of the milkweed, parts of which she has identified in many untitled Gorky drawings, as well as in the painting whose title names that flower, she writes: "They are the most difficult of all plants to dissect and draw, having a very complicated structure and it is amazing that the artist should discover such a rich source of hidden shapes"; letter to the author, March 9, 1982. Stones is not alone in her perception of plant forms in Gorky's work. According to Hayden Herrera, "Gorky's late abstract painting is a garden of flower parts: petals, pistils, stamens, and thorns. Even in the early years, he kept a paper flower at the foot of his easel to use as a referent in reality for his departure into fantasy"; see Hayden Herrera, "The Artist's Self Image: Self Portraits by Arshile Gorky," in *Arshile Gorky: Drawings to Paintings*, exhibition catalogue (Austin, Tex.: University Art Museum, University of Texas, 1975), p. 50.

131. Harry Rand, in his recent study of the iconography of Arshile Gorky's work, has identified an oft-repeated figure in the drawings for the pastoral series as a rooster. It had previously been identified as an insect (possibly a mantis) by Jim Jordan; see Harry Rand, *Arshile Gorky: The Implications of Symbols* (Montclair, N.J.: Allanheld & Schram, 1980), pp. 187–88.

132. In a letter to his sister Vartoosh, December 1944, Gorky writes: "At times I succeed in capturing the homeland's colors. At times I fail. But the effort is necessary. To capture on my canvas the rich colors of our fruits . . . the rich colors of our plants and vegetables, our grains and flowers. Always I try to duplicate the colors of Armenia on my works"; published in Karlen Mooradian, "The Letters of Arshile Gorky to Vartoosh, Moorad and Karlen Mooradian," *Ararat* (special issue on Arshile Gorky, ed. David Kherdian), 12 (Fall 1971), p. 33.

133. Quoted in Karlen Mooradian, "Remembrances of Gorky: Conversations with Milton Resnick, Robert Jonas, Willem de Kooning, Reuben Nakian, Max Schnitzler and Yenovk der Hagopian," ibid., p. 47.

134. Of the plant parts that Margaret Stones and her colleague David Field at the Royal Botanic Gardens, Kew, England, have observed in Gorky's work, she writes: "Nothing he draws can be seen by the casual eye. He ignores the larger, more obvious sepals and bracts"; letter to the author, March 9, 1982.

135. André Breton, "The Eye-Spring," in *Arshile Gorky*, exhibition catalogue (New York: Julien Levy Gallery, 1945).

136. Jennifer Bartlett, transcript of an interview with Richard Marshall, January 26, 1981, Artists' Files, Whitney Museum of American Art, New York.

137. Quoted in Eleanor Munro, *Originals: American Women Artists* (New York: Simon & Schuster, 1979), p. 408.

138. John Russell, Introduction to *Jennifer Bartlett: In the Garden* (New York: Harry N. Abrams, 1982), p. 7.

139. Looking back in 1896 over the "century's progress in science," John Fiske described the central contribution of the nineteenth century to be the evolutionary world view and its dynamic implications; see his "A Century's Progress in Science," *The Atlantic Monthly*, 78 (July 1896), p. 25.

140. Concerning the relationship of a work of art to nature, Ellsworth Kelly said, "It's nothing if it isn't about something you haven't seen before"; quoted in Elizabeth C. Baker, *Ellsworth Kelly: Recent Paintings and Sculptures*, exhibition catalogue (New York: The Metropolitan Museum of Art, 1979), p. 8.

141. Ellsworth Kelly, interview with the author, July 2, 1982.

Botanical Drawings

1. Charles F. Jenkins, "The Historical Background of Franklin's Tree," *The Pennsylvania Magazine of History and Biography*, 57, no. 3 (1933), p. 202.

2. Ibid.

3. I thank Mr. A. Chater, botanist at the British Museum (Natural History), for his adept and humorous taxonomic judgment.

4. Sprague's collection of watercolor drawings of birds and flowers, made from 1839 to 1842, during his trip with John James Audubon, is now in the Boston Athenaeum.

5. *Isaac Sprague Plates Prepared Between 1849 and 1859, to Accompany a Report on the Forest Trees of North America by Asa Gray* (Washington, D.C., 1891).

6. The relationship between the floral subject and its setting is explored further in the sections here on still-life and landscape compositions.

Floral Still Life

1. Ingvar Bergström, *Dutch Still-Life Painting in the Seventeenth Century*, trans. Christina Hedström and Gerald Taylor (New York: Thomas Yoseloff, 1956), p. 3.

2. Henry T. Tuckerman, *Book of the Artists: American Artist Life, Comprising Biographical and Critical Sketches of American Artists, Preceded by an Historical Account of the Rise and Progress of Art in America* (New York, 1867), p. 482.

3. George Cochran Lambdin, "The Charm of the Rose," *The Art Union Magazine*, 1 (June–July 1884), p. 137; quoted in William H. Gerdts, *Painters of the Humble Truth: Masterpieces of American Still Life, 1801–1939* (Columbia, Mo., and London: Philbrook Art Center with the University of Missouri Press, 1981), p. 125.

4. The rising popularity of chrysanthemums in late nineteenth-century American gardens and bouquets was noted by Peter Henderson, "Floriculture in the United States," *Garden and Forest: A Journal of Horticulture, Landscape Art and Forestry*, 1 (February 1888), p. 3: "There are fashions in flowers, and they continually change. Thirty years ago thousands of Camellia flowers were retailed in the holiday season for $1 each, while Rosebuds would not bring a dime. Now, many of the fancy Roses sell at $1 each, while Camellia flowers go begging at ten cents. The Chrysanthemum is now rivalling the Rose. . . ."

5. See Paul Hulton and Lawrence Smith, *Flowers in Art from East and West* (London: British Museum Publications, 1979), p. 91.

6. Henry McBride, *The Flow of Art: Essays and Criticisms of Henry McBride*, ed. Daniel Catton Rich (New York: Atheneum Publishers, 1975), p. 219.

7. John William Hill's son recorded that his father's reading of the first volume of Ruskin's *Modern Painters* "was a means of opening a new world for him"; John Hill, *John William Hill: An Artist's Memorial* (New York, 1888), p. 5.

Flowers and Landscape

1. *The New Path* (August 1863), p. 43, quoted in Linda S. Ferber, *William Trost Richards, American Landscape and Marine Painter, 1833–1905*, exhibition catalogue (Brooklyn: The Brooklyn Museum, 1973), p. 60.

2. Thomas Cole preferred to make penciled records of topographical details such as rocks and plants. Oil sketches, in his opinion, were "never more than half half true"; quoted in Theodore E. Stebbins, Jr., *Close Observation: Selected Oil Sketches by Frederic E. Church*, exhibition catalogue (Washington, D.C.: Smithsonian Institution Press for the Cooper-Hewitt Museum, 1978), p. 7.

3. Asher B. Durand, "Letters on Landscape Painting, 1855," Letter II, quoted in John W. McCoubrey, *American Art, 1700–1960: Sources and Documents* (Englewood Cliffs, N.J.: Prentice-Hall, 1965), p. 112.

4. John Ruskin, *Praeterita*, 3 vols. (London, 1899), vol. 2, p. 300. The passage quoted appears in chapter 10, "Crossmount," dated 1846–47.

5. Fidelia Bridges, letter to Anna Brown, August 3, 1863, quoted in May Brawley Hill, *Fidelia Bridges, American Pre-Raphaelite*, exhibition catalogue (New York: Berry-Hill Galleries, 1982), p. 13.

6. Celia Thaxter, *An Island Garden* (Boston and New York, 1894), p. 44.

7. Mabel Loomis Todd, "Background," section 3 of "Flower Painting in Oil-Colors" (unpublished manuscript, c. 1881), Mabel Loomis Todd Papers, Manuscripts Division, Sterling Memorial Library, Yale University, New Haven, Connecticut.

Twentieth-Century Flower Art

1. During the 1950s, the Abstract Expressionist movement prompted John I. H. Baur to explore the role of nature in nonrepresentational works of art. He reported that "an overwhelming majority [of artists] answered in the affirmative" to the question "Do you feel that nature has any serious relation to your own work?"; John I. H. Baur, *Nature in Abstraction: The Relation of Abstract Painting and Sculpture to Nature in Twentieth-Century American Art*, exhibition catalogue (New York: The Macmillan Co. for the Whitney Museum of American Art, 1958), p. 6.

2. Marsden Hartley, "John James Audubon as Artist, 1785–1851," in "The Spangle of Existence" (unpublished manuscript, 1942), Library, The Museum of Modern Art, New York.

3. Theodoros Stamos, "Why Nature and Art?" (unpublished manuscript, 1954), copy courtesy Barbara Cavaliere.

4. Henry McBride, review of a Morris Graves exhibition at the Whitney Museum of American Art, New York, in the *New York Sun*, February 3, 1945; reprinted in *The Flow of Art: Essays and Criticisms of Henry McBride*, ed. Daniel Catton Rich (New York: Atheneum Publishers, 1975), p. 404.

5. Charles Sheeler, unpublished autobiography, 1938, Archives of American Art, Smithsonian Institution, Washington, D.C.

6. Irma Jaffe, author of the definitive study *Joseph Stella* (Cambridge, Mass.: Harvard University Press, 1970), suggests that it was in connection with *Tree of My Life* that Stella began to make the flower studies which form such an extensive and important part of his oeuvre (p. 85).

7. Charles Burchfield, statement in Edith H. Jones, ed., *The Drawings of Charles Burchfield* (New York: Frederick A. Praeger in association with the Drawing Society, 1968), text facing pl. 5.

8. Georgia O'Keeffe, *Georgia O'Keeffe* (New York: The Viking Press, A Studio Book, 1976), text facing pl. 30.

9. Ellsworth Kelly, interview with the author, July 2, 1982.

10. The sayings of Kuo Hsi (c. 1020–1090) were repeated in the famous treatise of the Sung period called *The Great Message of Forests and Streams*; see Osvald Sirén, *The Chinese on the Art of Painting* (New York: Schocken Books, 1963), p. 46.

11. Lee Krasner, interview with the author, September 6, 1981.

12. Barbara Novak, "Excerpts from an Interview with Lee Krasner," in *Lee Krasner: Recent Work*, exhibition catalogue (New York: The Pace Gallery, 1981), unpaginated.

Bibliography

Flower Imagery: General

Adams, William Howard. "The Pleasures of Nature." In William Howard Adams, ed. *The Eye of Jefferson* (exhibition catalogue). Washington, D.C.: National Gallery of Art, 1976.

Anderson, Dennis R. *American Flower Painting*. New York: Watson-Guptill Publications, 1980.

Berrall, Julia S. *A History of Flower Arrangement*. New York: Studio Publications, 1953.

Born, Wolfgang. *Still-Life Painting in America*. New York: Hacker Books, 1973.

Bye, Arthur Edwin. *Pots and Pans; or, Studies in Still-Life Painting*. Princeton, N.J.: Princeton University Press, 1921.

Cain, J. Frederick. *An American Flower Show* (exhibition catalogue). Sandwich, Mass.: Heritage Plantation of Sandwich, 1980.

Coats, Alice M. *The Book of Flowers: Four Centuries of Flower Illustration*. London: Phaidon Press, 1973.

Gerdts, William H. *American Impressionism* (exhibition catalogue). Seattle: The Henry Art Gallery, University of Washington, 1980.
———. *Painters of the Humble Truth: Masterpieces of American Still Life, 1801–1939* (exhibition catalogue). Columbia, Mo., and London: Philbrook Art Center with the University of Missouri Press, 1981.

Gerdts, William H., and Russell Burke. *American Still-Life Painting*. New York: Praeger Publishers, 1971.

Grant, Maurice H. *Flower Paintings Through Four Centuries: A Descriptive Catalogue of the Collection Formed by Major the Honourable Henry Rogers Broughton*. Leigh-on-Sea, England: F. Lewis, 1952.

Honour, Hugh. *The European Vision of America* (exhibition catalogue). Cleveland: The Cleveland Museum of Art, 1975.

Hulton, Paul, and Lawrence Smith. *Flowers in Art from East and West*. London: British Museum Publications, 1979.

Kennedy, Ruth Wedgwood. *The Renaissance Painter's Garden*. New York: Oxford University Press, 1948.

Kirkham, E. Truce, and John W. Fink. *Indices to American Literary Annuals and Gift Books, 1825–1865*. New Haven, Conn.: Research Publications, 1975.

Langemeyer, Gerhard, and Hans-Albert Peters. *Stilleben in Europa* (exhibition catalogue). Münster: Landschaftsverband Westfalen-Lippe, 1979.

McShine, Kynaston, ed. *The Natural Paradise: Painting in America, 1800–1950* (exhibition catalogue). New York: The Museum of Modern Art, 1976.

Mitchell, Peter. *Great Flower Painters: Four Centuries of Floral Art*. Woodstock, N.Y.: The Overlook Press, 1973.

Norelli, Martina R. *American Wildlife Painting*. New York: Watson-Guptill Publications, 1975.

O'Doherty, Barbara Novak. *American Flowers: Loan Exhibition of Oils, Pastels, and Watercolors Assembled by Paul Magriel* (exhibition catalogue). New York: Wickersham Gallery, 1967.

Osgood, Frances S., ed. *The Poetry of Flowers and Flowers of Poetry: To Which Are Added, a Simple Treatise on Botany, with Familiar Examples, and a Copious Floral Dictionary*. New York, 1841.

Pächt, Otto. "Early Italian Nature Studies and the Early Calendar Landscape." *Journal of the Warburg and Courtauld Institutes*, 13 (January–June 1950), pp. 13–47.

Pavière, Sydney Herbert. *A Dictionary of Flower, Fruit and Still Life Painters.* Leigh-on-Sea, England: F. Lewis, 1964.

Sirèn, Osvald. *The Chinese on the Art of Painting.* New York: Schocken Books, 1963.

Staley, Allen. *The Pre-Raphaelite Landscape.* Oxford: Clarendon Press, 1973.

Sterling, Charles. *Still-Life Painting from Antiquity to the Twentieth Century.* 2nd ed. New York: Harper & Row, 1981.

Flower Painting: Artists Prior to 1900

Bergström, Ingvar. *Dutch Still-Life Painting in the Seventeenth Century.* Translated by Christina Hedström and Gerald Taylor. London: Faber & Faber; New York: Thomas Yoseloff, 1956.

Bienenstock, Jennifer Marein. "Portraits of Flowers: The Out-of-Door Still-Life Paintings of Maria Oakey Dewing." *American Art Review,* 4 (December 1977), pp. 48–55, 114–18.

Bol, L. J. *The Bosschaert Dynasty.* Leigh-on-Sea, England: F. Lewis, 1960.

Church, Frederic E. Church Diaries and Sketchbooks (photostats). The New-York Historical Society.

Church, Frederic E., and Martin Johnson Heade. Frederic E. Church/Martin Johnson Heade Correspondence. Archives of American Art, Smithsonian Institution, Washington, D.C.

Coffin, Annie R. "Audubon's Friend—Maria Martin." *The New-York Historical Society Quarterly,* 49 (January 1965), pp. 29–51.

Dewing, Maria Oakey. "Flower Painters and What the Flower Offers to Art." *American Magazine of Art: Art and Progress,* 6 (June 1915), pp. 255–62.

Dunthorne, Gordon. *Flower and Fruit Prints of the 18th and Early 19th Centuries.* New York: Da Capo Press, 1970.

Eldredge, Charles C. "Such a Strange Flower—*Calla moderna.*" Unpublished manuscript, undated. Author's copy.

Embury, Emma C. *American Wild Flowers in Their Native Haunts.* New York, 1845.

Ewan, Joseph, ed. *William Bartram: Botanical and Zoological Drawings, 1756–1788.* Philadelphia: The American Philosophical Society, 1968.

Ferber, Linda S. *William Trost Richards, American Landscape and Marine Painter, 1833–1905* (exhibition catalogue). Brooklyn: The Brooklyn Museum, 1973.

Foshay, Ella M. "Charles Darwin and the Development of American Flower Imagery." *Winterthur Portfolio: A Journal of American Material Culture,* 15 (Winter 1980), pp. 299–314.

Foster, Kathleen A. "The Still-Life Painting of John La Farge." *The American Art Journal,* 11 (July 1979), pp. 4–37.

Frankenstein, Alfred Victor. *After the Hunt: William Harnett and Other American Still Life Painters, 1870–1900.* Berkeley: University of California Press, 1953.

Gerdts, William H. "The Influence of Ruskin and Pre-Raphaelitism on American Still-Life Painting." *The American Art Journal,* 1 (Fall 1969), pp. 80–97.
——. "On the Tabletop: Europe and America." *Art in America,* 60 (September 1972), pp. 62–69.
——. "American Still-Life Painting: Severin Roesen's Fruitful Abundance." *Worcester Art Museum Journal,* 5 (1981–82), pp. 5–15.
——. "The Artist's Garden: American Floral Painting, 1850–1915." *Portfolio: The Magazine of the Fine Arts,* 4 (July–August 1982), pp. 44–51.

Grant, Maurice H. *Jan van Huysum, 1762–1749: Including a Catalogue Raisonné of the Artist's Fruit and Flower Paintings.* Leigh-on-Sea, England: F. Lewis, 1950.

Hassam, Frederick Childe. Catalogue raisonné now in preparation by Stuart P. Feld and Kathleen M. Burnside.

[Hill, John]. *A Series of Progressive Lessons, Intended to Elucidate the Art of Flower Painting in Water Colours.* Philadelphia, 1818.

Hill, May Brawley. *Fidelia Bridges, American Pre-Raphaelite* (exhibition catalogue). New York: Berry-Hill Galleries, 1982.

Hooper, Lucy, ed. *The Lady's Book of Flowers and Poetry: To Which Are Added, a Botanical Introduction, a Complete Floral Dictionary, and a Chapter on Plants in Rooms.* New York, 1842.

Hoopes, Donelson H., and Wend von Kalnein. *The Düsseldorf Academy and the Americans: An Exhibition of Drawings and Watercolors* (exhibition catalogue). Atlanta: The High Museum of Art, 1972.

Hulton, Paul. *The Work of Jacques Le Moyne de Morgues: A Huguenot Artist in France, Florida and England.* 2 vols. London: The Trustees of the British Museum, British Museum Publications, 1977.

Hulton, Paul, and David Beers Quinn. *The American Drawings of John White, 1577–1590: With Drawings of European and Oriental Subjects.* London: The Trustees of the British

Museum; Chapel Hill, N.C.: University of North Carolina Press, 1964.

"John van Huysum." *The Illustrated Magazine of Art*, 3 (February 1854), pp. 129–42.

Killerman, Sebastian. A. *Dürers Pflanzen- und Tierzeichnungen und Ihre Bedeutung für die Naturgeschichte*. Strassburg: J. H. E. Heitz [Heitz & Mündel], 1910.

La Farge, John. *An Artist's Letters from Japan*. New York, 1897.

Marcus, Lois Goldreich. *Severin Roesen: A Chronology* (exhibition catalogue). Williamsport, Pa.: Lycoming County Historical Society and Museum, 1976.

Martin, Jennifer A. "The Rediscovery of Maria Oakey Dewing." *The Feminist Art Journal*, 5 (Summer 1976), pp. 24–27.

McDermott, John Francis. "Early Sketches of T. R. Peale." *Nebraska History*, 33 (September 1952), pp. 186–89.

Mook, Maurice A. "S. Roesen, 'The Williamsport Painter.'" Allentown (Pa.) *Morning Call*, December 3, 1955. Reprint on file at the Art Division, New York Public Library, Astor, Lenox and Tilden Foundations.
———. "Severin Roesen, The Williamsport Painter." *Lycoming College Magazine*, 25 (June 1972), pp. 33–37.
———. "Severin Roesen: Also the Huntingdon Painter." *Lycoming College Magazine*, 26 (June 1973), pp. 13–20.

Norton, Bettina A. *Edwin Whitefield: Nineteenth-Century North American Scenery*. Barre, Mass.: Barre Publishing, 1977.

Novak, Barbara. *American Painting of the Nineteenth Century*. New York: Praeger Publishers, 1969. See especially chapter 7, "Martin Johnson Heade: Haystacks and Light."
———. *Nature and Culture: American Landscape and Painting, 1825–1875*. New York: Oxford University Press, 1980. See especially chapter 6, "The Organic Foreground: Plants."

Novak, Barbara, and Annette Blaugrund, eds. *Next to Nature: Landscape Paintings from the National Academy of Design* (exhibition catalogue). New York: National Academy of Design, 1980.

Peale, Charles Willson. "A Walk Through the Philadelphia Museum." Unpublished manuscript, undated. Charles Willson Peale Papers. Archives of American Art, Smithsonian Institution, Washington, D.C.
———. Charles Willson Peale Letterbooks. American Philosophical Society Library, Philadelphia.

Pedretti, Carlo. *Leonardo da Vinci Nature Studies from the Royal Library at Windsor Castle* (exhibition catalogue). Introduction by Kenneth Clark. New York: Johnson Reprint Corporation

for the J. Paul Getty Museum and the Metropolitan Museum of Art, 1980.

Schlie, Friedrich. "Sieben Briefe und eine Quittung von Jan van Huysum." *Oud-Holland*, 18 (1900), pp. 137–43.

Sellers, Charles Coleman. *Charles Willson Peale*. 2 vols. Philadelphia: The American Philosophical Society, 1947.
———. *Charles Willson Peale*. New York: Charles Scribner's Sons, 1969.

Sharf, Frederick A. "Fidelia Bridges, 1834–1923: Painter of Birds and Flowers." *Essex Institute: Historical Collections*, 104 (July 1968), pp. 217–38.

Sitwell, Sacheverell, and Wilfrid Blunt. *Great Flower Books, 1700–1900*. London: William Collins, 1956.

Stebbins, Theodore E., Jr. *Martin Johnson Heade*. College Park, Md.: University of Maryland, 1969.
———. *The Life and Works of Martin Johnson Heade*. New Haven, Conn.: Yale University Press, 1975.
———. *Close Observation: Selected Oil Sketches by Frederic E. Church* (exhibition catalogue). Washington, D.C.: Smithsonian Institution Press for the Cooper-Hewitt Museum, 1978.

Stone, Richard B. "Not Quite Forgotten: A Study of the Williamsport Painter, S. Roesen." *Lycoming Historical Society: Proceedings and Papers*, 9 (November 1951), pp. 2–40.

Todd, Mabel Loomis. "Flower Painting in Oil-Colors." Unpublished manuscript, undated (c. 1881). Mabel Loomis Todd Papers. Manuscripts Division, Sterling Memorial Library, Yale University, New Haven, Connecticut.

Weinberg, Helene B. Kallman. "The Decorative Work of John La Farge." Ph.D. dissertation, Columbia University, 1972.

Whitefield, Edwin. Edwin Whitefield Collection of Drawings, Prints, and Manuscripts. Print Room, Boston Public Library.

Flower Painting: Twentieth-Century Artists

Baker, Elizabeth C. *Ellsworth Kelly: Recent Paintings and Sculptures* (exhibition catalogue). New York: The Metropolitan Museum of Art, 1979.

Baur, John I. H. *Charles Burchfield*. New York: The Macmillan Co. for the Whitney Museum of American Art, 1956.
———. *Nature in Abstraction: The Relation of Abstract Painting and Sculpture to Nature in Twentieth-Century American Art* (exhibition catalogue). New York: The Macmillan Co. for the Whitney Museum of American Art, 1958.
———. *Joseph Stella*. New York: Frederick A. Praeger, 1971.

Baur, John I.H. *The Inlander: Life and Work of Charles Burchfield, 1893–1967*. Newark, Del.: University of Delaware Press; New York and London: Cornwall Books, 1982.

Burchfield, Charles. "On the Middle Border." *Creative Art*, 3 (September 1928), pp. xxv–xxxii.
———. Foreword to *Charles Burchfield*. New York: American Artists Group, 1945.

Cage, John. *The Drawings of Morris Graves*. Boston: Published for the Drawing Society by the New York Graphic Society, 1974.

Cavaliere, Barbara. "Theodore Stamos in Perspective." *Arts Magazine*, 52 (December 1977), pp. 104–15.

Debs, Barbara Knowles. "Ellsworth Kelly's Drawings." *The Print Collector's Newsletter*, 3 (September–October 1972), pp. 73–77.

Friedman, Martin. *Charles Sheeler*. New York: Watson-Guptill Publications, 1975.

Fuller, Mary. "The Water Becomes the Lily: An Interview with Joseph Raffael." *Currant*, 2 (August–October 1976), pp. 16–22.

Garver, Thomas H., and Robert Hughes. *Joseph Raffael: The California Years, 1969–1978* (exhibition catalogue). San Francisco: San Francisco Museum of Modern Art, 1978.

Gebhard, David, and Phyllis Plous. *Charles Demuth: The Mechanical Encrusted on the Living* (exhibition catalogue). Santa Barbara, Calif.: The Art Galleries, University of California, 1971.

Geldzahler, Henry. "Interview with Ellsworth Kelly." *Art International*, 8 (February 15, 1964), pp. 47–48.

Gerdts, William H. *Drawings of Joseph Stella from the Collection of Rabin & Krueger* (exhibition catalogue). Newark, N.J.: Rabin & Krueger Gallery, 1962.

Goossen, E. C. *Ellsworth Kelly* (exhibition catalogue). New York: The Museum of Modern Art, 1973.

Hartley, Marsden. "The Spangle of Existence." Unpublished manuscript, 1942. Library, The Museum of Modern Art, New York.

Jaffe, Irma. *Joseph Stella*. Cambridge, Mass.: Harvard University Press, 1970.

Jones, Edith, ed. *The Drawings of Charles Burchfield*. New York: Frederick A. Praeger in association with the Drawing Society, 1968.

Kherdian, David, ed. *Ararat* (special issue on Arshile Gorky), 12 (Fall 1971).

Lee, Sherman E. "Illustrative and Landscape Watercolors of Charles Demuth." *Art Quarterly*, 5, no. 2 (1942), pp. 158–75.

Milliken, William M. "*White Flower* by Georgia O'Keeffe." *The Bulletin of the Cleveland Museum of Art*, 24 (April 1937), pp. 51–53.

Norton, Thomas E., ed. *Homage to Charles Demuth: Still Life Painter of Lancaster*. Ephrata, Pa.: Science Press, 1978.

Novak, Barbara. "Excerpts from an Interview with Lee Krasner." In *Lee Krasner: Recent Work* (exhibition catalogue). New York: The Pace Gallery, 1981.

O'Keeffe, Georgia. *Georgia O'Keeffe*. New York: The Viking Press, A Studio Book, 1976.

Rand, Harry. *Arshile Gorky: The Implications of Symbols*. Montclair, N.J.: Allanheld & Schram, 1980.

Rubin, Ida E., ed. *The Drawings of Morris Graves with Comments by the Artist*. Boston: New York Graphic Society for the Drawing Society, 1974.

Russell, John. *Jennifer Bartlett: In the Garden*. New York: Harry N. Abrams, 1982.

Stamos, Theodoros. "Why Nature in Art?" Unpublished manuscript, 1954. Collection of Barbara Cavaliere.

Stella, Frank, and Donald Judd. "After Abstract Expressionism." In Barbara Rose, ed. *Readings in American Art Since 1900: A Documentary Survey*. New York and Washington, D.C.: Frederick A. Praeger, 1968.

Waldman, Diane. *Ellsworth Kelly: Drawings, Collages, Prints*. Greenwich, Conn.: New York Graphic Society, 1971.

Aesthetics and Philosophy

Emerson, Ralph Waldo. *The Complete Works of Ralph Waldo Emerson*. Vol. 1, *Nature: Addresses and Lectures*. Boston and New York: Houghton Mifflin Co., 1903.

Graham, John. *System and Dialectics of Art*. New York: Delphic Studios, 1937. Reprint, ed. Marcia Epstein Allentuck. Baltimore: The Johns Hopkins Press, 1971.

Greenberg, Clement. "Modernist Painting." In Gregory Battcock, ed. *The New Art: A Critical Anthology*. New York: E. P. Dutton & Co., 1966.

Jarves, James Jackson. *The Art-Idea*. New York, 1864. Reprint, ed. Benjamin Rowland, Jr. Cambridge, Mass.: Harvard University Press, Belknap Press, 1960.

La Farge, John. *Considerations on Painting: Lectures Given in the Year 1893 at the Metropolitan Museum.* New York, 1895.

McBride, Henry. *The Flow of Art: Essays and Criticisms of Henry McBride.* Edited by Daniel Catton Rich. New York: Atheneum Publishers, 1975.

Reynolds, Sir Joshua. *Discourses on Art.* London, 1797. Reprint, ed. Robert Wark. San Marino, Calif.: Huntington Library Publications, 1959. See especially chapter 4.

Ruskin, John. *Modern Painters.* 5 vols. 5th ed. London, 1851–60.
———. *Praeterita.* 3 vols. London, 1899.
———. *The Complete Works of John Ruskin.* Edited by E. T. Cook and Alexander Wedderburn. 39 vols. London: George Allen; New York: Longmans, Green & Co., 1903–12.

Stein, Roger B. *John Ruskin and Aesthetic Thought in America, 1840–1900.* Cambridge, Mass.: Harvard University Press, 1967.

Tuckerman, Henry T. "Flowers." *Godey's Lady's Book,* 40 (January 1850), pp. 13–18.
———. *Book of the Artists: American Artist Life, Comprising Biographical and Critical Sketches of American Artists, Preceded by an Historical Account of the Rise and Progress of Art in America.* New York, 1867.

Vinci, Leonardo da. *Treatise on Painting [Codex Urbinas Latinus 1270].* Translated and annotated by A. Philip McMahon. Princeton, N.J.: Princeton University Press, 1956.
———. *The Notebooks of Leonardo da Vinci.* Edited by Pamela Taylor. New York, London, and Scarborough, Ontario: Plume Books, 1960.

Wood, T. Martin. "Modern Flower-Painting and Its Character." *The International Studio,* 28 (May 1906), pp. 191–203.

Science, Natural History, Botany, and Horticulture

Allen, Garland E. *Life Science in the Twentieth Century.* New York and London: John Wiley & Sons, 1975.

Arber, Agnes. *Herbals, Their Origin and Evolution: A Chapter in the History of Botany, 1470–1670.* London: Cambridge University Press, 1938.

Audubon, John James. *Ornithological Biography; or, An Account of the Birds of the United States of America, Accompanied by Descriptions of the Objects Represented in the Work Entitled "The Birds of North America," and Interspersed with Delineations of American Scenery and Manners.* 5 vols. Edinburgh, 1831–39.
———. *Letters of John James Audubon, 1826–1840.* Edited by Howard Croning. 2 vols. Boston: The Club of Odd Volumes, 1930.
———. *The Original Water-Color Paintings by John James Audubon for the Birds of America.* Introduction by Marshall B. Davidson. 2 vols. New York: American Heritage Publishing Co., 1966.

Bartram, John. *Catalogue of American Trees, Herubs, and Herbacious Plants, Most of Which Are Now Growing, and Produce Ripe Seed in John Bartram's Garden, Near Philadelphia; The Seed and Growing Plants of Which Are Disposed of on the Most Reasonable Terms.* Philadelphia, c. 1780–83.

Bartram, John, and William Bartram. *John and William Bartram's America.* Edited by Helen Gere Cruickshank. New York: The Devin-Adair Co., 1957.
———. *Bartram Papers.* Bound, 4 vols. Historical Society of Pennsylvania, Philadelphia.

Bartram, William. *Travels Through North and South Carolina, Georgia, East and West Florida.* Philadelphia, 1791.

Berkeley, Edmund, and Dorothy S. Berkeley. *The Life and Travels of John Bartram: From Lake Ontario to the River St. John.* Tallahassee, Fla.: University Presses of Florida, 1982.

Betts, Edwin M., ed. *Thomas Jefferson's Garden Book, 1766–1824.* Philadelphia: The American Philosophical Society, 1944.

Blunt, Wilfrid, with the assistance of William Stearn. *The Art of Botanical Illustration.* London: William Collins, 1967.

Blunt, Wilfrid, and Sandra Raphael. *The Illustrated Herbal.* London: Frances Lincoln Publishers; New York: Thames & Hudson in association with the Metropolitan Museum of Art, 1979.

Boller, Paul F. *American Thought in Transition: The Impact of Evolutionary Naturalism, 1865–1900.* The Rand McNally Series on the History of American Thought and Culture, edited by David D. Van Tassel. Chicago: Rand McNally & Co., 1969.

Bridson, Gavin D. R., Valerie C. Phillips, and Anthony P. Harvey, comps. *Natural History Manuscript Resources in the British Isles.* New York: R. R. Bowker Co., 1980.

Catesby, Mark. *The Natural History of Carolina, Florida and the Bahama Islands.* 2 vols. London, 1731–43.

Coleman, William. *Biology in the Nineteenth Century: Problems of Form, Function, and Transformation.* New York: John Wiley & Sons, 1971.

"The Culture of Flowers." *Scientific American,* 1 (April 30, 1846), unpaginated.

Darlington, William, ed. *Memorials of John Bartram and Humphrey Marshall with Notices of Their Botanical Contemporaries.* Philadelphia, 1849.

Darwin, Charles. *On the Origin of Species by Means of Natural Selection; or, The Preservation of Favoured Races in the Struggle for Life.* London, 1859. Revised ed., New York, 1860.
———. *On the Various Contrivances by Which British and Foreign Orchids Are Fertilised by Insects.* London, 1862. 2nd ed., London, 1877.
———. "The Movements and Habits of Climbing Plants." *Journal of the Linnean Society,* 9 (1865). Revised ed. published as *The Movements and Habits of Climbing Plants.* London, 1876.
———. *Insectivorous Plants.* London, 1875.
———. *The Effects of Cross and Self Fertilisation in the Vegetable Kingdom.* London, 1876.
———. *The Different Forms of Flowers on Plants of the Same Species.* London, 1877.
———. *The Power of Movement in Plants.* London, 1880.

"Darwin on the Origin of Species." *North American Review and Miscellaneous Journal,* 90 (April 1860), pp. 474–506.

Dupree, A. Hunter, ed. *Science and the Emergence of Modern America, 1865–1916.* The Berkeley Series in American History. Chicago: Rand McNally & Co., 1963.

Ewan, Joseph, ed. *A Short History of Botany in the United States.* New York: Hafner Publishing Co., 1969.

Frick, George F. "Mark Catesby: The Discovery of a Naturalist." *Papers of the Bibliographical Society of America,* 54 (July–September 1960), pp. 163–75.

From Seed to Flower, Philadelphia, 1681–1876: A Horticultural Point of View (exhibition catalogue). Philadelphia: The Pennsylvania Horticultural Society, 1976.

Fulling, Edmund H. "Thomas Jefferson, His Interest in Plant Life as Revealed in His Writing." *Bulletin of the Torrey Botanical Club,* 72 (May–June 1945), pp. 248–70.

Glick, Thomas F., ed. *Conference on the Comparative Reception of Darwinism.* Austin, Tex.: University of Texas Press, 1972.

Goodale, George L. *The Wild Flowers of America: Illustrations by Isaac Sprague.* Boston, 1876.

Goode, George Brown. "The Beginnings of Natural History in America." *Proceedings of the Biological Society of Washington,* 3 (July 1, 1884–February 6, 1886), pp. 35–105; 4 (February 20, 1886–January 28, 1888), pp. 9–94.

Gould, Stephen Jay. *Ever Since Darwin: Reflections in Natural History.* New York: W. W. Norton & Co., 1977.

[Gray, Asa]. "Darwin on the Origin of Species." *The Atlantic Monthly,* 6 (July 1860), pp. 109–16; 6 (August 1860), pp. 229–39.
———. "Darwin and His Reviewers." *The Atlantic Monthly,* 6 (October 1860), pp. 406–25.

Green, J. Reynolds. *A History of Botany, 1860–1900.* New York: Russell & Russell, 1909. Reprint, New York: Russell & Russell, 1967.

Heade, Martin Johnson. "A Decade Wasted." *Forest and Stream,* 21 (August 2, 1883), p. 8.
———. "Taming Hummingbirds." *Forest and Stream,* 38 (April 14, 1892), p. 348.
———. Heade Papers and Notebooks. Archives of American Art, Smithsonian Institution, Washington, D.C.

Hedrick, Ulysses P. *A History of Horticulture in America to 1860.* New York: Oxford University Press, 1950.

Henrey, Blanche. *British Botanical and Horticultural Literature Before 1800.* 3 vols. London: Oxford University Press, 1975.

Hervey, Alpheus Baker. *Beautiful Wild Flowers of America: From Original Water-Color Drawings After Nature by Isaac Sprague, with Extracts from Longfellow, Whittier, Bryant, Holmes and Others.* Boston, 1882.
———. *Wayside Flowers and Ferns: From Original Water-Color Drawings by Isaac Sprague, with Selections from Poets.* Troy, N.Y., 1887.

Hindle, Brooke. *The Pursuit of Science in Revolutionary America, 1735–1789.* Chapel Hill, N.C.: Published for the Institute of Early American History and Culture, Williamsburg, Va., by the University of North Carolina Press, 1956.

"Introduction." *Bulletin of the Torrey Botanical Club,* 1 (January 1870), p. 1.

Jenkins, Charles F. "The Historical Background of Franklin's Tree." *The Pennsylvania Magazine of History and Biography,* 57, no. 3 (1933), pp. 193–208.

Kalm, Peter. *Travels into North America: Containing Its Natural History and a Circumstantial Account of Its Plantations and Agriculture in General.* Translated by John Reinhold Forster. 3 vols. Warrington, England, 1770.

Kepes, Gyorgy. *The New Landscape in Art and Science.* Chicago: Paul Theobald & Co., 1956.
———, ed. *Structure in Art and Science.* New York: George Braziller, 1965.

Kuhn, Thomas S. *The Structure of Scientific Revolutions.* International Encyclopedia of Unified Science series, edited by Otto Neurath. Chicago: University of Chicago Press, 1962. 2nd ed., Chicago: University of Chicago Press, 1970.

Latrobe, Benjamin Henry. *The Virginia Journals of Benjamin Henry Latrobe, 1795–1798.* Edited by Edward C. Carter II. 2 vols. New Haven, Conn.: Yale University Press for the Maryland Historical Society, 1977.

Linnaeus, Carl. *Systema naturae.* Leiden, 1735. Facsimile ed., with Introduction and English translation by M. S. J. Engel-Lederboer and H. Engel. Amsterdam: Nieuwkoop B. de Graaf, 1964.

Lockwood, Samuel. "Audubon's Lily Rediscovered." *Popular Science Monthly,* 10 (April 1877), pp. 675–78.

Mason, Stephen F. *Main Currents of Scientific Thought.* New York: The Macmillan Co. and Abelard-Schuman, 1956. Reprinted as *A History of the Sciences.* New York: Collier Books, 1973.

Mayr, Ernst. "Evolution." *Scientific American,* 239 (September 1978), pp. 47–55.

Meehan, Thomas. *The Native Flowers and Ferns of the United States in Their Botanical, Horticultural and Popular Aspects.* 2 vols., Boston: L. Prang & Co., 1878–79. 1 vol., Philadelphia: American Natural History Publishing Co., 1880.

"Mimicry as a Protection." *Forest and Stream,* 18 (June 20, 1882), pp. 486–87.

"New Publications." *Forest and Stream,* 1 (September 25, 1873), p. 110.

Nissen, Klaus. *Die botanische Buchillustration: Ihre Geschichte und Bibliographie.* Stuttgart: Hiersemann, 1951. Supplement, Stuttgart: Hiersemann, 1966.

Passe, Crispin van de, the Elder. *Hortus floridus.* Utrecht, 1614; Arnheim, 1616. *Hortus floridus: First Book, Flowers of Springe; Second Book, Flowers of Summer, Autumn and Winter.* Translated by Spencer Savage, Preface by Eleanour S. Rohde. 2 vols. London: The Cresset Press, 1928–29.

Peale, Charles Willson. *Discourse Introductory to a Course of Lectures on the Science of Nature: With Original Music, Composed for, and Sung on the Occasion* (delivered in the Hall of the University of Pennsylvania, November 8, 1800). Music by John Isaac Hawkins with words by Rembrandt Peale. Philadelphia, 1800.

Poesch, Jessie. *Titian Ramsay Peale and His Journals of the Wilkes Expedition.* Philadelphia: The American Philosophical Society, 1961.

Quimby, Jane, comp. *Catalogue of the Hunt Botanical Collection.* 3 vols. Pittsburgh: The Hunt Botanical Library, 1958.

The Rachel McMasters Miller Hunt Botanical Library, Carnegie Institute of Technology: Its Collections, Program and Staff. Pittsburgh: The Hunt Botanical Library, 1961.

Reingold, Nathan, ed. *Science in Nineteenth-Century America: A Documentary History.* New York: Hill & Wang, 1964.

Rensselaer, M. G. van. "Landscape Gardening—A Definition." *Garden and Forest,* 1 (February 29, 1888), p. 2.

Sandler, Henry Frederick Conrad. *Reichenbachia: Orchids Illustrated and Described by F. Sandler, with Assistance of Scientific Authority.* 2 vols. London, 1886–90.

Smallwood, William M., and Mabel S. C. Smallwood. *Natural History and the American Mind.* New York: Columbia University Press, 1941.

Smith, James Edward, ed. *A Selection of the Correspondence of Linnaeus and Other Naturalists, from the Original Manuscripts.* 2 vols. London, 1821.

Sprague, Isaac. Diary, 1843 (trip to the Missouri River with John James Audubon). Manuscript Division, Boston Athenaeum.

Stearns, Raymond Phineas. *Science in the British Colonies of America.* Urbana, Ill., Chicago, and London: University of Illinois Press, 1970.

Thaxter, Celia. *An Island Garden: With Pictures and Illuminations by Childe Hassam.* Boston and New York, 1894.
———. *Letters of Celia Thaxter.* Edited by A. F. and R. L. Boston, 1895.

Thoreau, Henry David. "Natural History of Massachusetts." *The Dial,* 3 (July 1842), pp. 19–40.

Thornton, Robert John. *New Illustration of the Sexual System of Carolus von Linnaeus; and the Temple of Flora, or Garden of Nature, Being Picturesque Botanical Coloured Plates, of Select Plants, Illustrative of the Same, with Descriptions.* 2 vols. London, 1812.

Ward, Lester F. "Darwin as a Botanist." *Proceedings of the Biological Society of Washington,* 1 (November 29, 1880–May 26, 1882), pp. 81–86.

"What Darwinism Means." *Popular Science Monthly,* 3 (September 1873), pp. 654–55.

Works in the Exhibition

Dimensions are given first in inches, then in centimeters, height preceding width. Dimensions for works on paper refer to sheet size, unless both image and sheet size are listed.

JOHN JAMES AUDUBON (1785–1851)

Key West Pigeon, Columba Montana, in *The Birds of America: From Original Drawings*, 1827–38. Hand-colored engraving and aquatint; image, 20¾ × 25⅞ (52.7 × 65.7); page, 26½ × 38 (67.3 × 96.5). Department of Library Services, The American Museum of Natural History, New York.

Ruby-throated Humming Bird, Trochilus Colubris, in *The Birds of America: From Original Drawings*, 1827–38. Hand-colored engraving and aquatint: image, 26 × 20¾ (66 × 52.7); page, 26½ × 38 (67.3 × 96.5). Department of Library Services, The American Museum of Natural History, New York.

JENNIFER BARTLETT (b. 1941)

In the Garden #10, 1980. Ink on paper, 19½ × 26 (49.5 × 66). Collection of Rose and Morton Landowne.

In the Garden #65, 1980. Pencil on paper, 26 × 19½ (66 × 49.5). Collection of Mr. and Mrs. Mason Adams.

In the Garden #112, 1980. Charcoal and gouache on paper, 19¾ × 26 (50.2 × 66). Collection of Wendy and Richard Hokin.

In the Garden #118, 1980. Watercolor and pastel on paper, 19¾ × 26 (50.2 × 66). Private collection.

In the Garden #174, 1980. Oil pastel on paper, 19¾ × 26 (50.2 × 66). Collection of Steven and Sue Antebi.

WILLIAM BARTRAM (1739–1823)

A Drawing of the Round Leafed Nymphaea as Flowering. Colocasia (American lotus), 1761–62. Pencil on paper, 15¼ × 9⅝ (38.7 × 24.4). The Trustees of the British Museum (Natural History), London; Fothergill Album.

Franklinia alatamaha, 1788. Watercolor on paper, 14⅜ × 11 (36.5 × 27.9). The Trustees of the British Museum (Natural History), London; Fothergill Album.

FIDELIA BRIDGES (1834–1923)

Studies for a Picture of Field Flowers Against an Evening Sky, c. 1865. Watercolor and pencil on paper, two sheets: left, 12½ × 8½ (31.8 × 21.6); right, 12 × 8½ (30.5 × 21.6). Collection of Judith and Wilbur Ross.

Queen Anne's Lace in a Landscape, c. 1870. Watercolor on paper, 14 × 10 (35.6 × 25.4). Private collection.

Untitled (Joe-pye weed), 1876. Watercolor on paper, 13⅞ × 9⁵⁄₁₆ (35.2 × 23.7). National Museum of American Art, Smithsonian Institution, Washington, D.C.; Gift in memory of Charles Downing Lay and Laura Gill Lay by their children.

CHARLES BURCHFIELD (1893–1967)

Wild Flower Study, 1911–12. Watercolor on paper, 20 × 14 (50.8 × 35.6). Kennedy Galleries, New York.

Dead Sunflower, 1917. Watercolor on paper, 19⅞ × 13⅞ (50.5 × 35.2). Munson-Williams-Proctor Institute, Utica, New York; Edward W. Root Bequest.

White Violets and Coal Mine, 1918. Watercolor on paper mounted on cardboard, 23¼ × 21¼ (59.1 × 54). The Cleveland Museum of Art; Purchased by Income Hinman B. Hurlbut Fund.

Cannas and Studio, c. 1931. Watercolor on paper, 22 × 28 (55.9 × 71.1). Collection of Mrs. William Green.

Dandelion Seed Heads and the Moon, 1961–65. Watercolor on paper, 54¼ × 38½ (137.8 × 97.8). Collection of Dr. Irwin Goldstein.

Mark Catesby (1679–1749)

Kalmia, c. 1726. Gouache on paper, 15 × 11¼ (38.1 × 28.6). The Pierpont Morgan Library, New York; Gift of Henry S. Morgan.

Magnolia Buds, c. 1726. Gouache and pencil on paper, 14¾ × 10½ (37.5 × 26.7). The Pierpont Morgan Library, New York; Gift of Henry S. Morgan.

Plumeria flore rosea, c. 1726. Gouache and pencil on vellum mounted on backing, 14 × 9 (35.6 × 22.9). The Pierpont Morgan Library, New York; Gift of Henry S. Morgan.

The Balsam-Tree, in *The Natural History of Carolina, Florida and the Bahama Islands*, 1731–43. Hand-colored engraving: image, 13½ × 10⅛ (34.3 × 25.7); page, 22 × 15¼ (55.9 × 38.7). Department of Library Services, The American Museum of Natural History, New York.

The Mock-bird, in *The Natural History of Carolina, Florida and the Bahama Islands*, 1731–43. Hand-colored engraving: image, 13½ × 10⅛ (34.3 × 25.7); page, 22 × 15¼ (55.9 × 38.7). Department of Library Services, The American Museum of Natural History, New York.

Frederic E. Church (1826–1900)

Cardamun (wild ginger), 1865. Oil and pencil on cardboard, 11 × 8½ (27.9 × 21.6). Cooper-Hewitt Museum, The Smithsonian Institution's National Museum of Design, New York.

Jamaican Flowers, 1865. Oil on paperboard, 13⅝ × 15⅝ (34.6 × 39.7). Cooper-Hewitt Museum, The Smithsonian Institution's National Museum of Design, New York.

Samuel Colman (1832–1920)

Azaleas, 1876. Watercolor and pencil on light brown paper, 14¼ × 22¼ (36.2 × 56.5). Cooper-Hewitt Museum, The Smithsonian Institution's National Museum of Design, New York.

Jasper F. Cropsey (1823–1900)

Hellebore, Iris and Violets, 1851. Oil on academy board mounted on canvas, 10⅝ × 7 (27 × 17.8). Munson-Williams-Proctor Institute, Utica, New York; Gift of Mr. and Mrs. Ferdinand H. Davis.

Skunk Cabbage, 1851. Oil on canvas, 8$\frac{1}{16}$ × 11½ (20.5 × 29.2). Newington-Cropsey Foundation, Hastings-on-Hudson, New York.

Leaf Study, n.d. Gouache and pencil on paper, 6⅞ × 9⅞ (17.5 × 25.1). Newington-Cropsey Foundation, Hastings-on-Hudson, New York.

George Walter Dawson (1870–1938)

Auratum Lilies, 1935. Watercolor on paper, 16 × 16 (40.6 × 40.6). Pennsylvania Academy of the Fine Arts, Philadelphia; Presented by friends of the artist.

Charles Demuth (1883–1935)

Yellow and Blue, 1915. Watercolor on paper, 14 × 10 (35.6 × 25.4). The Metropolitan Museum of Art, New York; The Alfred Stieglitz Collection.

Zinnias, 1921. Watercolor on paper, 11⅞ × 18 (30.2 × 45.7). Philadelphia Museum of Art; A. E. Gallatin Collection.

Poster Portrait: Georgia O'Keeffe, 1924. Oil on board, 20½ × 16½ (52.1 × 41.9). Collection of American Literature, Beinecke Rare Book and Manuscript Library, Yale University, New Haven, Connecticut.

Red and Yellow Gladioli, 1928. Watercolor on paper, 20 × 14 (50.8 × 35.6). Collection of Alan and Marianne Schwartz.

Red Poppies, 1929. Watercolor and pencil on paper, 13⅞ × 19¾ (35.2 × 50.2). The Metropolitan Museum of Art, New York; Gift of Mr. and Mrs. Henry A. Loeb.

Maria Oakey Dewing (1845–1927)

Garden in May, 1895. Oil on canvas, 23⅝ × 32½ (60 × 82.6). National Museum of American Art, Smithsonian Institution, Washington, D.C.; Gift of John Gellatly.

Bed of Poppies, 1909. Oil on canvas, 25 × 30 (63.5 × 76.2). Addison Gallery of American Art, Phillips Academy, Andover, Massachusetts.

Arthur G. Dove (1880–1946)

Plant Forms, 1915. Pastel on canvas, 17¼ × 23⅞ (43.8 × 60.6). Whitney Museum of American Art, New York; Gift of Mr. and Mrs. Roy R. Neuberger 51.20.

Arshile Gorky (1904–1948)

One Year the Milkweed, 1944. Oil on canvas, 37 × 47 (94 × 119.4). National Gallery of Art, Washington, D.C.; Ailsa Mellon Bruce Fund.

Morris Graves (b. 1910)

Iceland Poppies—A Triumph of Hybridization, 1970. Tempera on paper, 22½ × 16½ (57.2 × 41.9). Collection of Herschel and Caryl Roman.

GEORGE HENRY HALL (1825–1913)

Still Life: Vase of Flowers and Watermelon, 1865. Oil on canvas, 40⅝ × 30⅜ (103.2 × 77.2). Albrecht Art Museum, St. Joseph, Missouri; The Enid and Crosby Kemper Foundation Collection.

MARSDEN HARTLEY (1877–1943)

Flower Abstraction, 1914. Oil on canvas, 49⅜ × 42½ (125.4 × 108). Collection of Mr. and Mrs. Meyer P. Potamkin.

FREDERICK CHILDE HASSAM (1859–1935)

Gathering Flowers in a French Garden, 1888. Oil on canvas, 28 × 21⅝ (71.1 × 54.9). Worcester Art Museum, Massachusetts; Theodore T. and Mary G. Ellis Collection.
Celia Thaxter in Her Garden, 1892. Oil on canvas, 22⅛ × 18⅛ (56.2 × 46). National Museum of American Art, Smithsonian Institution, Washington, D.C.; Gift of John Gellatly.
The Island Garden, 1892. Watercolor on paper, 17½ × 14 (44.5 × 35.6). National Museum of American Art, Smithsonian Institution, Washington, D.C.; Gift of John Gellatly.

WILLIAM JACOB HAYS (1830–1875)

Bouquet of Orchids, 1871. Oil on fabric, 36 × 30 (91.4 × 76.2). Collection of Mr. James M. and Dr. Edith Hays Walton-Myers.

MARTIN JOHNSON HEADE (1819–1904)

A Vase of Corn Lilies and Heliotrope, 1863. Oil on canvas, 16⅜ × 12⅜ (41.6 × 31.4). The St. Louis Art Museum.
Study of "Lealia Purpurata" and Another Orchid, 1865–75. Oil on canvas, 8½ × 13 (21.6 × 33). St. Augustine Historical Society, Florida.
Tropical Landscape with Ten Hummingbirds, 1870. Oil on canvas, 18 × 30 (45.7 × 76.2). Private collection.
Hummingbird with a White Orchid, 1870s. Oil on canvas, 20 × 10½ (50.8 × 26.7). Shelburne Museum, Vermont.
Study of Varied Flowers with a Hummingbird, 1870s. Oil on canvas, 14¾ × 19½ (37.5 × 49.5). St. Augustine Historical Society, Florida.
Study of a Yellow Flower, 1871. Oil on canvas, 11¼ × 14¼ (28.6 × 36.2). St. Augustine Historical Society, Florida.
Jungle Orchids and Hummingbirds, 1872. Oil on canvas, 18 × 23 (45.7 × 58.4). Yale University Art Gallery, New Haven, Connecticut; Christian A. Zabriskie and Francis P. Garvan Funds.

Passion Flowers and Hummingbirds, c. 1875–85. Oil on canvas, 17¼ × 22⅛ (43.8 × 56.2). San Antonio Museum Association, Texas; Purchased with funds provided by the Robert J. Kleberg, Jr., and Helen C. Kleberg Foundation.
Branches of Cherokee Roses, c. 1880. Oil on canvas, 10 × 17 (25.4 × 43.2). St. Augustine Historical Society, Florida.
Study of Three Blossoms of Magnolia, c. 1880. Oil on canvas, 10¼ × 14½ (26 × 36.8). St. Augustine Historical Society, Florida.
Giant Magnolias, c. 1885–95. Oil on canvas, 15¼ × 24 (38.7 × 61). The R. W. Norton Art Gallery, Shreveport, Louisiana.

JOHN HENRY HILL (1839–1922)

Calla, 1888. Watercolor on paper, 13 × 9 (33 × 22.9). Collection of

JOHN WILLIAM HILL (1812–1879)

Bird's Nest and Dogroses, 1867. Watercolor on paper, 10¾ × 13⅞ (27.3 × 35.2). The New-York Historical Society.
Tearoses in Landscape, 1874. Watercolor on paper, 14 × 20 (35.6 × 50.8). Collection of Stephen Rubin.

JOHN E. HOLLEN (fl. 1842–1880)

Bouquet in Vase, c. 1842. Oil on canvas, 16½ × 12½ (41.9 × 31.8). Hunt Institute for Botanical Documentation, Carnegie-Mellon University, Pittsburgh.

WINSLOW HOMER (1836–1910)

Flower Garden and Bungalow, Bermuda, 1899. Watercolor on paper, 14 × 21 (35.6 × 53.3). The Metropolitan Museum of Art, New York; Amelia B. Lazarus Fund.

THOMAS HOVENDEN (1840–1895)

Peonies, 1886. Oil on canvas, 20 × 24 (50.8 × 61). Pennsylvania Academy of the Fine Arts, Philadelphia; Gift of Mrs. Edward H. Coates in memory of Mr. Coates.

ELLSWORTH KELLY (b. 1923)

Trunk with Leaves, 1949. Ink on paper, 10½ × 8⅛ (26.7 × 20.6). Private collection.
Corn, 1959. Watercolor on paper, 18½ × 22½ (47 × 57.2). Private collection.
Water Lily, 1968. Pencil on paper, 29 × 23 (73.7 × 58.4). Private collection.

Milkweed, 1969. Ink on paper, 29 × 23 (73.7 × 58.4). Private collection.

Lilies, 1980. Pencil on paper, 30 × 20 (76.2 × 50.8). Private collection.

LEE KRASNER (b. 1908)

Milkweed, 1955. Oil, paper, and canvas collage on canvas, 82⅜ × 57¾ (209.2 × 146.7). Albright-Knox Art Gallery, Buffalo; Gift of Seymour H. Knox.

JOHN LA FARGE (1835–1910)

Water Lilies in a White Bowl, 1859. Oil on academy board, 9½ × 13 (24.1 × 33). Private collection.

Flowers on a Window Ledge, c. 1862. Oil on canvas, 24 × 20 (61 × 50.8). The Corcoran Gallery of Art, Washington, D.C.; Museum Purchase, The Anna E. Clark Fund.

Wild Roses and Water Lily, 1882–85. Watercolor on paper, 10⅝ × 8⅞ (27 × 22.5). Collection of Mr. and Mrs. Raymond J. Horowitz.

Irises and Wild Roses, 1887. Watercolor on paper, 12⅝ × 10⅛ (32.1 × 25.7). The Metropolitan Museum of Art, New York; Gift of Priscilla A. B. Henderson in memory of her grandfather, Russell St. Sturgis, a founder of the Metropolitan Museum.

GEORGE COCHRAN LAMBDIN (1830–1896)

Calla Lilies, 1874. Oil on panel, 20 × 11⅞ (50.8 × 30.2). Berry-Hill Galleries, New York.

In the Greenhouse, n.d. Oil on canvas, 31³⁄₁₆ × 40 (79.2 × 101.6). The Metropolitan Museum of Art, New York; Gift of Mrs. J. Augustus Barnard.

BENJAMIN H. LATROBE (1764–1820)

Cyprepedium acaule (lady's slipper), c. 1798. Pencil, ink, and watercolor on paper, 7 × 10¼ (17.8 × 26). Benjamin Latrobe Papers, Museum and Library of Maryland History, Maryland Historical Society, Baltimore.

ERNEST LAWSON (1873–1939)

Garden Landscape, n.d. Oil on canvas, 20 × 24 (50.8 × 61). The Brooklyn Museum; Bequest of Laura L. Barnes.

HENRY RODERICK NEWMAN (1833–1918)

Anemones, 1876. Watercolor on paper, 18 × 11¾ (45.7 × 29.8). Private collection, courtesy Jeffrey R. Brown Fine Arts, North Amherst, Massachusetts.

GEORGIA O'KEEFFE (b. 1887)

Black Iris, 1926. Oil on canvas, 36 × 29⅞ (91.4 × 75.9). The Metropolitan Museum of Art, New York; The Alfred Stieglitz Collection.

Abstraction—White Rose III, 1927. Oil on canvas, 36 × 30 (91.4 × 76.2). Collection of the artist.

Two Calla Lilies on Pink, 1928. Oil on canvas, 40 × 30 (101.6 × 76.2). Collection of the artist.

Jack-in-the-Pulpit I, 1930. Oil on canvas, 12 × 9 (30.5 × 22.9). Private collection.

Jack-in-the-Pulpit II, 1930. Oil on canvas, 40 × 30 (101.6 × 76.2). Collection of the artist.

Jack-in-the-Pulpit III, 1930. Oil on canvas, 40 × 30 (101.6 × 76.2). Collection of the artist.

Jack-in-the-Pulpit IV, 1930. Oil on canvas, 40 × 30 (101.6 × 76.2). Collection of the artist.

Jack-in-the-Pulpit V, 1930. Oil on canvas, 48 × 30 (121.9 × 76.2). Collection of the artist.

Jack-in-the-Pulpit VI, 1930. Oil on canvas, 36 × 18 (91.4 × 45.7). Collection of the artist.

TITIAN RAMSAY PEALE (1799–1885)

Papeete, Island of Tahiti. Taken from Hill Back of the Town/Looking WNW, 1839. Ink and pencil on paper, 10⅞ × 15 (27.6 × 38.1). The American Museum of Natural History, New York.

JOSEPH RAFFAEL (b. 1933)

Large Mystic Lily, 1976. Watercolor on paper, 28½ × 38 (72.4 × 96.5). Collection of Frank and Betsy Goodyear.

JOSEPH RAPHAEL (1872–1950)

Rhododendron Field, 1915. Oil on canvas, 30 × 40 (76.2 × 101.6). The Oakland Museum; Gift of William S. Porter.

WILLIAM T. RICHARDS (1833–1905)

The Conservatory, 1860. Oil on wood, 10⅞ × 8⁹⁄₁₆ (27.6 × 21.7). Private collection.

ELLEN ROBBINS (1828–1905)

Flowers in a Wood, c. 1875. Watercolor on paper, 18½ × 28 (47 × 71.1). Collection of Mr. and Mrs. Arie L. Kopelman.

SEVERIN ROESEN (c. 1815–c. 1871)

Still Life: Flowers and Fruit, 1848. Oil on canvas, 36 × 26
(91.4 × 66). The Corcoran Gallery of Art, Washington,
D.C.; Museum Purchase through the gift of the Honorable
Orme Wilson.

Victorian Bouquet, c. 1850–55. Oil on canvas, 36½ × 29
(92.7 × 73.7). The Museum of Fine Arts, Houston; Museum
Purchase, Agnes Cullen Arnold Endowment Fund.

Still Life: Flowers and Fruit, c. 1855. Oil on canvas, 40 × 50⅜
(101.6 × 128). The Metropolitan Museum of Art, New York;
Charles Allen Munn Bequest; Fosburgh Fund, Inc. Gift; Mr.
and Mrs. J. William Middendorf II Gift; and Henry G.
Keasbey Bequest.

CHARLES SHEELER (1883–1965)

Chrysanthemums, 1912. Oil on canvas, 24 × 20 (61 × 50.8).
Whitney Museum of American Art, New York; Gift of the
artist   55.24.

Flower Forms, 1917. Oil on canvas, 23¼ × 19⅛ (59.1 × 48.6).
Private collection.

Flower in a Bowl, 1918. Watercolor on paper, 15 × 12
(38.1 × 30.5). Collection of Warren Adelson.

Geranium, c. 1926. Oil on canvas, 32 × 26 (81.3 × 66). Whitney
Museum of American Art, New York; Gift of Gertrude
Vanderbilt Whitney   31.343.

Cactus, 1931. Oil on canvas, 45⅛ × 30 (114.6 × 76.2).
Philadelphia Museum of Art; The Louise and Walter
Arensberg Collection.

ISAAC SPRAGUE (1811–1895)

Magnolia auriculata, Ear-lobed Umbrella Tree, 1849–52.
Watercolor on paper, 13⅞ × 14⅞ (35.2 × 37.8). Hunt
Institute for Botanical Documentation, Carnegie-Mellon
University, Pittsburgh.

THEODOROS STAMOS (b. 1922)

Movement of Plants, 1945. Oil on masonite, 16 × 20
(40.6 × 50.8). Munson-Williams-Proctor Institute, Utica,
New York; Edward W. Root Bequest.

JOSEPH STELLA (1877–1946)

Tree of My Life, 1919. Oil on canvas, 83½ × 75½
(212.1 × 191.8). Iowa State Education Association,
Des Moines.

Lupine, c. 1919. Pastel on paper, 27½ × 21½ (69.9 × 54.6).
Collection of Robert Tobin.

Lotus Flower, 1920. Oil on glass, 11 × 7¼ (27.9 × 18.4).
Collection of Dr. and Mrs. Martin Weissman.

Song of Barbados, 1938. Oil on canvas, 58 × 37 (147.3 × 94).
Collection of Mr. and Mrs. James A. Fisher.

JOHN HENRY TWACHTMAN (1853–1902)

Meadow Flowers, c. 1890–1900. Oil on canvas, 33¹⁄₁₆ × 22¹⁄₁₆
(84 × 56). The Brooklyn Museum; Caroline H. Polhemus
Fund.

In the Greenhouse, c. 1890–1902. Oil on canvas, 25 × 16
(63.5 × 40.6). North Carolina Museum of Art, Raleigh.

JOHN WHITE (fl. 1577–1593)

Horn Plantains on the Stalk (Platano or Planten), c. 1586.
Watercolor over black lead outlines on paper, 12¾ × 8¾
(32.4 × 22.2). The Trustees of the British Museum,
London.

Sabatia stellaris (rosegentian), c. 1586–90. Body color and
watercolor, touched with white (oxidized) over black lead
outlines on paper, 13¾ × 7 (34.9 × 17.8). The Trustees of the
British Museum, London.

WILLIAM YOUNG (fl. 1753–1784)

Nymphaea, Nymphaea, Nymphaea Leaf, 1766–67. Watercolor on
paper, 15 × 8½ (38.1 × 21.6). The Trustees of the British
Museum (Natural History), London.

Palmata digitalis, Aster, Tetandria Moss, 1766–67. Watercolor on
paper, 15 × 8½ (38.1 × 21.6). The Trustees of the British
Museum (Natural History), London.

Index

PHOTOGRAPH CREDITS

Photographs of works of art reproduced have been provided, in many cases, by the owners or custodians of the works, as cited in the captions. The following list applies to photographs for which an additional acknowledgment is due. Numbers refer to figures.

Larry Amato, 40, 102–105; Will Brown, 49; Geoffrey Clements, 41, 44, 55, 62, 67, 92, 96, 122, 125, 128, 145–149; Rick Echelmeyer, 144; eeva-inkeri, 141, 143; Roy M. Elkind, 98, 136; Mauro Galligani, 5; Helga Photo Studio, 93; Scott Hyde, 35, 37, 100, 101; Paul Macapia, 64, 99, 120; John Mahtesian Photography, 84; Edward Michel, 135; Nathan Rabin, 140; Taylor & Dull, 97; Malcolm Varon, frontispiece, 54, 56–60, 137

A NOTE ON THE TYPE

The text of this book has been set in Goudy Old Style, one of
the more than 100 type faces designed by Frederick William
Goudy (1865-1947). Although Goudy began his career as a
bookkeeper, he was so inspired by the appearance of several
newly published books from the Kelmscott Press that he devoted
the remainder of his life to typography in an attempt to bring a
better understanding of the movement led by William Morris to
the printers of the United States. Produced in 1914, Goudy Old
Style reflects the absorbtion of a generation of designers with
things "ancient." Its smooth, even color combined with its
generous curves and ample cut marks it as one of Goudy's finest
achievements.

Composed by Graphic Composition, Inc., Athens, Georgia
Printed and bound by Amilcare Pizzi S.P.A., Milan, Italy
Typography by Joe Marc Freedman